# Certified Coding Specialist–Physician-Based (CCS-P) Exam Preparation

## Sixth Edition

Anita C. Hazelwood,
MLS, RHIA, FAHIMA

Lynn Kuehn,
MS, RHIA, CCS-P, FAHIMA

Carol A. Venable,
MPH, RHIA, FAHIMA

AHIMA PRESS

ISBN: 978-1-58426-117-9

AHIMA Product No.: AC400214

AHIMA Staff:
Katherine M. Greenock, MS, Production Development Editor
Caitlin Wilson, Assistant Editor
Pamela Woolf, Director of Publications

**For more information, including updates, about AHIMA Press publications, visit http://www.ahima.org/publications/updates.aspx**

American Health Information Management Association
233 North Michigan Avenue, 21st Floor
Chicago, Illinois 60601-5809
ahima.org

# Contents

Exam 1 Multiple Choice and Multiple Select Questions and Answers
Exam 2 Multiple Choice and Multiple Select Questions and Answers
Exam 3 Multiple Choice and Multiple Select Questions and Answers
Exam 4 Multiple Choice and Multiple Select Questions and Answers
Practice Cases

# About the Authors

**Carol A. Venable, MPH, RHIA, FAHIMA**, is a retired professor and the former HIM department head from the University of Louisiana at Lafayette. **Anita C. Hazelwood, MLS, RHIA, FAHIMA**, is a professor and the HIM program director at the same university. Carol and Anita have co-authored two AHIMA books titled *Diagnostic Coding for Physician Services: ICD-10* and *ICD-10-CM Preview* and were contributing authors for the *Clinical Coding Workout* in 2011. Both were the recipient of the AHIMA Legacy Award for one of their publications, and both are Fellows of the American Health Information Management Association.

Both authors have conducted numerous coding workshops at the local, state, and national levels. Moreover, they have published articles in *Educational Perspectives in Health Information Management*, in addition to serving on its editorial review board, and in the *Journal of AHIMA*.

Active volunteers of AHIMA, Ms. Venable and Ms. Hazelwood were members of the Fellowship Committee and held various other AHIMA committee appointments.

**Lynn Kuehn, MS, RHIA, CCS-P, FAHIMA**, is president of Kuehn Consulting in Waukesha, Wisconsin. Previously, she was director of office operations for Children's Medical Group in Milwaukee. Additionally, she has served in health information management and coordination positions in a variety of healthcare settings. In her volunteer role, Ms. Kuehn has served as secretary and chair of the Ambulatory Care Section of AHIMA and the chair of several national committees. She was a member of the AHIMA Board of Directors for 2005–2007 and chair of the Board of Directors of the AHIMA Foundation from 2011–2012. Moreover, she has been active as a presenter at numerous meetings and seminars in the field of physician office management, coding, and reimbursement. Previous AHIMA publications include *Procedural Coding and Reimbursement for Physician Services, ICD-10-PCS: An Applied Approach 2014*; *Effective Management of Coding Services*, which she edited with Lou Ann Schraffenberger; *Documentation and Reimbursement for Physician Offices*, which she coauthored with LaVonne Wieland; and *The Learning Guide for Ambulatory Care*. Ms. Kuehn has been the recipient of the AHIMA Educator-Practitioner Award and the Wisconsin Health Information Management Association Distinguished Member Award. She holds an MS in health services administration and a BS in medical record administration, is a certified coding specialist–physician-based, and is a Fellow of the American Health Information Management Association.

# Preface

Welcome to the pages of *CCS–P Exam Preparation* manual, which is designed to help you study for the certified coding specialist–physician-based (CCS–P) exam. To become a physician-based coder, proficiency in assigning numeric codes for each diagnosis and procedure, in-depth knowledge of the Current Procedural Terminology (CPT) coding system, and familiarity with the *International Classification of Diseases, Tenth Revision, Clinical Modification* (ICD-10-CM) and Healthcare Common Procedure Coding System (HCPCS) Level II coding systems must be in place. This manual will help you identify less competent areas for further study. However, if at this point in your endeavor, this knowledge base is not as solidly understood as it should be, it is advisable to obtain copies of the following AHIMA publications for study,:

- *Diagnostic Coding for Physician Services*, 2014 Edition (Hazelwood and Venable)
- *Procedural Coding and Reimbursement for Physician Services: Applying Current Procedural Terminology and HCPCS*, 2015 Edition (Kuehn)

Other AHIMA publications cover topics such as health information documentation, data integrity and quality, and additional key areas of expertise required by the coder in the physician practice (available at AHIMA's webstore: ahimastore.org).

To fully prepare for the CCS–P exam, consult AHIMA's Certification website (ahima.org/certification) to check eligibility requirements, download and submit an exam application, see sample test questions and screenshots of the exam format, view a list of study resources, and find out more about exam day procedures, including which code books to bring.

The CCS–P exam assesses mastery-level knowledge or proficiency in coding rather than entry-level skills. The certification exam is based on an explicit set of competencies that have been determined by job analysis of coders in physician-based practices. Those competencies are subdivided into domains and tasks that include, in particular, health information documentation, ICD-10-CM diagnosis coding, CPT and HCPCS II coding, as well as reimbursement, data quality and analysis, information and communication technologies, and compliance and regulatory issues. Thorough preparation for taking the CCS–P exam requires that you have already successfully encountered questions in each of these domains. The practice medical case questions require diagnostic (ICD-10-CM) coding in all specialties and procedural (CPT and HCPCS Level II) coding for physician services.

Clearly, the best preparation for the exam is your education. We offer this manual as your guide to success on the CCS–P exam. We have used our collective expertise to compile questions that are aligned to the content areas currently featured in exam questions. The variety of questions ensures the reader of experience with all approaches.

Congratulations! You've chosen to earn credentials in what is forecast to be a favorable professional field. Get ready to study.

# About the CCS–P Exam

The CCS–P is a coding practitioner with expertise in physician-based settings such as physician offices, group practices, multispecialty clinics, or specialty centers. This coding practitioner reviews patients' records and assigns numeric codes for each diagnosis and procedure. To perform this task, an individual must possess in-depth knowledge of the CPT coding system and familiarity with the ICD-10-CM and HCPCS level II coding systems. The CCS–P is also expert in health information documentation, data integrity, and quality. Because patients' coded data are submitted to insurance companies or the government for expense reimbursement, the CCS–P plays a critical role in the health provider's business operation.

The CCS–P certification exam assesses mastery or proficiency in coding rather than entry-level skills. If you perform coding in a doctor's office, clinic, or similar setting, you should consider obtaining the CCS–P certification to attest to your ability.

To help you study for the exam, *CCS–P Exam Preparation* provides a practice exam and three additional exams that each include 8 medical records from the hospital, emergency room, operating room, and physician office/clinic settings for medical coding fill-in-the-blank practice. In addition, each of these exams includes 96 single-response multiple choice questions to model the exam experience.

The National Commission for Certifying Agencies (NCCA) has granted accreditation to AHIMA's CCS–P certification program for demonstrating compliance with the NCCA Standards for the Accreditation of Certification Programs. NCCA is the accrediting body of the Institute for Credentialing Excellence (formerly the National Organization for Competency Assurance).

The NCCA Standards were created in 1977 and updated in 2003 to ensure that certification programs adhere to modern standards of practice for the certification industry. AHIMA joins an elite group of more than 100 organizations representing more than 200 programs that have received and maintained NCCA accreditation. More information on the NCCA is available at www.credentialingexcellence.org/ncca.

## Exam Competency Statements

The CCS–P certification exam is based on an explicit set of competencies. These competencies were determined by job analysis surveys of physician-based coders. Exams test only content pertaining to the following competencies:

### Domain I: Health Information Documentation (8–12%)

1. Interpret health record documentation using knowledge of anatomy, physiology, clinical indicators and disease processes, pharmacology, and medical terminology to identify codeable diagnoses and/or procedures.
2. Determine when additional clinical documentation is needed to assign and/or validate the diagnosis and/or procedure code(s).
3. Consult with physicians and other healthcare providers to obtain further clinical documentation to assist with code assignment.
4. Consult reference materials to facilitate code assignment.
5. Identify patient encounter type.
6. Identify and post charges for healthcare services based on documentation.

## Domain II: Diagnosis and Procedure Coding (60–64%)

## Diagnosis:

1. Interpret conventions, formats, instructional notations, tables, and definitions of the classification system to select diagnoses, conditions, problems, or other reasons for the encounter that require coding.
2. Select the diagnoses that require coding according to current coding and reporting requirements for outpatient services.
3. Sequence diagnoses and other reasons to encounter according to notations and conventions of the classification system and standard data set definitions.
4. Apply the official ICD-10-CM coding guidelines.

## Procedure:

1. Interpret conventions, formats, instructional notations, and definitions of the classification system and/or nomenclature to select procedures/services that require coding.
2. Select the procedures that require coding according to current reporting requirements for professional services in any setting.
3. Sequence procedures according to notations and conventions of the classification system/ nomenclature and standard data set definitions.
4. Apply the official CPT/HCPCS Level II coding guidelines.

## Domain III: Regulatory Guidelines and Reporting Requirements for Outpatient Services (8–12%)

1. Select the reason for encounter, pertinent secondary conditions, primary procedure, and other procedures that require coding according to CPT Assistant, *Coding Clinic for ICD-10-CM*, and HCPCS.
2. Apply appropriate reporting requirements:
   a. Modifiers
   b. CPT/HCPCS Level II
   c. Evaluation and Management code assignment
3. Validate medical necessity for appropriate relationships between diagnosis and coded procedures/services.

## Domain IV: Data Quality and Management (5–7%)

1. Review the results of aggregate coded data as required.
2. Communicate with healthcare providers regarding reimbursement methodologies, documentation rules, and regulations related to coding.
3. Analyze health record documentation for quality and completeness of coding.
4. Review the accuracy of abstracted data elements for database integrity and claims processing.
5. Resolve coding edits such as National Correct Coding Initiative (NCCI).

## Domain V: Information and Communication Technologies (2–4%)

1. Use computer and mobile devices (tablet, hand-held, etc.) to ensure data collection, storage, analysis, and reporting of information.
2. Use common software applications and web-based applications in the execution of work processes.
3. Use specialized software in the completion of HIM processes.

## Domain VI: Privacy, Confidentiality, Legal, and Ethical Issues (4–6%)

1. Apply policies and procedures for access to and disclosure of personal health information.
2. Apply AHIMA Code of Ethics/Standards of Ethical Coding.
3. Report privacy and/or security concerns.
4. Protect data integrity and validity using software or hardware technology.

## Domain VII: Compliance (3–5%)

1. Evaluate the accuracy and completeness of the patient record as defined by organizational policy and external regulations and standards.
2. Monitor compliance with organization-wide coding guidelines.
3. Report compliance concerns.

## Exam Specifications

The current CCS–P certification exam consists of the following:
- 97 multiple choice questions covering all domains
- 8 medical record cases

The total testing time for the CCS–P exam is 4 hours with no breaks. Be sure to pace yourself during the exam and use your time wisely.

Review the Procedures for Coding the Medical Record Cases of the CCS–P Examination on page ix.

The Commission on Certification for Health Informatics and Information Management (CCHIIM) manages and sets the strategic direction for the certifications. Pearson Vue is the exclusive provider of AHIMA certification exams. To see sample questions and images of the new exam format, visit ahima.org/certification.

## What Books to Bring on Exam Day

Beginning October 19, 2015, candidates must bring the 2015 draft or 2016 edition of the ICD-10-CM code book and the 2015 version of the CPT code book and the HCPCS National Level II code book to the testing center. Only the American Medical Association CPT codebook is permitted. For a complete list of allowable ICD-10-CM code books, please see http://www.ahima.org/certification/ccsp. A medical dictionary is optional.

*Candidates without the required codebooks will not be permitted to test and will forfeit their application fee.* Candidates who do not bring all the required books or whose books do not have the correct year will not be allowed to test. **For the most up-to-date exam information, visit ahima.org/certification.**

# Procedures for Coding the Medical Record Cases of the CCS–P Examination

- Apply ICD-10-CM instructional notations and conventions and current approved Diagnostic Coding and Reporting Guidelines for Outpatient Services (Section IV of the official ICD-10-CM Guidelines for Coding and Reporting), to select diagnoses, conditions, problems, or other reasons for care that require ICD-10-CM coding in a physician-based encounter/visit either in a physician's office, clinic, outpatient area, emergency room, ambulatory surgery, or other ambulatory care setting. Code for professional services only.
- Sequencing is not required for the diagnoses or procedures.
- Apply the following directions to assign codes to secondary diagnoses:
  - Chronic diseases treated on an ongoing basis may be coded and reported as many times as the patient is receiving treatment and care for the condition(s).
  - Code all documented conditions that coexist at the time of the encounter/visit and that require or affect patient care, treatment, or management.
  - Conditions previously treated and no longer existing are not coded.
- Code for the professional services only and only for the physician designated on the cover sheet for each individual case.
- Assign two-character Level II (HCPCS/National) codes for all appropriate services.
- Assign CPT codes for anesthetic procedures listed in the anesthesia section only if indicated on the case cover sheet.
- Assign CPT codes for medical services/procedures based on current CPT guidelines.
- Confirm Evaluation and Management (E/M) codes based on the information provided in the box for each case.
  *For the purposes of this examination, do not challenge the level of key components chosen. You will not be expected to assign the level of history, examinations, and medical decision-making.*
- Assign CPT codes for radiology and pathology/laboratory procedures listed in the radiology and pathology/laboratory sections only when applicable.
- Assign CPT codes from the medicine section based on current CPT guidelines.
- Assign five-digit HCPCS Level II National (alphanumeric) codes, as appropriate.
- Do not assign ICD-10-CM External Causes of Morbidity codes (V00-V99 Chapter 20).
- Assign ICD-10-CM Factors Influencing Health Status and Contact with Health Services codes (Z00-Z99 Chapter 21) as appropriate.
- Do not assign ICD-10-PCS codes.
- Do not assign Category II or Category III CPT codes.

For the most up-to-date exam information, visit ahima.org/certification.

## How to Use This Book and Online Assessments

The CCS–P practice questions and practice exams in this book and on the accompanying online assessments test knowledge of content pertaining to the CCS–P competencies published by AHIMA. This book contains four complete practice exams, each made up of 96 single-response multiple choice questions and 8 medical cases. Each multiple choice question is identified by a CCS–P domain, so you will be able to determine whether you need knowledge or skill building in particular areas of the exam competencies. All answers include a rationale and corresponding reference. Pursuing these references will help you build your knowledge and skills in specific domains.

To most effectively use this book, work through each practice exam and try to do so in the allotted exam time—four hours. Identify areas in which you may need further preparation. For the questions that you answer incorrectly, read the associated references to help refresh your knowledge.

## About the Online Assessments

The self-scoring practice questions can be set to be presented in random order, or you may choose to go through the questions in sequential order by domain. You may also choose to practice or test your skills on specific domains. For example, if you would like to build your coding skills in domains II and III, you may choose only those domains' multiple choice and multiple select questions for a given practice session.

# Acknowledgments

The authors and AHIMA Press would like to acknowledge Jennifer Hornung Garvin, PhD, MBA, RHIA, CCS, CPHQ, CTR, FAHIMA, for contributing content to the Domain III questions included in this edition.

The authors would also like to thank Ann Barta, MSA, RHIA, CDIP; Theresa Rihanek, MHA, RHIA, CCS; and Kimberly A. Stevens CPC, CCS-P, CPCO, CPMA, CMSCS for their reviews.

# Introduction

This publication is designed to help the reader prepare for the AHIMA Certified Coding Specialist Physician-Based (CCS-P) examination. There are four practice exams which include practice questions and medical cases for each of the seven domains included in the exam:

1. Health Information Documentation (8–12%)
2. Diagnosis and/or Procedure Coding (60–64%)
3. Regulatory Guidelines and Reporting Requirements for Outpatient Services (8–12%)
4. Data Quality and Management (5–7%)
5. Information and Communication Technologies (2–4%)
6. Privacy, Confidentiality, Legal, and Ethical Issues (4–6%)
7. Compliance (3–5%)

The actual CCS-P exam includes ninety-seven (97) multiple choice questions and eight (8) medical record cases. This exam must be completed in four hours. The most difficult part of preparation is developing enough speed and stamina to answer the questions in the allotted time. Proper preparation should also include an assessment of the candidate's strengths and weaknesses throughout the domains. If weaknesses in a domain are already known, then a review of that material prior to the practice exams may be useful.

This CCS-P Exam Preparation book contains the following content:

1. Exam #1 - 96 multiple choice questions and 8 medical cases
2. Exam #2 - 96 multiple choice questions and 8 medical cases
3. Exam #3 - 96 multiple choice questions and 8 medical cases
4. Exam #4 - 96 multiple choice questions and 8 medical cases

This introduction also includes 20 additional practice medical cases.

After working through each of the four exams in the book, candidates should have an assessment of their knowledge of the material contained in the domains covered by the exam.

The following sections will review study topics for each domain covered by the exam. In addition, candidates should review the books and websites listed in the reference list located at the back of the book.

1. **Health Information Documentation (8–12%)**

   Students should be prepared to answer questions regarding the following types of tasks:

   a. Interpret health record documentation using knowledge of anatomy, physiology, clinical indicators and disease processes, pharmacology and medical terminology to identify codeable diagnoses and/or procedures
   b. Determine when additional clinical documentation is needed to assign the diagnosis or procedure code(s)
   c. Consult with physicians and other healthcare providers to obtain further clinical documentation to assist with code assignment
   d. Identify patient encounter type
   e. Identify and post charges for healthcare services based on documentation

2. **Diagnosis and/or Procedure Coding (60–64%)**

This portion of the exam is primarily focused on diagnosis and procedure coding which is done in a physician's office setting.

Students should be prepared to answer questions regarding the following types of tasks:

**Diagnosis:**

a.  Interpret conventions, formats, instructional notations, tables, and definitions of the classification system to select diagnoses, conditions, problems, or other reasons for the encounter that require coding

b.  Select the diagnoses that require coding according to current coding and reporting requirements for outpatient services

c.  Sequence diagnoses and other reasons for encounter according to notations and conventions of the classification system and standard date set definitions

d.  Apply the official ICD-10-CM coding guidelines

**Procedure:**

a.  Interpret conventions, formats, instructional notations, and definitions of the classification system and/or nomenclature to select procedures/services that require coding

b.  Select the procedures that require coding according to current reporting requirements for professional services in any setting

c.  Sequence procedures according to notations and conventions of the classification system/nomenclature and standard data set definitions

d.  Apply the official CPT/HCPCS Level II coding guidelines

3. **Regulatory Guidelines and Reporting Requirements for Outpatient Services (8–12%)**

Students should be prepared to answer questions regarding the following types of tasks:

a.  Select the reason for encounter, pertinent secondary conditions, primary procedure, and other procedures that require coding according to CPT Assistant, Coding Clinic, and HCPCS

b.  Apply appropriate reporting requirements:
    1.  Modifiers
    2.  CPT/HCPCS Level II
    3.  Evaluation and Management code assignment

c.  Validate medical necessity for appropriate relationships between diagnosis and coded procedures/services

4. **Data Quality and Management (5–7%)**

Students should be prepared to answer questions regarding the following types of tasks:

a.  Review the results of aggregate coded data as required

b.  Communicate with healthcare providers regarding reimbursement methodologies, documentation rules, and regulations related to coding

c.  Analyze health record documentation for quality and completeness of coding

d.  Review the accuracy of abstracted data elements for database integrity and claims processing

e.  Resolve coding edits such as National Correct Coding Initiative (NCCI)

5. **Information and Communication Technologies (2–4%)**
   Students should be prepared to answer questions regarding the following types of tasks:

   a. Use computer and mobile devices (tablet, handheld, etc.) to ensure data collection, storage, analysis, and reporting of information
   b. Use common software and web-based applications in the execution of work processes
   c. Use specialized software in the completion of HIM processes

6. **Privacy, Confidentiality, Legal, and Ethical Issues (4–6%)**
   Students should be prepared to answer questions regarding the following types of tasks:
   a. Apply policies and procedures for access and disclosure of protected health information
   b. Apply AHIMA Code of Ethics and Standards of Ethical Coding
   c. Report privacy or security concerns
   d. Protect data integrity and validity using software or hardware technology

7. **Compliance (3–5%)**
   Students should be prepared to answer questions regarding the following types of tasks:
   a. Evaluate the accuracy and completeness of the patient record as defined by organizational policy and external regulations and standards
   b. Monitor compliance with organization-wide coding guidelines
   c. Report compliance concerns
   In addition to a detailed reference list, an answer key is provided which fully explains the answers provided for all questions and medical record cases in the book.

# Additional Practice Cases

## PRACTICE—CASE 1

**PROCEDURE NOTE:**

**FINDINGS:** There was a 1.6 × 1.5-cm congenital defect of the right nasal sidewall that did not involve the alar cartilages. It did extend slightly onto the cheek.

**PROCEDURE:** After obtaining informed consent, the patient was taken into the operating room and placed in a supine position on the operating table. General anesthesia was induced via endotracheal intubation without difficulty. Approximately 2 mL of 1% lidocaine with 1:100,000 epinephrine was injected into the right conchal bowl and the right postauricular region. The face was prepped and draped in a sterile fashion. A surgical pause was performed to confirm the patient's identity and site of surgery.

A skin incision was made in the conchal bowl on the right-hand side, and a piece of conchal bowl cartilage measuring approximately 1 × 1.5 cm was harvested and placed in saline to be used as a strut along the right lateral sidewall. This incision was closed using 6-0 fast-absorbing gut.

A piece of foil was used to create a template of the defect in the nose. A full-thickness skin graft matching to the shape of a template was harvested from the right postauricular region. The cartilage was then placed along the lateral sidewall and secured in place with a single through-and-through fast-absorbing gut suture. The central portion of the full-thickness skin graft was also secured with a fast-absorbing gut suture to the central portion of the nasal defect. The perimeter of the graft was then sutured to the nose using interrupted 6-0 nylon suture.

Once the graft had been sutured in place, the harvested site in the postauricular region was expanded into an elliptical-shaped defect by removing some skin superior and inferior to the harvest site itself. Undermining was performed primarily in the posterior direction of the skin under the hairline. Minimal undermining was done of the skin anteriorly toward the pinna of the ear. Hemostasis was obtained after the undermining, and this harvest site incision was closed using 4-0 Vicryl and 5-0 nylon. A small pressure dressing was applied to the right side of the nose, and a Glasscock mastoid dressing was placed on the right ear.

The patient was then awakened from the anesthetic, extubated, and transported to the recovery room with stable vital signs and no evidence of stridor.

*Enter one diagnosis code and two procedure codes.*

**DX1**

**PR1**

**PR2**

## PRACTICE—CASE 2

**PREOPERATIVE DIAGNOSIS:** Nontraumatic right hip labral tear

**POSTOPERATIVE DIAGNOSIS:** Nontraumatic right hip labral tear

**ANESTHESIA:** General endotracheal

**PROCEDURE:** Right hip arthroscopic labral debridement

**COMPLICATIONS:** None

**DRAINS:** None

**ESTIMATED BLOOD LOSS:** Minimal

**PROPHYLAXIS:** Ancef

**OPERATIVE FINDINGS:** The patient was noted to have a labral tear in the superior portion of the acetabular labrum with a frayed portion of the labrum hanging down inferiorly. Also noted to have some tearing of the tissue along the pulvinar at the attachment of the ligamentum along the acetabular side as well. No articular lesions seen. No loose bodies seen. No other significant findings.

**INDICATION FOR PROCEDURE:** The patient is a 22-year-old female complaining of right hip pain. MRI confirms evidence of a labral tear. The patient also had a diagnostic injection with relief of pain and requires a right hip arthroscopic labral debridement versus repair. I discussed with the patient all risks, benefits, alternatives, and complications of the procedure including, but not limited to, infection, bleeding, damage to nerves or blood vessels, failure to relieve hip pain, decreased range of motion, reaction to anesthesia, etc. She understands and would like to proceed with operative intervention. All questions were answered. Consent is signed and on the chart prior to the start of the procedure.

**PROCEDURE IN DETAIL:** After the patient indicated that the right hip was the correct operative site, it was marked in the pre-op holding area by the surgeon. The patient was then taken to the operating room and placed in the supine position on the Chick table with all bony prominences adequately padded. Perineal post was placed. A Foley catheter was placed. The patient was placed in boots bilaterally, and traction was applied with the patient's hip in slight abduction and neutral rotation. Fluoroscopic images done by Radiology demonstrated an appropriate distraction. Traction was then let off. The right hip and lower extremity were then prepped and draped in the normal sterile fashion. Traction was applied, and time out was called in the room prior to incision. Next using fluoroscopic guidance, a spinal needle was passed at the anterolateral portal staying just anterior to the greater trochanter approximately 2 cm. Spinal needle was easily advanced into the hip joint. Hip articulation with an air arthrogram was achieved under fluoroscopy. Next, Nitinol wire was passed through this needle into the hip joint and after making an incision with an 11 blade and having infiltrated the joint with saline with good return, a trocar was then advanced into the hip articulation with a 5.5 cannula placed. Arthroscope was then placed, and diagnostic arthroscopy was performed with the above mentioned findings. Next, at the intersection of the greater trochanter and anterior superior iliac spine at the anterior portal needle localization under direct visualization was done, noting good placement within the hip joint. Through a percutaneous incision once again, another 5.5 cannula was placed and a soft tissue shaver and electrocautery were then used to debride the frayed tissue at the pulvinar, as well as address the superior labral tear. This was probed and noted to have a flap tear particularly on the undersurface. Using both the flexible probe cautery as well as a curve and straight meniscal shaver through these cannulas by alternating between the anterolateral and anterior portals visualization as well as addressing this labral tear with debridement was accomplished successfully, debriding the labrum back to a stable rim. Remaining labrum was then probed and noted to be stable. The debridement was carried down onto the bone just on the undersurface of the labrum without injuring articular cartilage to allow for healing. Final arthroscopic images were obtained. After removal of these cannulas, traction was let down and portal sites were closed with 3-0 Vicryl subcutaneous sutures followed by Steri-Strips. Sterile dressing was applied. The patient was extubated in the operating room and transported to the recovery room without complication. All needle, sponge, and instrument counts were correct.

*Enter one diagnosis code and one procedure code.*

**DX1**

**PR1**

## PRACTICE — CASE 3

**MR #:** 353901

**ENDOSCOPY REPORT**

**PREOPERATIVE DIAGNOSIS:** Generalized abdominal pain

**POSTOPERATIVE DIAGNOSIS:** Grossly normal colonoscopy

**RELEVANT HISTORY AND PHYSICAL FINDINGS:**

**Abdominal pain for years, much improved recently on activia**

**MEDICATIONS:** None

**DIET MODIFICATIONS:** Daily Activia

The procedures were explained to the patient, including the purpose, risks, and benefits, and possible alternatives procedures were discussed. Consent was obtained. The planned procedures were confirmed with staff, and the patient's identity was confirmed.

The patient was placed under general anesthesia with ET by an anesthesiologist. Photos were taken throughout the procedure. The PCF 160AL was passed via anus. The anus was normally placed. No fissures were observed. No fistulas were observed. No skin tags, no hemorrhoids or rash. The scope was passed. The preparation of the colon at this point was good. The anatomy of the rectum was normal. The mucosa was normal in color and vascularity. Biopsies were taken. The sigmoid anatomy was normal. The mucosa was normal in color and vascularity. Biopsies were taken. Transcending and ascending were both normal appearing. Biopsies taken in the transverse. The cecum was normal. The ICV was visualized and was normal. The terminal ileum was entered. It appeared normal.

**COMPLICATIONS:** None

The patient was repositioned. The GIF 140 was placed in the mouth and advanced through the mouth and hypopharynx under direct vision. The hypopharynx and cords were normal. Mucosa in the body of the esophagus was normal. The diaphragmatic indentation was visible. The Z line was identified. Biopsies were taken.

The scope was advanced into the stomach, which was insufflated with air. The anatomy was normal. Mucosa of the body, antrum, and pylorus were normal. Biopsies were taken of the antrum and body. A turnaround procedure was performed. The gastroesophageal junction was normal. Biopsies were taken in the cardia.

The endoscope was advanced to the third portion of the duodenum. The ampulla of Vater was observed. The duodenal folds were normal. The mucosa was normal and velvety. Biopsies × 4 were taken in standard fashion with minimal traction of the duodenal mucosa away from the muscular wall. The jejunum was normal. The endoscope was withdrawn into the stomach, which was evacuated of air. The endoscope was removed.

**COMPLICATIONS:** None

**RESULTS:** Grossly normal colonoscopy and upper endoscopy

**DISPOSITION:** The patient was informed of the gross results of the exam. Biopsy results will be reported when received.

*Enter one diagnosis code and two procedure codes.*

**DX1**

**PR1**

**PR2**

## PRACTICE—CASE 4

**PREOPERATIVE DIAGNOSIS:** Acute respiratory failure, intracranial hemorrhage

**POSTOPERATIVE DIAGNOSIS:** Acute respiratory failure, intracranial hemorrhage

**PROCEDURE PERFORMED:** Tracheostomy

**ANESTHESIA TYPE:** General

**ESTIMATED BLOOD LOSS:** 10 mL

**HISTORY:** This is a 58-year-old female who presented with acute respiratory failure and intracranial hemorrhage. She has been on the ventilator and unable to support her ventilation without a mechanical ventilator. She is unable to be weaned from a ventilator and thus in need of a tracheostomy. The risks and benefits were explained to the family, and they consented to the procedure.

**PROCEDURE:** The patient was brought to the operating room and had preoperative antibiotics given prior to any incision. She had come down with the ET-tube, and this was hooked up to the ventilator by the anesthesia staff. She was prepped and draped in normal sterile fashion, and the anatomic landmarks of the thyroid cartilage and sternal notch were identified, as well as the cricothyroid membrane. About 1 fingerbreadth below the cricothyroid membrane, incision was made down to the level of the subcu tissue. Bovie electrocautery was used to dissect down through the platysma. Any venous bleeders were identified and tied off with silk suture. We then had good exposure of the trachea. We identified the third tracheal ring. We had the ICU staff deflate the balloon and we placed stay sutures laterally on both sides of the third tracheal ring. This was carried down from skin to the tracheal ring back up to the skin. We then reinflated the balloon and then when we were ready we deflate the balloon again and made a square incision around the third tracheal ring and removed this portion in a square fashion. We brought our ET-tube out proximally just proximal to this and used a tracheal spreader to dilate the trachea. We then placed a #8 Shiley tracheostomy tube without any difficulty, and the balloon was inflated. We then hooked our tracheostomy to the ventilator and received good end tidal C02. The patient was oxygenating at 100%, and her tidal volumes were equivalent to what they were preop with the ET-tube. There were no signs of bleeding, and good, hemostasis was achieved. The skin around the tracheostomy incision was closed in running fashion, and the tracheostomy was secured in four places with nylon suture. The Vicryl stay sutures were secured to the chest wall with Steri-Strips. The patient tolerated the procedure well and was taken to ICU in stable condition.

*Enter two diagnosis codes and one procedure code.*

**DX1**

**DX2**

**PR1**

## PRACTICE—CASE 5

**PREOPERATIVE DIAGNOSIS:** Carcinoma of the right breast, status post neoadjuvant chemotherapy

**POSTOPERATIVE DIAGNOSIS:** Carcinoma of the right breast, status post neoadjuvant chemotherapy

**PROCEDURE PERFORMED:** Right modified radical mastectomy, subsequent reconstruction

**PREOPERATIVE HISTORY:** The patient is an unfortunate 37-year-old woman who had a pregnancy-associated breast cancer of the right breast with extensive involvement of the breast, clinically a stage III breast cancer. She underwent neoadjuvant chemotherapy with a complete clinical response to therapy with no residual palpable tumor in the breast and no palpable adenopathy. She has elected to undergo a right modified radical mastectomy with reconstruction, and we are taking her to the operating room now.

**OPERATIVE NOTE:** The patient was taken to the operating room. General anesthesia was induced. A Foley catheter was inserted. Her arms were placed on pads. Her legs were placed on pads. Bear hugger was applied, and her entire upper torso was sterilely prepped and draped in usual fashion. Symmetric skin sparing mastectomy was planned incorporating the nipple-areolar complex. An elliptical incision was created incorporating the nipple-areolar complex. Flaps were raised from superior infraclavicular and a portion of the breast circumferentially to the midline and subsequently to the inframammary fold and subsequently out to the latissimus dorsi muscle. The breast was removed from the pectoralis major muscle incorporating the fascia, reflected laterally. The clavipectoral fascia was opened, and a level I and level II axillary lymph node dissection was performed, sparing the long thoracic and the thoracodorsal neurovascular bundle, as well as at least 1 intercostal brachial cutaneous nerve. There was no palpable adenopathy in level III. We dissected lymph nodes out from underneath the pectoralis major muscle and also from underneath the brachial vessels. The axillary dissection was truncated at its lowest extent. The breast and axilla were marked for orientation, weighed, and sent to pathology. Irrigation was performed. Hemostasis was achieved where necessary using some Surgiclips and electrocautery. There was no evidence of bleeding at the end of the case. At this point Dr. X took over for the reconstructive portion of the procedure. This completes our operative dictation.

*Enter two diagnosis codes and one procedure code.*

**DX1**

**DX2**

**PR1**

## PRACTICE—CASE 6

*Please code for the services of the physician.*

**INPATIENT PULMONARY CONSULTATION:**

The patient was seen and examined by the intensive care unit house staff. Please see their note for further details. He is post-trauma day 7. Some of his injuries include right acetabulum fracture, right open talus, manubrium rib fracture, mediastinal hematoma, and pulmonary contusion.

This morning, the patient was initially a GCS of 7. We held his sedation. He did wake up and followed some intermittent commands. He is currently on morphine at 2 mg/hour and Ativan at 2 mg/hour.

His lungs are coarse bilaterally. He is on assist control, rate of 12, tidal volume 600, PEEP of 10, FIO2 of 0.4. His saturations have been greater than 96%. He persists in acute respiratory failure; however, his AA gradient has been improving and we will attempt to decrease his PEEP today. Patient has a pulmonary contusion which I will continue to monitor.

**CARDIOVASCULAR:** His pulse is 80 to 115, blood pressure 100 to 130/60 to 80. He is in sinus tachycardia on examination.

**RENAL/FLUID/ELECTROLYTES:** He had 3.4 liters in and 2.4 liters out. His glucoses have been well controlled with EndoTool. His electrolytes are all within normal limits. His abdomen is much less distended than it has been over the previous several days. He is receiving tube feeds at 65 cc/hour. He has had four bowel movements.

**HEMATOLOGY:** His hemoglobin is stable at 10. His platelet count is 225. He has on SCDs and is receiving Lovenox for DVT prophylaxis. T-max is 101.3. There is a much improved temperature curve and his white blood cell count is down to 11 from 12. He is currently on Linezolid and tobramycin. His BAL from 09/09 grew out *Haemophilus influenzae* and now yeast. His urine and blood cultures from 09/12 are negative. We will start Diflucan today. We will also send stool for C-diff. We will await final cultures from BAL prior to discontinuing Linezolid. We will continue tobramycin for treatment of his *Haemophilus influenzae*.

I spent over 30 minutes at this patient's bedside assessing him and making critical care decisions.

**ASSESSMENT:**

1. *Haemeophilus influenza*
2. Candida of lung

---

*Enter four diagnosis codes and one procedure code.*

DX1 [                    ]

DX2 [                    ]

DX3 [                    ]

DX4 [                    ]

PR1 [                    ]

## PRACTICE—CASE 7

*Please code for the services of the surgeon.*

**DATE OF BIRTH:** 08/30/1949

**ADMISSION DATE:** 12/13/20XX

**SURGERY DATE:** 12/13/20XX

**PREOPERATIVE DIAGNOSIS:** Thyroid nodule

**POSTOPERATIVE DIAGNOSIS:** Necrotic thyroid nodule, Hashimoto's thyroiditis based on frozen section.

**PROCEDURE:** Right thyroid lobectomy and frozen section

**ESTIMATED BLOOD LOSS:** 30 mL

With adequate sedation in the operating room, the patient was given a general anesthetic. The patient was positioned and prepared and draped for thyroidectomy. A collar incision was performed after the skin was appropriately marked for symmetry. The skin, subcutaneous tissue, and platysmal muscle were divided, and then superior-inferior flaps were developed behind the platysmal muscle. The strap muscles were separated in the midline. There was a dominant nodule in the right lobe of the thyroid. The left lobe appeared grossly normal, although slightly enlarged and fleshy. Previous imaging had demonstrated some cystic change in the left lobe as well, but this was not apparent on gross examination. The right thyroid lobe was mobilized first by double ligating the superior thyroid vessels and then transected, and the thyroid gland mobilized. The parathyroid glands were not definitely visualized, but care was taken to dissect exactly on the capsule of the thyroid lobe. The recurrent laryngeal nerve was carefully identified and preserved. The inferior thyroidal vessels were clamped, transected, and ligated. Other bleeders were identified and secured with ligatures of 3-0 silk as well. The isthmus was transected and transfixed with two transfixion stitches of 3-0 silk. Hemostasis was then satisfactory. Frozen section revealed a mass with a necrotic center and a thin wall, which showed no malignant change. Permanent sections pending. The strap muscles were then approximated in the midline with a running simple stitch of 3-0 Vicryl. The platysmal muscle was approximated with interrupted simple stitches of 3-0 Vicryl and the skin was closed with 4-0 Vicryl. A sterile dressing was applied, and the patient left the operating room in satisfactory condition having tolerated the procedure satisfactorily.

*Enter one diagnosis code and one procedure code.*

**DX1**

**PR1**

## PRACTICE—CASE 8

*Please code for the services of the surgeon.*

**PREOPERATIVE DIAGNOSIS:** End-stage renal disease; Dialysis dependence

**POSTOPERATIVE DIAGNOSIS:** End-stage renal disease; Dialysis dependence

**OPERATION:** Left brachiocephalic arteriovenous fistula

**ESTIMATED BLOOD LOSS:** Less than 25 cc

**COMPLICATIONS:** None

**PROCEDURE:** The patient was taken to the operating room and placed in the supine position, where his left arm was placed on an arm board and prepared and draped in the usual sterile fashion. He was given intravenous sedation and a local anesthetic using 1% lidocaine. After infiltration of the area just above the antecubital fossa, an incision was made between the brachial artery and the cephalic vein and approximately 1 cm beyond the antecubital fossa proximally toward the shoulder. This was carried down through the skin and subcutaneous tissues to the level of the fascia. The fascia was identified, and dissection was continued laterally and medially to expose the cephalic vein, which was noted to have a medial branch that was large and clotted and a lateral branch that was a little smaller but clearly open. We traced the cephalic vein distally and proximally and developed enough mobility of the vein with ligation of branches and surrounding tissues to be able to move it toward the brachial artery for close approximation for anastomosis. Attention was then turned to the brachial artery, which was identified in a somewhat deep position in the medial aspect of the elbow and was noted to be relatively small with a diameter of around 4 to 5 mm. It had some mild disease in the arterial wall; however, after ligation of a single small branch, we were able to get elevation of approximately 2.5 cm of the artery. This provided adequate exposure for the arteriotomy and for proximal and distal occlusion. The patient then had amputation and ligation of the cephalic vein distally with the cut end being brought over to the artery. The artery itself was opened with a #11 blade after proximal and distal occlusion, and approximately 6 mm of anastomosis was performed in running fashion with 6-0 Prolene using the end of the spatulated cephalic vein to the side of the brachial artery. The patient tolerated this procedure very well. The anastomosis, once completed, did not bleed, and there was a good thrill in the vein. After inspection, there was no evidence of any significant obstruction to the vein course and no kinking that would cause any problems with development of the fistula.

At this point, we infiltrated the wounds with 0.25% Marcaine for postoperative anesthesia and closed the wounds with interrupted 3-0 Vicryl for the subcutaneous tissues and running 4-0 Monocryl for the skin. Sponge and needle counts were correct, and the patient was taken to recovery without incident with plan for discharge.

---

*Enter two diagnosis codes and one procedure code.*

**DX1**

**DX2**

**PR1**

## PRACTICE—CASE 9

*Please code for the services of the physician and the office.*

**DATE OF PROCEDURE:** 03/07/20XX

**HISTORY:** This is a 59-year-old man with metastatic lung cancer who presented for EEG in the office with a diagnosis of status epilepticus on March 3, 20XX.

**CONDITIONS:** This is an 18-channel EEG done using the 10–20 system electrode placement. During the study, the patient was not able to follow commands and at times he groaned and yawned throughout this examination.

**FINDINGS:** The EEG begins with the patient's eyes closed and there is a posterior dominant rhythm of 7 on the left and 7 on the right. Photic stimulation and hyperventilation were not done. Sleep was not obtained. There was some left temporal slowing shown in leads T5-01 and FP1-F3. There was no epileptiform activity seen.

**IMPRESSION:** This is an abnormal EEG due to the slowing seen on the left temporofrontal area.

---

*Enter three diagnosis codes and one procedure code.*

**DX1**

**DX2**

**DX3**

**PR1**

## PRACTICE—CASE 10

*Please code for the services of the physician (professional) but do not assign a modifier.*

**REASON FOR EXAMINATION:** Fourth nerve palsy

**RESULTS:**

**CLINICAL HISTORY:** Left fourth nerve palsy

**EXAMINATION:** MRI brain with and without contrast 1/18/20XX

**COMPARISON:** None

**TECHNIQUE:** Thin section axial T1, axial T2, T2, FLAIR, diffusion, ADC, and coronal T2, T1. Postcontrast T1 axial, thin section T1, sagittal, and coronal. 3 cc of gadolinium was used.

Sedation was provided by anesthesia.

**FINDINGS:** No midline shift. No mass in the brain or brainstem. No abnormal signal in the brainstem. No abnormal signal or enhancement in the expected course of the fourth cranial nerves. Mild prominence of the supratentorial subarachnoid spaces. Third ventricle is mildly prominent. Lateral and fourth ventricles are normal. No mass or obstructing lesion in the aqueduct or tectum.

There are two ovoid, cystic foci in the periventricular white matter measuring 10 mm × 3 mm adjacent to the atria of the left lateral ventricle, likely prominent perivascular spaces.

No evidence of acute infarct on diffusion-weighted sequences.

No Chiari malformation. Normal corpus callosum. Normal myelination for age.

Paranasal sinuses and orbits are normal. There is diffuse high T2 signal in the mastoid air cells.

**IMPRESSION:**

1. Fourth cranial nerve palsy. No mass or abnormal signal in the brainstem. No abnormal signal or enhancement in the expected course of the fourth cranial nerves.

2. Mild prominence of the supratentorial subarachnoid spaces with mildly enlarged third ventricle and normal lateral and fourth ventricles. No obstructing mass identified, although communicating hydrocephalus could have this appearance.

*Enter one diagnosis code and one procedure code.*

**DX1**

**PR1**

## PRACTICE—CASE 11

*Please code for the services of the physician.*

**ESTABLISHED PATIENT**

**HISTORY OF PRESENT ILLNESS:** The patient is a 7-year-old boy who presents today with his mother due to jamming his finger in the door this morning. He caught his right middle finger in the door leading to his garage. It occurred about 40 minutes prior to his arrival at the clinic.

**PHYSICAL EXAMINATION:** Temperature 98.4, pulse 79, respirations 14, blood pressure 90/60. Heart has a regular rate and rhythm. Lungs are clear to auscultation. Abdomen is soft. The patient is alert and resting on his back on the examination table. Examination of the right middle finger shows some swelling and a flap of skin to the distal right middle finger that is raised. There appears to be no involvement of the nail bed itself, no subungual hematoma present. Distal extremity is neurovascularly intact.

**RADIOGRAPHS:** X-rays done on the right middle finger done at the imaging center do not demonstrate any fracture to the distal tip. Await official report of radiology.

**PROCEDURE:** The patient was taken to the procedure room. Informed consent was obtained from the patient's mother, and she gave permission for laceration repair. He was placed in a supine position, and a digital block was performed with 2 mL of 2% lidocaine. The area was then cleansed and irrigated with copious amounts of sterile saline. The area was then draped in a sterile fashion and three 5-0 Ethilon interrupted sutures were placed to realign the 1-cm flap. Dressing was applied and patient tolerated it well.

**ASSESSMENT:** Laceration of the right middle finger

**PLAN:**

1.  Status post repair.

2.  Wound care directions were given. The patient will follow up in 7 to 10 days for suture removal or sooner if any condition worsens or problems arise.

**HISTORY:** Problem-focused

**EXAMINATION:** Detailed

**MEDICAL DECISION MAKING:** Low

*Enter one diagnosis code and two procedure codes.*

**DX1**

**PR1**

**PR2**

## PRACTICE—CASE 12

*Please code for the services of the physician.*

**CHIEF COMPLAINT:** Hematuria in a new patient

**HISTORY OF PRESENT ILLNESS:** Patient is a 36-year-old woman who presents to my office with acute onset of hematuria within the last 6 to 8 hours. However, over the last 2 days the patient has noted urinary pressure, urinary frequency, dysuria, and chills, although she denies any true rigors. She has not had any identifiable fever. She has mild low central abdominal discomfort but has had no nausea or vomiting. She has not noted changes in her bowel habits.

**PAST MEDICAL HISTORY:** Notable for arthritis in her right foot. There is no history of diabetes, ischemic heart disease, or hypertension. Has a significant history of schizophrenia.

**SURGICAL HISTORY:** She is status post corrective surgery on her right foot, status post operative procedure on her cervix, and status post cyst removal at her right ankle.

**CURRENT MEDICATIONS:** Ibuprofen p.r.n.

**ALLERGIES:** Noted to PENICILLIN and SULFA

**SOCIAL HISTORY:** The patient lives independently. She smokes approximately 1/2 pack of cigarettes per day and denies excessive ethanol use.

**REVIEW OF SYSTEMS:**

**GENERAL:** Negative for any documented fevers, but the patient does report some chills. Her p.o. intake has been normal, and no weight loss described.

**GI:** See HPI

**GU:** See HPI

**GYN:** No unusual vaginal discharge or bleeding. The patient is sexually active. Does not believe she is pregnant.

**PHYSICAL EXAMINATION:**

**VITAL SIGNS:** Blood pressure 111/68. Pulse is 86, Respiration is 20, Temperature is 97.8

**GENERAL:** The patient is awake, alert, nontoxic, in no acute distress.

**HEENT:** Was unremarkable

**NECK:** Supple

**LUNGS:** Breath sounds clear and symmetric

**CARDIAC:** Regular S2, S2. No murmur or gallop appreciated.

**ABDOMEN:** Soft, nontender in the upper regions with some minimal suprapubic tenderness. There are no masses, organomegaly, or peritoneal signs present, and no tenderness present.

**EXTREMITIES:** No deformities, clubbing, or edema. Pulses full and symmetric throughout.

**SKIN:** Warm and dry. No jaundice, pallor, or cyanosis noted. No skin rash is present.

**NEUROLOGIC:** The patient is alert, fully oriented. Pupils equal, round, and reactive to light. The remainder of her examination is nonfocal.

## PRACTICE—CASE 12 (*continued*)

A voided urine specimen was obtained for pregnancy testing, and an automated urinalysis was done. Pregnancy test was negative, and the urinalysis demonstrated specific gravity of less than 1.005 with large occult blood and a large leukocyte esterase. Microscopy revealed 3 to 5 red blood cells were seen with greater than 100 red blood cells, and only an occasional squamous cell noted.

The results of her urinalysis and my findings and recommendations were discussed with the patient in detail. She was given Levaquin 500 mg orally in the office and a prescription for 5 additional days worth. I recommended she drink plenty of fluids. Pyridium 100 mg, 1 to 2 q. 8 hours p.r.n. was prescribed for discomfort, and two tablets of Pyridium given to the patient for her use overnight. Patient was significantly agitated due to her ongoing schizophrenia. Patient was recommended to follow up with me in 3 to 5 days if not significantly improved.

**DIAGNOSES:** Acute urinary tract infection. Schizophrenia.

**HISTORY:** Extended problem-focused

**EXAMINATION:** Comprehensive

**MEDICAL DECISION MAKING:** Moderate

---

*Enter two diagnosis codes and three procedure codes.*

**DX1**

**DX2**

**PR1**

**PR2**

**PR3**

## PRACTICE—CASE 13

*Please code for the services of the surgeon.*

**DATE OF OPERATION:** 09/25/20XX

**PREOPERATIVE DIAGNOSES:**

1. Left facial skin tag

2. Left preauricular sinus

**POSTOPERATIVE DIAGNOSES:**

1. Left facial skin tag

2. Left preauricular sinus

**OPERATION:**

1. Excision of left facial skin tag

2. Excision of left preauricular sinus tract with wound closure 1.1 cm

**ANESTHESIA:** General endotracheal anesthesia

**FLUIDS:** Approximately 100 cc crystalloid

**ESTIMATED BLOOD LOSS:** Less than 5 cc

**URINE OUTPUT:** None

**CULTURES:** None

**DRAINS:** None

**SPECIMENS:**

1. Left facial skin tag

2. Left preauricular sinus

**FINDINGS:** 1.1 cm left preauricular sinus and approximately 1 cm left facial skin tag

**DESCRIPTION OF PROCEDURE:** The patient was brought to the operating room. General endotracheal anesthesia was introduced. The table was turned 90° counterclockwise. The skin and subcutaneous tissue around the sinus, as well as the left facial skin tag, were infiltrated with 0.5% Marcaine with 1:100,000 epinephrine. A total of 1.5 cc was used. The patient was then prepared and draped in the usual sterile fashion.

Attention was first turned to the sinus and a lacrimal probe was used to determine the extent and direction of the sinus. The tract was approximately 1.1 cm, and the outline was made with a marking pen followed by incision through the skin and dermis with a Weck blade. Sharpie scissors were then used to dissect down to the sinus capsule and dissect out the capsule until it was removed and blocked. Hemostasis was then achieved, and the wound was closed in three layers; one to obliterate the subcutaneous tissues with 4-0 Vicryl simple interrupted followed by a single deep dermal of 4-0 Vicryl and finally the skin was reapproximated with a 6-0 fast absorbing gut running subcuticular suture.

Attention was then turned to the skin tag, and it was removed with a single snip of tenotomy scissors. The resulting wound was then reapproximated with a single 6-0 fast absorbing gut simple interrupted suture. The wound was dressed with Tegaderm and care of the patient returned to the anesthesia team.

**COMPLICATIONS:** None

**DISPOSITION:** To the postanesthesia care unit

## PRACTICE—CASE 13 (*continued*)

**PATHOLOGY REPORT—EXAM 3 CASE 10**

**CLINICAL INFORMATION**

**PROCEDURE:** Excision of left preauricular skin tag and sinus

**PREOPERATIVE DIAGNOSIS:** Preauricular skin tag and sinus, left

**CLINICAL HISTORY:** None given

**GROSS DESCRIPTION:**

1. Received in formalin for routine examination designated LEFT PREAURICULAR SINUS is a tan irregular fragment of tissue measuring 0.8 × 0.3 × 0.2 cm. The entire specimen is submitted in cassette A.

2. Received in formalin for routine examination designated SKIN TAG, LEFT PRE-AURICULAR is a cone-shaped fragment of tissue lined by skin measuring 0.5 cm in length with a variable diameter from 0.2 cm at the base to 0.1 cm at the tip. The cut margin is inked black. The specimen is bisected, wrapped, and submitted in cassette B.

**MICROSCOPIC DESCRIPTION:**

1. Microscopic sections examined; description omitted.

2. The facial skin tag is covered by keratinizing squamous epithelium with underlying intact adnexal structures and a central core of skeletal muscle.

**DIAGNOSIS:**

1. LEFT PREAURICULAR SINUS, EXCISION: DERMOID SINUS

2. LEFT PREAURICULAR SKIN TAG, EXCISION: HAMARTOMATOUS MALFORMATION OF SKIN AND SKELETAL MUSCLE. SEE COMMENT

**COMMENT:** Although the pathology requisition identifies the resected skin tag as coming from the left preauricular region, the clinic note from 8/24/20XX instead indicates that this skin tag was located posterolateral to the lateral canthus of the left eye.

*Enter two diagnosis codes and three procedure codes.*

**DX1** [                    ]

**DX2** [                    ]

**PR1** [                    ]

**PR2** [                    ]

**PR3** [                    ]

## PRACTICE—CASE 14

*Please code for the services of the physician.*

**DIAGNOSIS:** s/p Tetralogy of Fallot repair

**INDICATIONS:** Palpitations

A two-channel Holter monitor was recorded for 23:59 hours. The predominant rhythm was sinus rhythm with sinus arrhythmia and wandering atrial pacemaker. Analysis of the recording revealed that the heart rate ranged from 70 to 145 bpm with an average heart rate of 99 bpm.

Supraventricular arrhythmias occurred. The mean frequency of supraventricular premature depolarizations was 0.7 beats per hour. The frequency ranged from 0 to 6 for a total of 16 beats. This represents <0.01% of the rhythm.

Supraventricular tachycardia occurred. 1 episode(s) occurred. The longest run was 3 beats. The fastest run was 118 bpm.

Ventricular arrhythmia did not occur. Ventricular couplets did not occur. Ventricular tachycardia did not occur. AV block did not occur. Bradycardia for patient's age was not recorded.

**ECG INTERVALS:** PR = 120 – 160 msec QRS = 120 msec QTc = 436–481 msec

No symptoms were recorded during the monitoring period.

**IMPRESSION:**

The quality of the tracing was good.

1. The predominant rhythm was normal sinus rhythm with sinus arrhythmia and wandering atrial pacemaker. Physiologic and circadian heart rate variation were mildly diminished. The heart rate ranged from 70 to 145 bpm, averaging 99 bpm.

2. Rare supraventricular premature beats occurred, comprising <0.01% of the total rhythm. There was 1 supraventricular couplet with a coupling interval of 0.560 msec.

3. Ventricular ectopy will not occur. Neither ventricular couplets nor runs occurred. VT did not occur.

4. Bradycardia did not occur. AV block did not occur.

5. No definite diagnosis identified.

*Enter three diagnosis codes and one procedure code.*

**DX1**

**DX2**

**DX3**

**PR1**

## PRACTICE—CASE 15

*Please code for the services of the laboratory.*

**LABORATORY RESULTS**

**CLINICAL HISTORY:** Hyperemesis gravidarum with electrolyte imbalance at 19 weeks' gestation

Drawn here today:

| 03/10/20XX 13:00 Basic Metabolic Panel For more Final Results Received | | | | |
|---|---|---|---|---|
| **Specimen Comment** | **1 SERUM SEPARATOR TUBE (SST)** | | | **Final** |
| Sodium | 137 | | [136–145 mmol/L] | Final |
| Potassium | 3.3 | L | [3.8–5.4 mmol/L] | Final |
| Chloride | 95 | L | [98–106 mmol/L] | Final |
| Carbon Dioxide | 36 | H | [20–26 mmol/L] | Final |
| BUN | 14 | | [7–18 mg/dL] | Final |
| Creatinine | 0.8 | | [0.4–1.0 mg/dL] | Final |
| Glucose | 114 | H | [70–106 mg/dL] | Final |
| Calcium (total) | 7.7 | L | [8.8–10.1 mg/dL] | Final |

| 03/10/20XX 13:00 CBC with Auto Diff For more Final Results Received | | | | |
|---|---|---|---|---|
| White Blood Cell Count | 10.8 | | [4.5–13.5 THOU/uL] | Final |
| Red Blood Cell Count | 3.56 | L | [4.5–5.3 MIL/uL] | Final |
| Hemoglobin | 10.8 | L | [13.0–16.0 g/dL] | Final |
| Hematocrit | 31.3 | L | [37.0–49.0%] | Final |
| Mean Corpuscular Volume | 87.8 | | [78.0–98.0 fL] | Final |
| Mean Corpuscular Hgb | 30.4 | | [25.0–35.0 pg] | Final |
| Mean Corpus Hgb Conc | 34.5 | | [31.0–37.0 g/dL] | Final |
| Red Distribution Width | 15.7 | H | [11.5–14.5%] | Final |
| Platelet Count | 95 | LL | [150–400 THOU/uL] | Final |

| CONSISTENT WITH PREVIOUS RESULTS | | | | |
|---|---|---|---|---|
| Mean Platelet Volume | 7.3 | L | [7.4–10.4 fL] | Final |
| Segmented Neutrophils | 95.7 | H | [40–59%] | Final |
| Absolute Neutrophil Count | 10336 | | [THOU/uL] | Final |
| Eosinophils Count | 0.6 | | [0–4%] | Final |
| Basophils | 0 | | [0–1%] | Final |
| Lymphocytes | 1.4 | L | [34–48%] | Final |
| Monocytes | 2.3 | L | [3–8%] | Final |
| Platelet Estimate | Not Done | | | Final |
| Differential Method | AUTOMATED | | | Final |

*Enter one diagnosis code and three procedure codes.*

**DX1** [                    ]

**PR1** [                    ]

**PR2** [                    ]

**PR3** [                    ]

## PRACTICE—CASE 16

*Please code for the services of the physician.*

**DATE OF SERVICE:** 12/29/20XX

**CHIEF COMPLAINT:** Acute left-sided weakness

**HISTORY OF PRESENT ILLNESS:** The patient is a 47-year-old woman who was on the phone talking to a friend when she had acute weakness to her left arm and left leg. She states her leg and arm felt like an extremity feels when you sleep on it. There was decreased strength, but she states the symptoms and also the sensation is slightly decreased. Her husband noted some slight slurring of her speech. The patient denies any visual changes, loss of vision, double vision. She has not had any headache. She gives no history of any chest pain or palpitations. She presents here stating that her symptoms have somewhat improved.

**PAST MEDICAL AND SURGICAL HISTORY:**

1. Appendectomy
2. Mitral valve prolapse

**CURRENT MEDICATIONS:** Ranitidine

**SOCIAL HISTORY:** She does not smoke. She is a missionary. She has no primary care provider.

**FAMILY HISTORY:** Negative for early stroke or coronary artery disease.

**REVIEW OF SYSTEMS:** See HPI, otherwise negative.

**PHYSICAL EXAMINATION:**

**VITAL SIGNS:** Temperature 98.1; Blood pressure 120/69; Pulse 76 and regular, respirations 17; Saturation 99% on room air

**GENERAL:** Awake, alert, nontoxic-appearing female

**HEENT:** Head is a traumatic, normocephalic. Pupils are equal and round. Extraocular muscles are intact. Cranial nerves II-XII are intact. The palate raises symmetrically.

**NECK:** Supple, no JVD, no bruits

**CHEST:** Clear and equal breath sounds bilaterally without any wheezes, rales, or rhonchi

**CARDIOVASCULAR:** S1 and S2 normal. Regular rate and rhythm. Occasional ectopic beat is noted. I do not appreciate any murmur.

**ABDOMEN:** Soft

**EXTREMITIES:** Warm and dry, well perfused

**NEUROLOGICAL:** She is awake, alert, oriented ×3. Her strength is 5/5 and symmetric. Finger-to-nose normal. Heel-to-shin normal.

**EMERGENCY DEPARTMENT COURSE:** The patient underwent extensive diagnostics. A continuous three-lead monitor demonstrated a sinus rhythm with occasional PVC. Twelve-lead electrocardiogram revealed a sinus rhythm, occasional PVC, no ST-segment elevation or depression. CT scan of her head was found to be unremarkable. Her white blood cell count was 4.7, normal hemoglobin and hematocrit, normal differential. Comprehensive metabolic and CK were all normal as well. The patient was given aspirin orally here in the department. Given that she is 47 years of age, has mitral valve prolapse, and has rather classic symptoms of a TIA and thought to be at high risk, the patient will be placed in the hospital for further inpatient workup for acute transient ischemic attack, which appears to be improved.

## PRACTICE—CASE 16 (*continued*)

**DIAGNOSES:**

1. Acute transient ischemic attack
2. Mitral valve prolapse by history

**INSTRUCTIONS:** The patient's case was discussed with cardiology. The patient will be admitted to a telemetry bed for further care and treatment.

**HISTORY:** Comprehensive

**EXAMINATION:** Comprehensive

**MEDICAL DECISION MAKING:** High

*Enter two diagnosis codes and two procedure codes.*

**DX1**

**DX2**

**PR1**

**PR2**

## PRACTICE—CASE 17

*Please code for the services of the physician.*

**HISTORY OF PRESENT ILLNESS:** This is a 4-year-old Hispanic girl who is presenting new to me today and is 6 weeks after a left comminuted supracondylar fracture ×3, which occurred on 06/16/20XX status post closed reduction and percutaneous pinning by another physician on 06/17. The patient has Still's syndrome.

X-rays today show a well-healing fracture with pins in place. Long-arm cast was removed today prior to films.

Patient had pain for the first couple days after the injury and after the procedure and then patient denied pain. Her mom said that she had been complaining of pain after those first couple of days.

**PAST MEDICAL HISTORY:** She has no past medical history.

**MEDICATIONS:** No medications.

**ALLERGIES:** No allergies.

**PHYSICAL EXAMINATION:** On examination she has 3 percutaneous pins that are protruding from the dorsal aspect of the elbow. There are no signs of infection, no warmth, redness, or edema. She has normal sensation and motor function of the left hand and 2+ radial pulses.

**IMPRESSION:** Well-healing supracondylar fracture with percutaneous pins.

**PLAN:** Pins were removed today in clinic, and sterile dressing was applied. We will see this patient back in 4 weeks for follow-up with x-rays at that time. We counseled the mother regarding the limited activity for the patient over the next 4 weeks including no monkey bars, no running, no bicycling, and no activity where the patient would be at risk for a fall.

**HISTORY:** Problem-focused

**EXAMINATION:** Expanded problem-focused

**MEDICAL DECISION MAKING:** Moderate

---

*Enter two diagnosis codes and two procedure codes.*

**DX1**

**DX2**

**PR1**

**PR2**

## PRACTICE—CASE 18

*Please code for the services of the surgeon.*

**DATE OF OPERATION:** 11/08/20XX

**PREOPERATIVE DIAGNOSIS:** Mucocele, inside right lower lip

**POSTOPERATIVE DIAGNOSIS:** Mucocele, inside right lower lip

**OPERATION:** Excision of right lower lip mucocele

**ANESTHESIA:** General via laryngeal mask airway (LMA)

**SPECIMENS:** Mucocele from right lower lip

**OPERATIVE FINDINGS:** Consistent with above

**ESTIMATED BLOOD LOSS:** Less than 10 mL

**COMPLICATIONS:** None

**INDICATIONS:** The patient is a healthy 6-year-old girl who was referred to our clinic from an outside medical clinic for evaluation of a lower lip mucocele. This small lesion has been present for several months and is indicated for removal. Prior to going to the operating room, the details of the procedure along with all risks and all questions were invited and answered with the mother with interpreter present. They elected to have this procedure performed in the operating room under general anesthesia.

**PROCEDURE:** The patient was properly identified in the preanesthesia holding area, and her consent, NPO status, and history and physical examination were updated, reviewed, and verified. At this time she was brought to operating theater #10 where she was placed in the supine position. Next, the anesthesia team induced and intubated the patient without complication. The tube was secured, and the patient was maintained under general anesthesia throughout the entire procedure. At this time a time-out and patient and procedure verification took place. Next, the patient was prepared, draped, and padded in the usual fashion for a procedure of this type. At this time approximately 2 cc of 0.25% Marcaine with epinephrine 1:200,000 was infiltrated in the right lower lip in the area of the medial nerve. Next, a #15 blade was used to make an elliptical incision around the 3 mm × 3 mm mucocele on the inside of the right lower lip. This was taken just through mucosa. Next, a superficial sub-mucosal dissection was undertaken and the mucocele was removed in its entirety. The surgeon was careful to remain just under the mucosa so that no damage to the medial nerve or its branches would take place. Following this, the wound was irrigated and closed with 5-0 Vicryl in multiple running horizontal mattress sutures. The patient was then awakened, extubated, and taken to the postanesthesia care unit (PACU) in stable condition. There were no complications. All sponge and needle counts were correct ×2.

**CLINICAL INFORMATION:**

**PROCEDURE:** Excision of mucocele lower lip

**PREOP DIAGNOSIS:** Mucocele lower lip

**CLINICAL HISTORY:** Not given

**GROSS DESCRIPTION:** Received in formalin for routine examination designated MUCOCELE RIGHT LOWER LIP are two fragments of tissue measuring 0.6 cm and 0.2 cm in maximal dimension. The tissue is wrapped and entirely submitted in one cassette.

## PRACTICE—CASE 18 (*continued*)

**PATHOLOGY REPORT—EXAM 4 CASE 8**

**MICROSCOPIC DESCRIPTION:** Sections contain oral epithelium with underlying glandular tissue that has both serous and acinar cells. The gland has intact architecture, although lumen of the excretory duct is dilated. The stroma immediately under the oral epithelium contains an irregularly shaped cystic space that contains proteinaceous fluid and neutrophils. The adjacent stroma contains reactive capillaries and venules with mild chronic inflammation. No definite mucous is present. Additional step sections were examined.

**DIAGNOSIS:** ORAL MUCOSA, LOWER LIP, EXCISION: MUCOUS RETENTION CYST

*Enter one diagnosis code and one procedure code.*

**DX1**

**PR1**

## PRACTICE—CASE 19

*Please code for the services of the surgeon.*

**DATE OF OPERATION:** 12/08/20XX

**PREOPERATIVE DIAGNOSES:**

1. Stage IV metastatic renal cell carcinoma

2. Metastatic disease involving the left femoral neck, left peritrochanteric proximal femur with nondisplaced pathologic fracture of the neck of the femur

3. Metastatic disease involving the left supracondylar femur with impending pathologic fracture

**PROCEDURE:**

1. Resection of the left femoral head and metastatic neck, renal cell carcinoma

2. Long-stem cemented hemiarthroplasty utilizing the Smith & Nephew Echelon cemented 175-mm #12 stem with a 48-mm 0 neck endo-head

3. Extended curettage and methylmethaculate of the left supracondylar femur

4. Open reduction internal fixation of left distal femur utilizing a Synthes nine-hole 3.5 plate and screws

**ANESTHESIA:** General

**ESTIMATED BLOOD LOSS:** For the distal femur was less than 50 cc. For the hip was 150 cc.

**INDICATIONS FOR PROCEDURE:** This is a 58-year-old man in whom a large renal cell carcinoma was diagnosed earlier this year, has undergone multiple other orthopedic procedures for bone disease, has had radiation therapy for a subtrochanteric lesion in the left femur, developed a new lytic lesion in the femoral neck, has gone on to progression and pain. Additionally, he was noted to have a separate discrete lesion in the distal supracondylar femur on the left. After preoperative embolization performed yesterday, the patient is brought to the operating room for the above-stated surgical procedures.

**FINDINGS AT SURGERY:** At the time of surgery, the left distal femur underwent an eventful curettage, methylmethaculate and open reduction internal fixation, given very stable fixation, ready for immediate weightbearing. The patient's proximal left femur was noted to have a nondisplaced but complete fracture at the base of the neck, therefore is not deemed a candidate for a spiral blade intermedullary fixation and therefore opted for a head and neck resection followed by a long-stemmed cemented hemiarthroplasty that also gave a very stable and excellent fixation ready for immediate weightbearing.

**DESCRIPTION OF PROCEDURE:** The patient was identified, brought to the operating room, and placed on the operating room table in the supine position, where general anesthesia was induced. The patient was oroendotracheally intubated. After he was stabilized, he was carefully and gently placed on the O.S.I. fracture table with a bump beneath the left hip. He received antibiotic prophylaxis, and the left hindquarter was prepared and draped in the usual sterile fashion. Under C-arm fluoroscopy, we ranged his hip and noted that the femoral head was not moving in unison with the femoral neck and therefore opted out of antegrade intermedullary nailing. We therefore proceeded with the distal femur first, which was approached with a direct lateral approach to the femur. The vastus lateralis was elevated. The underlying lytic lesion, which measured approximately 2 cm × 4 cm, was identified, entered with a sharp knife, then a burr, and curetted extensively throughout the intermedullary canal back to normal cortical bone. This was irrigated and dried with peroxide and saline. Methylmethaculate was mixed to a doughy state, digitally impacted to fill this defect. A nine-hole 3.5 Synthes plate was then bent and twisted to contour the lateral femur and fixed in the usual standard fashion with 35 screws. This gave excellent rigid fixation. Routine closure was obtained utilizing 0, 2-0 Vicryl followed by skin staples and sterile Tegaderm.

## PRACTICE—CASE 19 (*continued*)

At this time the patient was again prepared and draped in the right lateral decubitus position with care taken to pad bony prominences, neurovascular structures for a posterior approach to his left hip. Through a standard posterolateral approach to his hip, the proximal femur was identified, hip arthrotomy performed, and findings as noted above osteotomizing the proximal femur just above the lesser trochanter. Femoral head and neck were excised and found to be extensively involved with malignancy. These were passed off as specimen. The proximal femur was curetted back to stable bone. Then it was reamed and broached to accept a 175-mm, #12 stem. Length was verified as satisfactory under C-arm fluoroscopy. The canal was prepared, dried, distal cement restrictor placed and the #12 stem was cemented into standard anteversion utilizing excellent cement technique. After it had dried, a 48-mm 0 neck was impacted onto the prosthesis having been previously measured. This was reduced and noted to give excellent stable reduction. The wound was then copiously irrigated with antibiotic-containing saline solution and closed with 0 Vicryl interrupted, short external rotators reattached to the gluteus medius tendon, fascia closed with 0 Vicryl interrupted, 2-0 Vicryl inverted and skin staples. A medium Hemovac drain was used in the hip wound.

The patient was then returned to the supine position, awakened and extubated in the operating room, and moved to the recovery room in stable condition.

**POSTOPERATIVE PLAN:** For routine posterior hip precautions, weight-bearing as tolerated.

---

*Enter three diagnosis codes and three procedure codes.*

DX1

DX2

DX3

PR1

PR2

PR3

## PRACTICE—CASE 20

*Please code for the services of the surgeon.*

**DATE OF OPERATION:** 12/15/20XX

**PREOPERATIVE DIAGNOSIS:** Right middle ear cholesteatoma

**POSTOPERATIVE DIAGNOSIS:** Right middle ear cholesteatoma

**OPERATION:** Right mastoidectomy, tympanoplasty

**FINDINGS:** Cholesteatoma, right anterior middle ear epitympanum, intact ossicular chain

**INDICATIONS:** The patient is an 18-year-old woman with previous ear surgery elsewhere and then a right tympanoplasty here in 2001 for anterior-superior middle ear cholesteatoma. She was seen recently with enlarging right anterior-superior whitish mass within the tympanic membrane.

**OPERATIVE PROCEDURE:** After endotracheal intubation and administration of general anesthesia, the right ear was prepared and draped in the usual fashion. The ear was inspected with a microscope. The patient was known to have a whitish mass within an intact tympanic membrane in the anterior-superior quadrant of the middle ear. A canal incision was made 4 mm behind the posterior bony annulus with a 7200 blade from 6 o'clock to 12 o'clock. A postauricular incision was made with a 15-blade knife, and the periosteum was divided under the linea temporalis and behind the ear canal. At this point, the patient was found to have no accessible temporalis fascia. The temporalis muscle was then retracted superiorly with a Senn rake, and a 1.5 cm × 1.5 cm periosteal graft was harvested from underneath the temporalis fascia. This was cleaned and placed on the Mayo stand for drying. The ear canal was brought forward with a Freer elevator down to the previously made incision.

At this point, the patient was known to have a cholesteatoma that was within the posterior-superior ear canal in an area of scalloped-out bone. This cholesteatoma pearl was removed with a duckbill and then stapes curet. This was not contiguous with any other process. The tympanomeatal flap was elevated down to bony annulus, and then the middle ear was entered under the membranous annulus with a Rosen needle and annulus elevator. It was reflected forward to the malleus handle. At this point, the patient was known to have cholesteatoma extending along the medial surface of the malleus handle and body of malleus involving the anterior portion of tensor tympani tendon and filling the entire anterior middle ear and anterior epitympanum. The tympanic membrane was dissected off the malleus handle in its entirety with a 5910 Beaver blade and then reflected up to the anterior ear canal. The cholesteatoma mass was removed from the anterior hypotympanum, anterior-superior middle ear, and anterior epitympanum with a combination of duckbills and cupped forceps. It was difficult to visualize the tensor tympani tendon. The tensor tympani tendon was therefore cut at its attachment to the neck of the malleus with a 5910 blade and, with gentle lateral retraction on the malleus, the cholesteatoma could be followed up and dissected off the anterior surface of the body of the malleus. At this point, no other cholesteatoma was noted in the middle ear or epitympanum.

A mastoidectomy was carried out by removing the lateral cortex with a 3-mm burr to expose the posterior epitympanum. Dissection was carried further up to the short process of the malleus with a stapes curet. The mucosa in the posterior epitympanum was clean. No other cholesteatoma was noted under the incus. Irrigation at that point flowed freely over the facial ridge into the middle ear.

## PRACTICE—CASE 20 (*continued*)

Next, the middle ear was inspected again. A small amount of granulation tissue was dissected from around the long process of the incus and the incudostapedial joint, which was intact. No cholesteatoma was noted in that area. At this point, inspection of the middle ear and epitympanum yielded no evidence of recurrent cholesteatoma. A portion of the anterior tympanic membrane from the malleus handle up to the annulus was resected, where that had been contiguous with the main portion of the inflamed cholesteatoma mass. This resulted in about a 35% anterior marginal perforation. The anterior annulus was raised at the level of the perforation with a round 90-degree canal knife, and a Rosen needle was then used to make an adjacent tunnel under anterior ear canal skin. The previously harvested periosteal graft was placed under the malleus handle so that the anterior edge was positioned just at the mouth of the eustachian tube. A microcup forceps was placed into the previously made tunnel, and the anterior edge of the graft was pulled up anterior and underneath the anterior membranous annulus in order to hold the graft in place on the anterior canal wall. The posterior aspect of the graft and the tympanomeatal flap were reflected forward, and several pieces of Gelfoam were placed in the middle ear and pushed forward into the middle ear, instilled with Gelfoam, and the graft was elevated to meet the surrounding tympanic membrane. The posterior aspect of the graft was placed on the posterior ear canal along the remainder of the tympanomeatal flap, and Gelfoam was placed starting anteriorly to reconstitute the anterior sulcus and then over the entire tympanic membrane and graft.

The postauricular incision was closed in three layers with periosteum, auricular muscle, and dermis with 3-0 and 4-0 chromic. Steri-Strips were applied, and Gelfoam was then used to pack the remainder of the external ear canal. Estimated blood loss was approximately 100 cc. The final status of the middle ear is intact mobile ossicular chain, medial periosteal graft to anterior marginal 35% perforation.

**PLAN:** I explained to the patient's parents that if we get a significant recurrence along the ossicles, then the plan in the future will probably be to divide the incudostapedial joint and remove the head of the malleus and incus for better access to the epitympanum.

---

*Enter one diagnosis code and one procedure code.*

**DX1**

**PR1**

# EXAM 1

*For the following questions, choose the* best *answer. A blank answer sheet for these multiple choice questions can be found on page 25.*

| **Domain I** | ***Health Information Documentation*** |

1. The paper record format in which the entire record is arranged in strict chronological order is called a(n):

   a. Clinical-entry health record

   b. Integrated health record

   c. Source-oriented health record

   d. Problem-oriented health record

2. In ICD-10-CM, which one of the following is *not* considered a complication of labor and delivery?

   a. Obstructed labor due to incomplete rotation of fetal head

   b. Cephalic or occipital presentation with spontaneous, vaginal delivery

   c. Anal sphincter tear, not associated with third-degree perineal laceration

   d. Trauma to perineum and vulva during delivery

3. Sometimes referred to as a "superbug," this organism is a major cause of hospital-acquired infection:

   a. Friedlander's bacillus

   b. *Pseudomonas*

   c. Methicillin-resistant *Staphylococcus aureus*

   d. Coxsackie virus

4. Which of the following is considered a prion disease, a family of rare progressive neurodegenerative disorders?

   a. Creutzfeldt-Jakob disease

   b. ECHO virus

   c. Cat-scratch disease

   d. Asymptomatic neurosyphilis

5. The coder notes that the physician has prescribed Levothyroxine (Synthroid) for the patient. The coder might find which of the following on the patient's problem list?

   a. Acromegaly

   b. Hypothyroidism

   c. Dwarfism

   d. Cushing's disease

6. A male patient is seen by the physician and diagnosed with pneumonia. The doctor took cultures to try to determine which organism was causing the pneumonia. Which of the following organisms would alert the coder to code it as a gram-negative pneumonia?

    a. *Staphylococcus*

    b. *Clostridium*

    c. *Klebsiella*

    d. *Streptococcus*

7. Which of the following data elements is needed to accurately assign a CPT preventive medicine code?

    a. Time spent with the patient

    b. Age of the patient

    c. History, examination, and medical decision making

    d. Place of service

8. The physician visits his patient in the hospital and indicates that the patient has diabetes. Insulin is prescribed for and given to the patient. What is the best decision that the coding professional can make in this situation?

    a. Assign a code for type 1 diabetes mellitus because insulin was given

    b. Assign a code for drug-induced diabetes mellitus

    c. Assign a code for type 2 diabetes mellitus with complications

    d. Assign a code for type 2 diabetes mellitus along with a code for the insulin use

9. Documentation in the health record that relates to the patient's diagnoses and treatment is considered what type of data?

    a. Demographic

    b. Clinical

    c. Financial

    d. Personal

10. The clinical statement, "sections contain oral epithelium with underlying glandular tissue that has both serous and acinar cells" would be documented on which record form?

    a. Physical examination

    b. Operative report

    c. Pathology report

    d. Discharge summary

11. Which of the following types of asthma is due to environmental allergens?

    a. Intrinsic asthma

    b. Extrinsic asthma

    c. Exercise-induced bronchospasm

    d. Cough variant asthma

## Domain II  *Diagnosis and Procedure Coding*

12. The patient is seen in the emergency department (ED) with acute lumbar pain. The ED physician documents possible kidney stones and orders an x-ray. The radiologist documents bilateral nephrolithiasis. The coder would assign a code for which of the following conditions?

    a. Acute lumbar pain

    b. Bilateral nephrolithiasis

    c. Possible kidney stones

    d. Abnormal x-ray findings

13. Of the following ICD-10-CM codes, which one can serve as a "stand-alone" code?

    a. Z38.00, Single liveborn infant, born in hospital, delivered without mention of cesarean section

    b. V00.321, Fall from snow-skis

    c. Z37.0, Outcome of delivery, single liveborn

    d. Y92.020, Kitchen in mobile home as the place of occurrence of the external cause

14. A fetal death is defined as a:

    a. Death of a fetus of less than 500 g

    b. Death of a fetus of 20 or more weeks of gestation

    c. Death of a fetus as defined by the physician

    d. Death of a fetus where state law determines weight and weeks of gestation

15. Using the illustration below from the Table of Drugs and Chemicals in the ICD-10-CM codebook, which code would a coder select for the following diagnsosis: "Initial presentation for excessive drowsiness due to sensitivity to Periactin taken as prescribed"?

| Table of Drugs and Chemicals | | | | | | |
|---|---|---|---|---|---|---|
| Substance | Poisoning, accidental | Poisoning, Intentional | Poisoning Assault | Poisoning Undetermined | Adverse Effect | Underdosing |
| Periactin | T45.0X1 | T45.0X2 | T45.0X3 | T45.0X4 | T45.0X5 | T45.0X6 |

Note: 7th character "A" is assigned to indicate initial encounter

    a. T45.0X2A

    b. T45.0X6A

    c. T45.0X4A

    d. T45.0X5A

16. Wide excision of a 0.65-cm malignant melanoma (margins included) from right forearm. Which of the following diagnosis and procedure codes are reported?

| | |
|---|---|
| C43.61 | Malignant melanoma of skin; right upper limb, including shoulder |
| C76.41 | Malignant neoplasm of right upper limb |
| 11401 | Excision, benign lesion including margins, except skin tag (unless listed elsewhere), trunk, arms, or legs; excised diameter 0.6 to 1.0 cm |
| 11601 | Excision, malignant lesion including margins, trunk, arms, or legs; excised diameter 0.6 to 1.0 cm |
| 25075 | Excision, tumor, soft tissue of forearm and/or wrist area; subcutaneous, less than 3 cm |

   a. C76.41, 11401

   b. C76.41, 11601

   c. C43.61, 11601

   d. C43.61, 25075

17. A "missed abortion" refers to:

   a. Fetal death prior to completion of 20 weeks of gestation with retention in the uterus

   b. Fetal death prior to actual delivery date with retention in the uterus

   c. Fetal death prior to completion of 22 weeks of gestation with retention in the uterus

   d. Fetal death prior to 15 weeks of gestation with retention in the uterus

18. A diagnosis of elevated blood pressure reading, without a diagnosis of hypertension is assigned code:

   a. I99.8

   b. I10

   c. R03.0

   d. O10

19. A female infant was born in the hospital at term and at a normal birth weight. It was a vaginal delivery with a vertex presentation. In the hours after birth, jaundice was noted and eventually a diagnosis of erythroblastosis fetalis due to an ABO incompatibility was made. How would this admission be coded?

| | |
|---|---|
| Z38.00 | Single liveborn, born in hospital, delivered vaginally |
| P55.0 | Hemolytic disease due to RH isoimmunization |
| P55.1 | Hemolytic disease due to ABO incompatibility |
| P55.8 | Other hemolytic diseases of newborn |
| P55.9 | Hemolytic disease of newborn, unspecified |

   a. Z38.00, P55.0

   b. Z38.00, P55.1

   c. Z38.00, P55.8

   d. Z38.00, P55.9

20. What is the correct code assignment for the following scenario: 39 week intrauterine pregnancy presenting in right occiptoanterior position which resulted in vaginal delivery of liveborn female infant, second-degree lacerations of perineum?

    a. O70.1, Z37.0, Z3A.39

    b. Z37.0, O70.0, Z3A.30

    c. O70.1, Z37.9, Z3A.00

    d. O70.2, Z37.9, Z3A.40

21. A patient visits his physician's office and indicates that he has left arm paralysis due to a case of poliomyelitis that he suffered as a young child. What diagnosis codes would be assigned for this diagnosis?

| | |
|---|---|
| A80.9 | Acute poliomyelitis, unspecified |
| B91 | Sequelae of poliomyelitis, (acute) |
| G81.90 | Hemiplegia, unspecified affecting unspecified side |
| G83.20 | Monoplegia of upper limb affecting unspecified side |
| G83.22 | Monoplegia of upper limb affecting left dominant side |
| G83.24 | Monoplegia of upper limb affecting left nondominant side |

    a. G83.24, B91

    b. B91, G83.22

    c. G81.90, A80.9

    d. B91, G83.20

22. The physician sees a patient in the hospital with a diagnosis of "metastasis to the brain admitted in a comatose state." In ICD-10-CM, how would this diagnosis be coded?

    a. Code only the brain metastasis (C79.31)

    b. Code only the unknown primary site (C80.1)

    c. Code the metastasis (C79.31) followed by a code for the coma (R40.20)

    d. Code only the coma (R40.20)

23. What ICD-10-CM code is used to represent "an encounter for contraceptive sterilization?"

    a. Z30.2, Encounter for sterilization

    b. Underlying medical condition

    c. Code for the incidental pregnancy

    d. Underlying psychological condition

24. The patient is seen in his ophthalmologist's office and treated for bilateral open angle glaucoma, moderate stage. How would this encounter be coded?

| | |
|---|---|
| H40.10X2 | Unspecified open-angle glaucoma, moderate stage |
| H40.11X1 | Primary, open-angle glaucoma, mild stage |
| H40.11X2 | Primary open-angle glaucoma, moderate stage |
| H40.9 | Unspecified glaucoma |

   a. H40.10X2

   b. H40.11X1

   c. H40.9

   d. H40.11X2

25. Which is the correct way to report the encounter for a patient who is menopausal due to natural aging and is asymptomatic?

| | |
|---|---|
| E28.39 | Other primary ovarian failure |
| E89.40 | Postprocedural Asymptomatic postprocedural ovarian failure |
| N95.1 | Menopausal state and female climacteric states |
| Z78.0 | Asymptomatic menopausal state |

   a. Z78.0, E28.39

   b. Z78.0, N95.1

   c. Z78.0

   d. E89.40

26. A 26-year-old female delivers a 36-week, full-term infant per the physician's documentation. The young mother has previously diagnosed AIDS. What is the correct diagnosis code assignment for the physician's services?

| | |
|---|---|
| O98.72 | Human immunodeficiency virus [HIV] disease complicating childbirth |
| B20 | AIDS |
| O60.13X0 | Preterm labor second trimester with preterm delivery third trimester |
| Z37.0 | Single live birth |
| Z21 | Asymptomatic HIV status |
| Z3A.36 | Thirty-six weeks gestation of pregnancy |

   a. O98.72, O60.13X0, B20, Z37.0, Z3A.36

   b. O98.72, B20, Z37.0, Z3A.36

   c. O98.72, Z21, Z37.0, Z3A.36

   d. O98.72, O60.13X0, Z21, Z3A.36

27. In which of the following situations is the code C34.90, Primary malignant neoplasm of the lung, unspecified, appropriate to code?

   a. Metastatic carcinoma of the colon to the lung

   b. Carcinoma of the brain from the left lower lobe of the lung

   c. Renal cell carcinoma to the lung

   d. Secondary malignant neoplasm of the lung

28. The patient is seen in the wound clinic with bilateral decubitus ulcers of the buttocks. The physician documents the stage of the ulcers as stage 3. What diagnosis codes would be submitted for this encounter?

| | |
|---|---|
| L89.313 | Pressure ulcer of right buttock, stage 3 |
| L89.323 | Pressure ulcer of left buttock, stage 3 |
| L89.303 | Pressure ulcer of unspecified buttock, stage 3 |
| L98.499 | Non-pressure chronic ulcer of the skin of other sites with unspecified severity |

   a.  L89.313, L89.323

   b.  L89.313, L89.313

   c.  L98.499, L89.303

   d.  L89.323, L89.323

29. In which of the following situations would acute respiratory failure be considered as the secondary diagnosis?

   a.  A patient with emphysema develops acute respiratory failure and is admitted for treatment.

   b.  A patient with congestive heart failure is brought to the emergency department in acute respiratory failure and is intubated and admitted.

   c.  A patient overdoses on crack cocaine and is admitted to the hospital in acute respiratory failure.

   d.  A patient with chronic myasthenia gravis suffers an acute exacerbation and develops acute respiratory failure. The patient is admitted to treat the respiratory failure.

30. A patient is admitted with MRSA pneumonia. The physician also documents MRSA colonization. What codes are reported for this admission?

| | |
|---|---|
| A49.02 | Methicillin resistant Staphylococcus aureus |
| J15.212 | Pneumonia due to methicillin resistant Staphylococcus aureus |
| Z22.322 | Carrier or suspected carrier of Methicillin resistant Staphylococcus aureus |

   a.  A49.02, Z22.322

   b.  J15.212, A49.02, Z22.322

   c.  J15.212

   d.  J15.212, Z22.322

31. The infant is admitted to the hospital for correction of a narrowed aorta. The physician would likely document which of the following?

   a.  Coarctation of the aorta

   b.  Transposition of great vessels

   c.  Ventricular septal defect

   d.  Aortic valve stenosis

32. The patient is admitted to the hospital for a third round of chemotherapy for her acute lymphoblastic leukemia. On the second day of hospitalization, the patient develops severe nausea and vomiting. Which of the following codes would be reported as the principal diagnosis?

    a. Z51.11, Encounter for antineoplastic chemotherapy

    b. C91.00, Acute lymphoblastic leukemia not having achieved remission

    c. R11.2, Nausea with vomiting

    d. Z51.12, Encounter for antineoplastic immunotherapy

33. Down syndrome, Patau's syndrome, and Edward's syndrome are all:

    a. Musculoskeletal conditions

    b. Chromosomal anomalies

    c. Digestive system disorders

    d. Genitourinary tract diseases

34. A liveborn infant was born vaginally in the hospital and shortly thereafter was diagnosed with fetal alcohol syndrome. The infant's mother was alcohol-dependent. How would this case be coded?

    a. Z38.00, Q86.0

    b. Z38.01, Q86.0

    c. Z38.00, F10.20

    d. Z38.01, F10.20

35. Urinary frequency, urgency, nocturia, incontinence, and hesitancy are all symptoms of:

    a. Benign Prostatic Hypertrophy

    b. End-stage renal disease

    c. Salpingitis

    d. Genital prolapse

36. Which of the following terms is not a mechanical complication of an internal prosthetic device?

    a. Protrusion

    b. Leakage

    c. Perforation

    d. Hemorrhage

37. A patient is seen in the emergency room and diagnosed with a subsequent anterior wall myocardial infarction 3 weeks after he had a myocardial infarction. Which of the following codes would you use to correctly code this encounter?

    a. I20.9, Angina pectoris, unspecified

    b. I22.0, Subsequent ST elevation (STEMI) myocardial infarction of anterior wall; I21.3, Acute myocardial infarction

    c. I25.2, Old myocardial infarction

    d. I24.1, Postmyocardial infarction syndrome

38. Status migrainosus generally refers to a severe migraine that lasts for more than _____ hours.

    a. 72

    b. 100

    c. 96

    d. 84

39. Which of the following terms refers to the active management of withdrawal symptoms in a patient who is physically dependent on alcohol or drugs:

    a. Therapy

    b. Intoxication

    c. Detoxification

    d. Rehabilitation

40. Which of the following statements represents the appropriate use of Category Z85, Personal history of malignant neoplasms?

    a. Primary malignancy has recurred at the original site and chemotherapy is now directed at the site

    b. Primary malignancy has been removed or eradicated and no adjunct treatment is being given at this time

    c. Secondary malignancy has been removed or eradicated and the patient is admitted for adjunct radiotherapy to the secondary site

    d. Secondary malignancy is partially removed and treatment is refused by the patient even though the physician explains that there is some remaining malignant tissue

41. When CPT codes have resequenced (appear out of the normal order), the code is preceded by which of the following symbols?

    a. ▲

    b. ○

    c. #

    d. •

42. A 2-month-old baby presents to the emergency department (ED) with a high fever. The ED physician performs a detailed history, a detailed examination, and uses high-level medical decision making. The physician also performs a lumbar puncture to remove cerebrospinal fluid sample for culture. How are the ED physician's services coded?

| | |
|---|---|
| 99284 | Emergency department visit for the evaluation and management of a patient, which requires these 3 key components: A detailed history; a detailed examination; and medical decision making of moderate complexity |
| 99285 | Emergency department visit for the evaluation and management of a patient, which requires these 3 key components: A comprehensive history; a comprehensive examination; and medical decision making of high complexity |
| 62270 | Spinal puncture, lumbar, diagnostic |
| 62272 | Spinal puncture, therapeutic, for drainage of cerebrospinal fluid (by needle or catheter) |
| –25 | Significant, separately identifiable Evaluation and Management service by the same physician on the same day of the procedure or other service |

   a. 99284–25, 62270

   b. 99285–25, 62270

   c. 99284–25, 62272

   d. 99285–25, 62272

43. The physician removes an autograft of iliac crest bone to be used as crushed bone during a lumbar arthrodesis procedure. How is this autograft coded?

   a. 20900, Bone graft, any donor area; minor small (eg, dowel or button)

   b. 20902, Bone graft, any donor area; major or large

   c. 20936, Autograft for spine surgery only (includes harvesting the graft); local (eg, ribs, spinous process, or laminar fragments) obtained from same incision (List separately in addition to code for primary procedure.)

   d. 20937, Autograft for spine surgery only (includes harvesting the graft); morselized (through separate skin or fascial incision) (List separately in addition to code for primary procedure.)

44. The physician treats a patient who has osteomyelitis of the left shoulder blade following a past injury. A piece of dead bone is removed from the body of the shoulder blade, and the physician removes surrounding bone to return the shoulder blade to its natural contour. How is this coded?

| | |
|---|---|
| 23140 | Excision or curettage of bone cyst or benign tumor of clavicle or scapula |
| 23170 | Sequestrectomy (eg, for osteomyelitis or bone abscess), clavicle |
| 23172 | Sequestrectomy (eg, for osteomyelitis or bone abscess), scapula |
| 23180 | Partial excision (craterization, saucerization, or diaphysectomy) bone (eg, osteomyelitis), clavicle |
| 23182 | Partial excision (craterization, saucerization, or diaphysectomy) bone (eg, osteomyelitis), scapula |
| 23190 | Ostectomy of scapula, partial (eg, superior medial angle) |

   a. 23170–LT, 23140–51–LT

   b. 23172–LT, 23140–51–LT

   c. 23172–LT, 23182–51–LT

   d. 23190–LT, 23180–51–LT

45. The physician curettes three lesions off the patient's back. The lesions are keratotic and measure 0.5 cm each. How is this service coded?

| | |
|---|---|
| 11400 | Excision, benign lesion including margins, except skin tag (unless listed elsewhere), trunk, arms, or legs; excised diameter 0.5 cm or less |
| 11402 | excised diameter 1.1 to 2.0 cm |
| 17000 | Destruction (eg, laser surgery, electrosurgery, cryosurgery, chemosurgery, surgical curettement), premalignant lesions (eg, actinic keratoses); first lesion |
| 17003 | second through 14 lesions, each (List separately in addition to code for first lesion.) |

   a. 11400, 11400–51, 11400–51

   b. 11402

   c. 17000

   d. 17000, 17003

46. A 32-year-old female patient presents to the urgent care center after eating a fish sandwich, stating that she has a stabbing pain in the throat as she swallows or clears her throat. The physician examines her larynx using a mirror, locates a small fish bone lodged in the muscular wall of the larynx, and removes it using a long-nosed forceps. How are these services coded?

| | |
|---|---|
| 31505 | Laryngoscopy, indirect; diagnostic (separate procedure) |
| 31511 | with removal of foreign body |
| 31515 | Laryngoscopy direct, with or without tracheoscopy; for aspiration |
| 31530 | Laryngoscopy, direct, operative, with foreign body removal |
| –51 | Multiple procedures |

   a. 31511

   b. 31505, 31511–51

   c. 31515

   d. 31530

47. The physician performs therapeutic injections of both the patient's facet joints at L1–L2 and L2–L3, using fluoroscopic guidance. How is this coded?

| | |
|---|---|
| 64490 | Injection, diagnostic or therapeutic agent, paravertebral facet (zygapophyseal) joint (or nerves innervating that joint) with image guidance (fluoroscopy or CT), cervical or thoracic; single level |
| 64493 | Injection, diagnostic or therapeutic agent, paravertebral facet (zygapophyseal) joint (or nerves innervating that joint) with image guidance (fluoroscopy or CT), lumbar or sacral; single level |
| 64494 | second level (List separately in addition to code for primary procedure.) |
| 64495 | third and any additional level(s) (List separately in addition to code for primary procedure.) |
| –50 | Bilateral procedure |

   a. 64493–50, 64494–50

   b. 64490–50, 64494–50

   c. 64493, 64493

   d. 64495

48. The physician performs a median sternotomy and places the patient on cardiopulmonary bypass to repair the patient's aortopulmonary window, or a connection between the aorta and pulmonary artery just above the semilunar valves. The physician opens the pulmonary artery and locates the window, closing it with a Dacron fabric patch. The patient is taken off bypass, and the sternal incision is closed. How is this procedure coded?

    a. 33645, Direct or patch closure, sinus venosus, with or without anomalous pulmonary venous drainage

    b. 33813, Obliteration of aortopulmonary septal defect; without cardiopulmonary bypass

    c. 33814, Obliteration of aortopulmonary septal defect; with cardiopulmonary bypass

    d. 33917, Repair of pulmonary artery stenosis by reconstruction with patch or graft

49. The physician debrides and dresses second degree burns on the patient's entire left leg and foot. How is this coded?

    a. 11000, Debridement of extensive eczematous or infected skin; up to 10% of body surface

    b. 11042, Debridement, subcutaneous tissue (includes epidermis and dermis, if performed); first 20 sq cm or less

    c. 16025, Dressings and/or debridement of partial-thickness burns, initial or subsequent; medium (eg, whole face or whole extremity, or 5% to 10% total body surface area)

    d. 16030, Dressings and/or debridement of partial-thickness burns, initial or subsequent; large (eg, more than 1 extremity, or greater than 10% total body surface area)

50. The patient undergoes a CT colonography using contrast material to diagnose and stage colon cancer. How is this procedure coded?

    a. 45378, Colonoscopy, flexible; diagnostic, including collection of specimen(s) by brushing or washing, when performed (separate procedure)

    b. 74262, Computed tomographic (CT) colonography, diagnostic, including image postprocessing; with contrast material(s), including non-contrast images, if performed

    c. 74263, Computer tomographic (CT) colonography, screening, including image postprocessing

    d. 91299, Unlisted diagnostic gastroenterology procedure

51. The physician orders the following blood tests, which are performed together at the office: Carbon dioxide, Chloride, Potassium, Sodium. How are these tests coded?

| | |
|---|---|
| 80051 | Electrolyte panel: Carbon dioxide; Chloride; Potassium; Sodium |
| 80053 | Comprehensive metabolic panel: Albumin; Bilirubin, total; Calcium, total; Carbon dioxide; Chloride; Creatinine; Glucose; Phosphatase, alkaline; Potassium; Protein, total; Sodium; ALT/SGPT; AST/SGOT; Urea nitrogen |
| 82374 | Carbon dioxide (bicarbonate) |
| 82435 | Chloride; blood |
| 82436 | Urine |
| 84132 | Potassium; serum, plasma or whole blood |
| 84133 | Urine |
| 84295 | Sodium; serum, plasma or whole blood |
| 84302 | Other source |

    a. 82374, 82435, 84132, 84295

    b. 82374, 82436, 84133, 84302

    c. 80051

    d. 80053

52. During a 50-minute follow-up office visit, the physician provides psychotherapy and spends 5 minutes reviewing medications and adjusting dosages. How is this service coded?

| | |
|---|---|
| 90834 | Psychotherapy, 45 minutes with the patient and/or family member |
| 90863 | Pharmacologic management, including prescription and review of medication, when performed with psychotherapy services (List separately in addition to the code for primary procedure.) |
| 99215 | Office or other outpatient visit for the evaluation and management of an established patient, which requires at least 2 of these 3 key components: A comprehensive history; comprehensive examination; medical decision making of high complexity. Physicians typically spend 40 minutes face-to-face with the patient and/or family. |
| 99354 | Prolonged physician service in the office or other outpatient setting requiring direct (face-to-face) patient contact beyond the usual service; first hour (List separately in addition to code for office or other outpatient Evaluation and Management service.) |

a. 99215

b. 99215, 99354

c. 90834

d. 90834, 90863

53. After completion of allergy testing, the allergist prepares and provides allergenic extracts in 20 single-dose vials to begin desensitization. These vials are sent to the patient's primary care physician, who will administer the injections according to the prescribed schedule. How are the services of the allergist coded?

| | |
|---|---|
| 95117 | Professional services for allergen immunotherapy not including provision of allergenic extracts; 2 or more injections |
| 95144 | Professional services for the supervision of preparation and provision of antigens for allergen immunotherapy, single dose vial(s) (Specify number of vials.) |
| 95165 | Professional services for the supervision of preparation and provision of antigens for allergen immunotherapy; single or multiple antigens (Specify number of doses.) |
| 95199 | Unlisted allergy/clinical immunologic service or procedure |

a. 95117 × 10

b. 95144 × 20

c. 95165 × 20

d. 95199

54. A 9-year-old boy is seen in the emergency department and receives 560 units of rabies immune globulin and rabies vaccine as intramuscular injections after being bitten by a squirrel that exhibited signs of being infected. The documentation contains an expanded problem-focused history, a detailed examination, and high-level medical decision making. How are these services coded?

| | |
|---|---|
| 99283 | Emergency department visit with an expanded problem focused history, an expanded problem focused examination, and medical decision making of moderate complexity |
| 99284 | Emergency department visit with a detailed history, a detailed examination, and medical decision making of moderate complexity |
| 99285 | Emergency department visit with a comprehensive history, a comprehensive examination, and medical decision making of high complexity |
| 90375 | Rabies immune globulin (RIg), human, for intramuscular and/or subcutaneous use |
| 90471 | Immunization administration (includes percutaneous, intradermal, subcutaneous, or intramuscular injections); 1 vaccine (single or combination vaccine/toxoid) |
| 90675 | Rabies vaccine, for intramuscular use |
| 90676 | Rabies vaccine, for intradermal use |
| 96372 | Therapeutic, prophylactic, or diagnostic injection (specify substance or drug); subcutaneous or intramuscular |

   a. 99283, 90676, 90675

   b. 99283, 90375, 90675, 90471, 96372

   c. 99284, 90375 x 560 units, 90675, 96372 x2

   d. 99285, 90375, 90676, 90471, 96372

55. The nephrologist performs a needle biopsy of the liver using imaging guidance provided by the radiologist. How are the services of the nephrologist coded?

   a. 10022, Fine needle aspiration, with imaging guidance

   b. 47000, Biopsy of liver, percutaneous

   c. 47100, Biopsy of liver, wedge

   d. 47399, Unlisted procedure, liver

56. A patient covered by Medicare underwent an anterior keratoplasty. The patient's eye was prepared with a laser prior to the placement of the graft. How is this coded?

| | |
|---|---|
| 65710 | Keratoplasty, (corneal transplant); anterior lamellar |
| 65730 | penetrating (except in aphakia or pseudophakia) |
| 65756 | endothelial |
| 0290T | Corneal incisions in the recipient cornea created using a laser, in preparation for penetrating or lamellar keratoplasty (List separately in addition to code for primary procedure.) |

   a. 65710

   b. 65710, 0290T

   c. 65730, 0290T

   d. 65756

57. The patient has L2–3 spinal stenosis. The surgeon removes the lower portion of the L2 spinous process and the upper portion of the L3 spinous process, as well as the inter-spinous ligament to provide access to the space. A spinous process distraction device is then inserted using imaging guidance. How is this service coded?

| | |
|---|---|
| 22102 | Partial excision of posterior vertebral component (eg, spinous process, lamina or facet) for intrinsic bony lesion, single vertebral segment, lumbar |
| 22612 | Arthrodesis, posterior or posterolateral technique, single level; lumbar (with lateral transverse technique, when performed) |
| 22841 | Internal spinal fixation by wiring of spinous processes (List separately in addition to code for primary procedure.) |
| 0171T | Insertion of posterior spinous process distraction device (including necessary removal of bone or ligament for insertion and imaging guidance), lumbar; single level |

a. 22102, 22841

b. 22612, 22841

c. 0171T

d. 22102, 0171T

58. The physician orders and administers 600 mg of IV levofloxacin. How many units of code J1956 would be billed?

| | |
|---|---|
| J1956 | Levofloxacin, 250 mg |

a. 1

b. 2

c. 3

d. 4

59. The patient undergoes a complex cystometrogram with bladder voiding pressure studies at the hospital, completed by their urologist. How does the urologist code for this service?

| | |
|---|---|
| 51726 | Complex cystometrogram (ie, calibrated electronic equipment) |
| 51728 | Complex cystometrogram (ie, calibrated electronic equipment); with voiding pressure studies (ie, bladder voiding pressure), any technique |
| 51729 | Complex cystometrogram (ie, calibrated electronic equipment); with voiding pressure studies (ie, bladder voiding pressure) and urethral pressure profile studies (ie, urethral closure pressure profile), any technique |
| 51798 | Measurement of post-voiding residual urine and/or bladder capacity by ultrasound, non-imaging |
| –26 | Professional component |

a. 51726–26

b. 51728–26

c. 51729

d. 51728–26, 51798

60. Drs. Blank and Null are in the same cardiovascular practice. Dr. Blank is a cardiologist and Dr. Null is a cardiovascular surgeon. Dr. Blank has been seeing this Medicare patient for several years and now sends the patient to Dr. Null for consideration of a CABG procedure. What series of codes would Dr. Null use to code the services provided to this patient?

    a. Office or Other Outpatient Consultations, 99241–99245

    b. Inpatient Consultations, 99251–99255

    c. Office or Other Outpatient Services, New Patient, 99201–99205

    d. Office or Other Outpatient Services, Established Patient, 99211–99215

61. Ventilating tubes are inserted into the ear drums of a 3-year-old child under general anesthesia. In addition, a tonsillectomy and adenoidectomy are performed. How are these services coded?

    a. 69433, 42825, 42830

    b. 69433–50, 42820

    c. 69436–50, 42820

    d. 69436–50, 42820–50

62. An infant is born with a large gastroschisis. The intestines are mechanically eased into the abdomen using a prosthesis. Surgical closure is completed after 1 week. What is the correct CPT coding for the final closure?

    a. 49600, Repair of small omphalocele, with primary closure

    b. 49605, Repair of large omphalocele or gastroschisis; with or without prosthesis

    c. 49606, Repair of large omphalocele or gastroschisis; with removal of prosthesis, final reduction and closure, in operating room

    d. 49611, Repair of omphalocele (Gross type operation); second stage

63. The patient undergoes a completely endoscopic, off-pump coronary artery bypass procedure using a daVinci robot. Three ports are placed in the thorax for the robotic arms and the camera. The physician uses the system to obtain the internal mammary artery and graft it to the left anterior descending coronary artery. How is this procedure coded?

    a. 33533

    b. 33533, 33999

    c. 33534

    d. 33999

64. The physician destroys a choroid lesion using photocoagulation. What is the correct code assignment for this procedure?

    a. 67208

    b. 67210

    c. 67220

    d. 67221

65. The patient undergoes a vaginal hysterectomy with a 230-gram uterus, bilateral salpingectomy, and unilateral oophorectomy. How is this coded?

    a. 58260, 58720
    b. 58260, 58700–50, 58940
    c. 58262
    d. 58285

66. The patient is seen after the nursing staff reports that an A-V dialysis fistula cannot be accessed. The physician performs an open thrombectomy of the brachial artery side of the fistula. How is this procedure coded?

    a. 34101
    b. 35875
    c. 36831
    d. 36870

67. The patient had a total ethmoidectomy 5 days ago and now presents with headache and a clear nasal discharge. The surgeon performs a nasal endoscopy looking for a CSF leak and repairs the leak at the prior procedure site. What is the correct code assignment for this repair?

    a. 31238
    b. 31290
    c. 31291
    d. 31299

68. A 48-year-old female patient undergoes a transurethral incision of the bladder neck. What is the proper code assignment for this procedure?

    a. 52214
    b. 52224
    c. 52500
    d. 53899

69. The patient was the victim of an attack and received several deep stab wounds to the anterolateral chest wall with injury to the cardiac muscle of the right atrium, the inferior vena cava, and the right middle lobe of the lung. The surgeon repairs the cardiac wound, sutures the vena cava, and performs a wedge resection of the damaged portion of the lung. Surgical drains are placed, and the chest wall requires major reconstruction using flaps to complete the closure. What is the correct code assignment for this case?

    a. 15734, 32505, 33300, 33320
    b. 32440, 32820, 33300, 33320
    c. 32505, 32820, 33330, 33320
    d. 32505, 33305, 33322

70. A repeat thyroidectomy is performed after a previous left partial thyroidectomy was completed several years ago. All thyroid tissue is removed from the left side and a total right thyroidectomy is performed. Two parathyroid glands are spared and autotransplanted into the exposed sternocleidomastoid muscle. What is the correct code assignment for this case?

    a. 60212, 60512

    b. 60240, 60500

    c. 60260, 60220

    d. 60260, 60220, 60512

71. The physician destroys three large lesions on the patient's labia majora using cryosurgery and performs a biopsy of two suspicious looking lesions on the mons pubis. How is this service coded?

    a. 11100, 11101, 17000

    b. 56605, 56606, 56515

    c. 11420, 11420, 17000, 17003

    d. 56605, 56606, 17000, 17003

72. A patient with carcinoma of the breast now undergoes a sentinel node biopsy. After injection of a radioactive tracer, a deep axillary lymph node glows bright blue. This node is excised through an open approach. What is the correct code assignment for this procedure?

    a. 38505, 38790

    b. 38525, 38792

    c. 38500, 38790

    d. 38308, 38525

73. **Inpatient admission:** The patient is a 78-year-old woman with heart palpitations and abdominal pain who was brought to the ED by her grandson. The physician ordered an EKG, a complete blood count and upper GI series. The GI revealed significant gastritis. The EKG was not significantly abnormal. The CBC revealed the following: Hct: 23%; Hgb 6.5; and WBC: 6,000. The cardiologist who admitted the patient into the hospital indicated that he felt the palpitations were a symptom of the patient's significant anemia. Social services were notified because the physician felt that the patient was not receiving the proper nutritional support causing the hemoglobin deficiency. The patient received 2 units of packed cells and was discharged the following day. The discharge diagnoses included nutritional anemia and gastritis. What codes would be reported for this encounter?

    a. D53.9, K29.70

    b. D53.9, K29.70, R00.2

    c. D53.9, K29.70, R10.9

    d. D53.9, K29.70, R00.2, R10.9

74. The patient is a 59-year-old African-American female who presented to an outside hospital with shortness of breath. She underwent imaging that revealed a pleural effusion and a thoracentesis that was consistent with adenocarcinoma. Given her desire for definitive diagnosis and opting for a surgical debulking, she was brought to the operating room today.

    **Findings:** External genitalia was atrophic, as was the vaginal canal. There was no blood, discharge, or lesions noted in the vaginal vault. There was a palpable mass across the superior portion of the abdominal cavity. Intraoperatively there was extensive tumor with a large omental cake adherent to the entire transverse colon in addition to the inferior portion of the stomach. There was carcinomatosis throughout the entire abdominal cavity extending from the hemidiaphragm down to the pelvis. There were bilateral adnexal masses. There was tumor along the surface of both the large bowel and small bowel. At the end of the procedure, there was an extensive amount of tumor remaining.

    **Preoperative Diagnosis:** Ovarian carcinoma

    **Postoperative Diagnosis:** Ovarian carcinoma, metastasis to pelvic organs

    Which of the following codes would be selected?

    a. C56.1, C79.89, J91.0

    b. C56.9, C79.89, J91.0

    c. C56.9, C79.89, J90

    d. C56.9, C80.0, J91.0

75. The patient was seen today for a postsurgical wound infection (Escherichia coli) following surgery for an open, type 1, right tibial shaft fracture. There is routine healing of the fracture. Which of the following diagnosis codes would be reported by the physician? Choose the correct coding selection

    a. T81.4XXA, B96.21, S82.201E

    b. T81.4XXA, B96.20, S82.201S

    c. T81.4XXA, B96.20, S82.201E

    d. T81.4XXD, B96.20, S82.201E

76. A 77-year-old white woman is seen with interstitial pneumonitis. Hospital course here has been complicated by hypoxemia, renal insufficiency, and steroid-induced diabetes mellitus. The patient has been taking steroids as prescribed for quite some time for her rheumatoid arthritis. The patient reports having episodes of small volume painless hematochezia at home secondary to hemorrhoids. Last evening and this morning experienced larger volume bright red blood per rectum. The patient reports having colonoscopy roughly 3 years ago performed elsewhere revealing diverticulosis and her aforementioned hemorrhoids. She does state that she has had sequential colonoscopies performed in the past. However, she is unclear on the findings.

    **Final Diagnoses Upon Discharge:**

    1. Hematochezia
    2. Interstitial pneumonitis
    3. Steroid-induced diabetes mellitus
    4. Chronic renal insufficiency

    What codes are reported for this condition?

    a. E11.9, J84.9, R09.02, K92.1, M06.9, N18.9, T38.0X5A, Z79.4

    b. E09.9, J84.9, R09.02, K92.1, M06.9, N18.9, T38.0X5A

    c. E09.9, J84.9, K92.1, M06.9, N18.6, T38.0X5A

    d. E09.9, J84.9, K92.1, M06.9, N18.9, T38.0X5A

77. Medicare's allowed fee for an in-office procedure is $200. Dr. Smith is a PAR physician, and Dr. Jones is a nonPAR physician who does not accept assignment. How much will Dr. Smith and Dr. Jones, respectively, receive from CMS?

    a. $160, $152

    b. $200, $152

    c. $160, $0

    d. $200, $0

78. Medicare's allowed fee for an in-office procedure is $200. Dr. Smith is a PAR physician, and Dr. Jones is a nonPAR physician who does not accept assignment. How much will Dr. Smith and Dr. Jones receive, respectively, in total for this procedure?

    a. $200, $200

    b. $160, $152

    c. $200, $218.50

    d. $200, $230

79. When a patient is covered by Medicare, which of the following services will be reimbursed?

    a. General Health laboratory panel

    b. Consultation E/M codes

    c. A preventive medicine service at the start of coverage

    d. Certain transplant services such as pancreas and cornea

80. The physician performs, interprets, and reports a 12-lead EKG in the office. Later in the day, the same physician interprets and reports a 64-lead EKG in the heart center at the hospital. Referencing these NCCI Column 1 and Column 2 edits, which code requires a −59 modifier for payment?

| Column 1 | Column 2 |
|----------|----------|
| 0180T | 0179T |
| 0180T | 93000 |
| 0180T | 93005 |
| 0180T | 93010 |
| 0180T | 93040 |
| 0180T | 93041 |
| 0180T | 93042 |

    a. 93000, Electrocardiogram, routine ECG with at least 12 leads; with interpretation and report

    b. 93010, Electrocardiogram, routine ECG with at least 12 leads; interpretation and report only

    c. 0178T, Electrocardiogram, 64 leads or greater, with graphic presentation and analysis; with interpretation and report

    d. 0180T, Electrocardiogram, 64 leads or greater, with graphic presentation and analysis; interpretation and report only

## Domain IV  *Data Quality and Management*

81. A physician requests that the office manager identify any potentially significant issues in the ICD-9-CM code assignment for the 2013 fiscal year. The best report to review would be the:

    a. Diagnosis distribution report

    b. Service distribution report

    c. Revenue production report

    d. Charge summary report

82. There are several characteristics of data quality. Which of the following is *not* one of these characteristics?

    a. Consistency

    b. Analysis

    c. Precision

    d. Timeliness

83. A patient covered by Medicare is admitted on the evening of 1-14-2014. The attending physician completes the Initial Hospital Service while rounding and submits the following codes to describe the service. What education should take place regarding this claim?

    | Date | CPT Code | ICD-9-CM Code |
    | --- | --- | --- |
    | 1-15-2014 | 99223, Level 3 initial hospital service | 820.20, Fracture of neck of femur, pretrochanteric fracture, closed, unspecified |

    a. Level 3 initial hospital service codes are frequently the subject of government audits.

    b. The ICD-9-CM code does not appear specific.

    c. Modifier –AI, Principle physician of record, was not assigned.

    d. The date of service is incorrect.

## Domain V  *Information and Communication Technologies*

84. A physician wants to graphically show the increase in numbers of patients he has treated over the last 15 years. Which of the following would best be used to depict these data?

    a. Bar chart

    b. Pie chart

    c. Line graph

    d. Histogram

85. Which of the following is a barrier to effective computer-assisted coding?

    a. Capability of the computer to apply coding rules

    b. Resistance by physicians

    c. Lack of complete clinical documentation

    d. Resistance by coders

86. Storing duplicate data at a distant location is an example of:

    a. Data mapping

    b. Data mining

    c. Data storage for recovery

    d. Data redundancy

87. The _____ is a type of coding that uses software to automatically generate a set of medical codes based on documentation by the healthcare provider.

    a. Natural language processing

    b. Encoder

    c. Automated codebook

    d. Computer-assisted coding

## Domain VI  *Privacy, Confidentiality, Legal, and Ethical Issues*

88. Under HIPAA's Privacy and Security Rules, which one of the following is *not* considered a covered entity?

    a. Healthcare providers

    b. Healthcare clearinghouse

    c. Life insurance company

    d. Health plan

89. A legal, written document that specifies patient preferences regarding future healthcare or designates a person to assume authority for the patient is known as a(n):

    a. Court order

    b. Subpoena *duces tecum*

    c. Covered entity

    d. Advance directive

90. In a hospital, the Business/Accounting department has a legitimate access to a patient's health record without the patient's authorization. This statement is based on what HIPAA principle or standard?

    a. Preemption

    b. Minimum necessary

    c. Disclosure accounting

    d. Statute of limitations

91. Minors are generally unable to access, use, or disclose their personal health information. What resource should be cited as to who may legally authorize disclosure of a minor's health record?

    a. Chief information officer for the hospital

    b. Individual state law(s) since HIPAA defers to state law on such matters

    c. Hospital attorney hired by the facility

    d. HIPAA because of the strict rules regarding minors

92. Upon reviewing her record Sally finds that her physician stated in the discharge summary that she exhibited symptoms of extreme paranoia. Sally does not feel this statement is accurate and requests to amend her record. Which of the following would be a valid reason for Sally's physician to deny her request for amendment?

    a. Sally's physician feels the statement was accurate at the time

    b. It is inappropriate to amend entries related to mental health

    c. The request to amend the record was made greater than 7 days post-discharge

    d. Accepting the amendment may lessen the physician's reimbursement

93. Which of the following is not a required element of an authorization for release of PHI under HIPAA?

    a. The description of the information to be disclosed

    b. The purpose of the disclosure

    c. The signature of the individual

    d. A statement that the information may not be disclosed and must be destroyed upon completion of its use

## Domain VII *Compliance*

94. HIM coding professionals and the organizations that employ them have the responsibility to not tolerate behavior that adversely affects data quality. Which of the following is an example of behavior that should *not* be tolerated?

    a. Assign codes to an incomplete record without organizational policies in place to ensure codes are reviewed after the records are complete

    b. Follow up on and monitor identified problems

    c. Evaluate and trend diagnoses and procedures code selections

    d. Report data quality review results to organizational leadership, compliance staff, and the medical staff

95. An exception to the required consent requirement for treatment includes a(n):

    a. Implied consent

    b. Informed consent

    c. Physician discretion

    d. Medical emergency

96. Coding policies and procedures in any HIM Coding Compliance Manual should include all of the following components *except:*

    a. AHIMA Code of Ethics

    b. Official Coding Guidelines

    c. AHIMA Standards of Ethical Coding

    d. Bylaws and Regulations of the Medical Staff

# Multiple Choice Exam 1 Answers

| | | | |
|---|---|---|---|
| 1. | 25. | 49. | 73. |
| 2. | 26. | 50. | 74. |
| 3. | 27. | 51. | 75. |
| 4. | 28. | 52. | 76. |
| 5. | 29. | 53. | 77. |
| 6. | 30. | 54. | 78. |
| 7. | 31. | 55. | 79. |
| 8. | 32. | 56. | 80. |
| 9. | 33. | 57. | 81. |
| 10. | 34. | 58. | 82. |
| 11. | 35. | 59. | 83. |
| 12. | 36. | 60. | 84. |
| 13. | 37. | 61. | 85. |
| 14. | 38. | 62. | 86. |
| 15. | 39. | 63. | 87. |
| 16. | 40. | 64. | 88. |
| 17. | 41. | 65. | 89. |
| 18. | 42. | 66. | 90. |
| 19. | 43. | 67. | 91. |
| 20. | 44. | 68. | 92. |
| 21. | 45. | 69. | 93. |
| 22. | 46. | 70. | 94. |
| 23. | 47. | 71. | 95. |
| 24. | 48. | 72. | 96. |

# EXAM 1 MEDICAL CASES

## EXAM 1—CASE 1

**PICU PROGRESS NOTE**

**CHIEF COMPLAINT:** Wheezing

**HISTORY OF PRESENT ILLNESS:** The patient is a 25-month-old boy, transported here yesterday from the community hospital with a history of acute onset of respiratory distress and desaturation on room air. Clinical picture is initially consistent with first episode of wheezing. His respiratory distress has responded to Albuterol, Atrovent, Solu-Medrol, and Magnesium sulfate. However, he has persistent elevated anion gap that is not well explained.

**OVERNIGHT EVENTS:** The patient was initially treated with continuous Albuterol at 10 mg/hr, Atrovent q 6 hours, Solu-Medrol × 6 hours, and he was given one dose of Magnesium sulfate IV for continued respiratory distress, with resulting decrease in tachypnea and improvement in wheezing. However, he showed a persistent metabolic acidosis with an elevated anion gap. Given that metabolic acidosis did not improve after aggressive fluid rehydration, and the anion gap was elevated, a search was carried out for possible etiologies. His initial serum glucose prior to initiation of steroid therapy was 178, and he did begin spilling ketones and glucose in his urine. We therefore elected to treat for possible diabetic ketoacidosis. His hyperglycemia rapidly resolved on Insulin 0.05 units/kg/hour and aggressive fluid and electrolyte replacement. He was quiet from a neurologic standpoint overnight, responding with appropriate distress to multiple blood draws and verbally interacting with parents. On further history, there is a family history of diabetes type 2 in grandmother. There is no antecedent polyuria or polydipsia. No weight loss. He had been completely well until 3 days prior to admission when he developed URI symptoms, which developed into acute respiratory distress yesterday, necessitating ED visit to outside hospital and subsequent transfer here.

**VITAL SIGNS:**

    **TEMPERATURE:** 37.4

    **HEART RATE:** 147–199

    **MBP:** 60–95, R: 28–52

    **OXYGEN SATURATION:** 96–100%

    **INPUT:** 1,087

    **OUTPUT:** 853

**GENERAL:** Alert, says "No" or "Okay," appears more tired than yesterday's exam on admission, somewhat pale

**HEENT:** NCAT, TM's mildly red and partially wax impacted, no rhinorrhea, neck supple, no LAD

**CARDIOVASCULAR:** Tachycardia, regular sinus rhythm, no m/r/g

**PULMONARY:** Tachypnea, bilateral expiratory wheeze and prolonged expiratory phase, retractions

**ABDOMEN:** Soft, ND/NT, 1BS, no masses or HSM

## EXAM 1—CASE 1 (*continued*)

**EXTREMITIES:** WWP, symmetrical movements, CFT, 2 sec

**NEURO:** Somewhat more tired appearing than yesterday but still responds "Okay" to questions, symmetric movements UE and LE b/1, normal muscle bulk and tone, good strength when fighting blood draw today, EOMI, PERRL at 3 mm.

**LABS:** Serum ketones 10 (elevated), urine glucose 250–800

**CXR:** Hyperinflation, PBT, no infiltrate

**PHYSICAL EXAMINATION**

**ASSESSMENT:** Previously healthy 25-month-old boy with history of rapid onset of acute respiratory distress and wheezing. His pulmonary clinical picture is consistent with first-time reactive airway disease exacerbation with good response to typical asthma meds. However, he has persistent elevated anion gap acidosis and treatment for diabetic ketoacidosis is just beginning. Is on step 1 of new diabetes clinical pathway.

**PLAN:**

1. Diabetes mellitus, type 1, new onset. Follow clinical pathway, advancing diet to clears and assess tolerance. Follow I/Os. Get chem.–8 BID and CBC with lytes q 6 hours. Parents to step 1 education this afternoon.

2. Reactive airway disease, still with tachycardia and slightly tachypneic. Continue to observe as ketoacidosis resolves. Continue albuterol q 4 hrs prn. Transitioned from Solu-Medrol to Prednisone 2 mg/kg/day and will continue for total of 5-day course. Discontinue Atrovent. Repeat CXR prn for increasing respiratory distress.

3. Social work consult. Patient and parents are from out of state and visiting grandparents here. Mom in particular is quite worried about patient and his ability to complete travel plans to return home. Social work to assist with airline changes.

**HISTORY:** Detailed

**EXAMINATION:** Comprehensive

**MEDICAL DECISION MAKING:** Moderate

---

*Enter two diagnosis codes and one procedure code.*

---

**DX1**

**DX2**

**PR1**

## EXAM 1—CASE 2

**PROCEDURE NOTE**

**PREOPERATIVE DIAGNOSIS:** Classical Hodgkins, nodular sclerosis

**POSTOPERATIVE DIAGNOSIS:** Same

**PROCEDURE:** Bone marrow aspirates

Procedure performed in OR under anesthesia. Patient identified and consent obtained. Bone marrow studies performed today as patient is having a Mediport placed by general surgery during same operative session. 11-gauge Jamshidi biopsy needle used. Bone marrow biopsy sample obtained from right posterior iliac crest and sent to pathology.

Tolerated procedure without complications and was handed to surgery team for placement of port.

*Enter one diagnosis code and one procedure code.*

**DX1**

**PR1**

## EXAM 1—CASE 3

**PSYCHIATRY PROGRESS NOTE**

**DATE:** 2/15/XX

**LENGTH OF SERVICE:** 55 minutes

**LOCATION:** Office

**NOTES:** The patient has continued to work on "Oceans of Emotions" workbook to help identify and understand her emotions better. Worked on short- and long-term goals—socially, academically, emotionally. She denies any difficulty with school with organization or concentration. She does endorse wanting more friends.

**MSE:** Alert, casually groomed wearing jeans and fleece; cooperative, good eye contact

**SPEECH:** Normal

**THOUGHT PROCESS:** Linear

**THOUGHT CONTENT:** Appropriate

**MOOD:** "Fine"

**AFFECT:** Somewhat anxious at times

**INSIGHT AND JUDGMENT:** Fair/good

**ATTENTION:** Fair

**CHANGES TO MEDS SINCE LAST VISIT:** None. No side effects reported. Good compliance.

**CURRENT MEDS:**

Risperdal 1 mg TID

Adderall XR 30 mg q a.m., Adderall 15 mg at 2 p.m.

Celexa 5 mg q day

Bactrim for acne

**DIAGNOSES:**

1. ADHD

2. Reactive adjustment disorder with anxiety

**PLAN:**

1. Continue current meds

2. Mother met with therapist for family therapy, patient to be scheduled in March

3. Insurance has approved up to 8 more visits

## EXAM 1—CASE 3 (*continued*)

**TREATMENT PLAN GOALS:**

1. Decrease mood dysregulation
2. Decrease self-injurious behaviors
3. Decrease anxiety
4. Improve socialization
5. Improve self-esteem
6. Improve academic performance

*Enter two diagnosis codes and one procedure code.*

**DX1**

**DX2**

**PR1**

## EXAM 1—CASE 4

**PROCEDURE:** Implantation of spinal cord stimulator lead under fluoroscopic guidance

**DIAGNOSES:** Chronic low back pain, lumbar radiculopathy, and multiple lumbar disc protrusions

The patient is well known to me, originally referred by Dr. X for management of chronic low back pain. The patient has tried multiple analgesics with partial relief. The patient has had epidural steroid injections also, which have given her temporary relief. The patient requested aggressive treatment, as the patient had a spinal cord stimulator trial done previously and was extremely happy with the degree of pain relief. The patient was happy that she was able to sleep well and also that she did not have to take her pain medications. The patient is very eager to get this permanent lead placement. It was decided to do a permanent spinal cord stimulator in lead as well as an implanted IPG. The patient also saw Dr. Y, who will be doing IPG implantation and the patient also has gone through the brochure as well as the video for the procedure. The patient understands the risks and benefits of the procedure. The patient understands its possible side effects, including headache from posterior puncture and also the possibility of weakness in the legs and epidural hematoma. The patient also understands that she should call me and also the representative from Bionics as often as needed, if she has any side effects to call us, and if needed, to go to ER. The patient also understands the restrictions advised to be followed sincerely.

**PROCEDURE:** Under monitored anesthesia care, the patient was positioned prone with arms extended upwards away from the surgical field. The patient's back was prepped aseptically. The patient was stable, spontaneously breathing, and communicating throughout the procedure. Radiographic C-arm was positioned directly over the thoracolumbar junction. Ll-L2 interspace was identified using fluoroscopy. Then 2 mL each of 1% lidocaine with 0.25 mL preservative free Marcaine was mixed and infiltrated using a 25-gauge needle to the inter laminar space. A #14-gauge Bionix epidural needle was then advanced toward the epidural space using paramedian approach by loss of resistance technique to air with 30- to 45-degree angle of entry. Epidural space was identified by lateral fluoroscopy continuously. On aspiration, no CSF or heme. No paraesthesia at any point. The electrode was then advanced through the needle cephalad in epidural space directed to remain in the midline in the dorsal epidural space. The electrode was finally positioned at T8–T9 level. The patient appreciated appropriate paresthesia for stimulation covering her back and both the legs, especially the left lower extremity and back area. Further procedure was taken over by Dr. X, who implanted the pulse generator and secured the lead as well as the pulse generator. In the recovery room, the patient complained of frontal headache, no nausea, or vomiting. The patient also complained of mild stiffness in the neck, which was partially reduced by Demerol 25 mg as well as 30 mg of Toradol. I again went over the patient with possible side effects of the procedure including posterior puncture headache, which may be the possible reason that she was having headache as well as neck stiffness. In detail, I explained to the patient the conservative management including analgesics, hydration, use of caffeine, and pain killers. I also explained the possibility of posterior puncture headache, treatment with blood patch. The patient will call me as needed and if the pain is significant will consider further aggressive treatment. The patient was discharged uneventfully. The patient has been prescribed Keflex. The patient has my number and the Bionics representative's telephone number to reach as needed.

Enter two diagnosis codes and one procedure code.

**DX1**

**DX2**

**PR1**

## EXAM 1—CASE 5

**PREOPERATIVE DIAGNOSIS:** Metastatic prostate cancer.

**POSTOPERATIVE DIAGNOSIS:** Bilateral orchiectomy.

**PROCEDURE PERFORMED:** Bilateral orchiectomy.

**INDICATIONS:** This 71-year-old white male developed leg swelling, and a CT scan revealed retroperitoneal lymphadenopathy. Biopsy of these lymph nodes was positive for adenocarcinoma, PSA positive, suggesting prostate cancer. His PSA was 105 nanograms.

The options of treatment were discussed with the patient. He was advised to have bilateral orchiectomy. He has been started on Casodex. The patient agreed to surgery.

After satisfactory general anesthesia, the patient was prepped and draped in supine position. Incision was made in the median raphe of the scrotum. The testicular tunics were incised on the left side and the left testicle delivered from the wound. Spermatic cord was doubly clamped and excised. The spermatic cord was controlled with a proximal tie of #1 chromic catgut and a distal suture ligature of #1 chromic catgut. In similar fashion, the right testicle was removed. No complications were encountered. Wound was closed routinely in layers and sterile dressings applied, as well as a scrotal support. The patient was taken to the recovery room in good condition.

*Enter two diagnosis codes and one procedure code.*

**DX1**

**DX2**

**PR1**

## EXAM 1—CASE 6

**DATE OF EMERGENCY DEPARTMENT VISIT:** 07/24/XX

**CHIEF COMPLAINT:** Right-sided chest pain

**HISTORY OF PRESENT ILLNESS:** The patient is a 47-year-old female who reports the onset of severe, sharp pain on her right side after an extended bout of coughing this afternoon. She reports the pain becoming acutely worse at approximately 5:30 p.m., again after another round of coughing. The patient is asthmatic and only in fair control. This last round of coughing resulted in post-tussive emesis. She reports that she is not short of breath but is breathing shallowly to avoid increasing the pain. There is no left-sided chest pain or pressure. She describes this pain as far different than any asthma-related pain. She tried her albuterol inhaler for the cough, but this had no relief of the pain. The pain is worse with deep inspiration and with movement of the chest. Other than the initial coughing episodes, there has been no focal trauma or direct injury to the area. She does report that she just returned from vacation yesterday, after a 5-hour plane flight. She has not experienced any lower extremity pain or edema and is not actually short of breath. She has no history of deep vein thrombosis or pulmonary embolism.

**PAST MEDICAL HISTORY:**

1. Asthma

2. Gastroesophageal reflux

3. Migraine headaches

**PAST SURGICAL HISTORY:** Tubal ligation and bone spur removal from left foot in the remote past.

**MEDICATIONS:** Albuterol inhaler, Claritin, Prilosec, Singular, and Verapamil for headache prevention

**ALLERGIES:** Codeine

**FAMILY HISTORY:** Significant for asthma in mother and COPD in maternal grandfather.

**SOCIAL HISTORY:** She denies tobacco, alcohol, or drug abuse. She is accompanied to the ED by her husband.

**REVIEW OF SYSTEMS:** As per HPI and additionally, she denies fever, chills, or nausea. There is no diffuse weakness and no recent URI. There is no chest pressure, tightness, or palpitations. No sputum production with cough. No abdominal pain or diarrhea. No tingling or numbness. There are no rashes. Does not report any depression.

**PHYSICAL EXAM:** 141/96, Pulse 81, Respirations 24, Temp 97.6. The patient is awake and fully oriented. However, there appears to be moderate to severe distress from pain described above. Pupils: ERRLA bilaterally. The sclerae are white. Conjunctiva are pink. The oral mucosa is moist. The neck is supple with full ROM. No evidence of JVD. Lungs are clear to auscultation with breath sounds equal bilaterally. Heart is RRR, S1, S2 without murmur. Back is tender over the anterior or lower one third of the rib cage, including the lateral aspect of the left side of her chest. The sternum is nontender. There are no rashes. Abdomen is moderately obese but otherwise soft, nontender, and not distended with normal bowel sounds. Extremities are without cyanosis, clubbing, or edema. Homans sign is negative bilaterally. The calves are nontender. The radial and dorsalis pedis pulses are 2+ and equal bilaterally.

**ED FINDINGS:** A BMP revealed sodium of 137, potassium of 3.4, chloride 102, C02 27, BUN 11, Creatinine 0.5, and glucose of 102. The D-Dimer was normal at 0.24. Chest x-ray revealed mild elevation of the diaphragm on the right side but no evidence of pneumothorax. Otherwise, clear lung fields with a normal-appearing heart. CT of the chest to rule out PE revealed a little area of atelectasis with some fat and normal size lymph nodes in the Hila, but no definitive evidence of PE.

## EXAM 1—CASE 6 (*continued*)

**ED COURSE:** Initial suspicions were for pneumonia, pneumothorax, pulmonary embolism, costochondritis, or musculoskeletal pain. In light of her recent airplane flight, I felt that she was above a low risk for PE and obtained the above listed studies. The radiologist recommended the D-dimer, which returned normal.

The patient's pain was controlled with IV Toradol and IV Morphine in the ED, and she had no evidence of tachycardia, tachypnea, or hypoxia on repeat evaluation. She felt comfortable with discharge and the diagnosis of costochondritis. She was given Vicodin for discomfort and will take ibuprofen 400 mg for anti-inflammatory, as tolerated by her GERD.

**HISTORY:** Comprehensive

**EXAMINATION:** Comprehensive

**MEDICAL DECISION MAKING:** High

*Enter four diagnosis codes and one procedure code.*

**DX1**

**DX2**

**DX3**

**DX4**

**PR1**

## EXAM 1—CASE 7

**PREOPERATIVE DIAGNOSIS:** Right upper lung tumor.

**POSTOPERATIVE DIAGNOSIS:** Right upper lung tumor.

**OPERATION:** Flexible bronchoscopy.

**ANESTHESIA:** 2% Xylocaine gel, Xylocaine spray, and IV sedation.

**DESCRIPTION OF PROCEDURE:** The patient was placed in the supine position. The right nostril was anesthetized with 2% Xylocaine gel and the pharynx with Xylocaine spray and 4% Xylocaine liquid. After proper anesthesia the flexible bronchoscope was inserted into the right nostril without any difficulty. The pharynx and vocal cords looked normal. There were copious secretions over the cords and in the trachea; however, the trachea looks normal, the carina and the entire endobronchial tree, both the left side and the right side, looks normal. Because of the lesions on the right upper lobe and possibly the right lower lobe superior segment noted on imaging, the bronchoscope was passed and then wedged in the right upper lobe, where multiple endobronchial biopsies were taken. Also, biopsies from the right lower lobe superior segment were also taken. However, no lesions were seen. The old lumina looks open. The patient tolerated the procedure very well. Estimated blood loss was about 2 mL. The patient was taken to the recovery room in satisfactory condition, where a chest x-ray will be taken to rule out any pneumothorax.

*Enter one diagnosis codes and one procedure code.*

**DX1**

**PR1**

## EXAM 1—CASE 8

**ADMISSION DATE:** 10/21/XX

**DISCHARGE DATE:** 10/24/XX

**ADMISSION CHIEF COMPLAINT:** Pneumonia

**DISCHARGE DIAGNOSES:** Pneumonia

**PROCEDURES:** Chest radiography

**HOSPITAL COURSE:** 7-week-old girl, ex 34 week preemie, presenting with 5 days of cough and runny nose and 1 day of fever to 100.8, vomiting X4. Patient went to the local community hospital for a full sepsis workup and was transferred here for further treatment. Chest radiograph consistent with hyperinflation and lower respiratory infection. Patient was started on ampicillin and cefotaxime. She was also started on azithromycin given recent local pertussis epidemic. However, she did not clinically have signs or symptoms of pertussis during this admission. Her blood culture from the local hospital grew non-anthrax bacillus species on aerobic media, thought to potentially be a contaminant. Repeat blood culture after antibiotics before discharge showed no growth. Pertussis PCR negative.

Patient otherwise continued to stay afebrile throughout admission. She was monitored on IV antibiotics until discharge. She was discharged home when afebrile >24 hours, stable on RA and tolerating POs well. CBC one day prior to discharge was within normal limits. CSF culture is pending.

**DISCHARGE STATUS:** Recovered

**DISCHARGE PLAN:** I spent 45 minutes in education with the mother and grandmother, as well as treatment planning with primary care for follow-up after the CSF culture results return.

---

*Enter one diagnosis code and one procedure code.*

---

**DX1**

**PR1**

# EXAM 2

*For the following questions, choose the* best *answer. A blank answer sheet for these multiple choice questions can be found on page 63.*

## Domain I    Health Information Documentation

1. The physician removes, in his office, a skin lesion from the patient's cheek and submits it to a pathologist for review. The physician documents "skin lesion" in the chart but prior to billing the pathologist reports that it is a basal cell carcinoma. What does the coder submit on the claim form?

   a. Basal cell carcinoma of the skin

   b. Skin lesion

   c. Benign skin lesion

   d. The coder must query the physician because of conflicting data

2. What information is necessary to assign the correct Evaluation and Management (E/M) code for preventive medicine services?

   a. The level of history and examination performed

   b. The counseling provided

   c. The risk factor reduction intervention

   d. The age of the patient

3. What is the best source of documentation to determine the size of a removed malignant lesion?

   a. Pathology report

   b. Postacute care unit record

   c. Operative report

   d. Physical examination

4. A coder might find which of the following on a patient's problem list if the medication list contains the drug Protonix?

   a. High blood pressure

   b. Esophagitis

   c. Congestive heart failure

   d. AIDS

5. The coder notes that the patient is taking prescribed Haldol. The final diagnoses on the progress notes include diabetes mellitus, acute pharyngitis, and malnutrition. What condition might the coder suspect the patient has and should query the physician?

   a. Insomnia

   b. Hypertension

   c. Schizophrenia

   d. Rheumatoid arthritis

6. According to CPT guidelines, a colonoscopy includes:

    a. Examination of the rectum and sigmoid colon

    b. Examination of the entire rectum, sigmoid colon, and may include examination of a portion of the descending colon

    c. Examination of the entire colon from the rectum to the cecum

    d. Examination of the entire colon, from the rectum to the cecum, and may include the examination of the terminal ileum

7. A biopsy revealed serous papillary adenocarcinoma. The coder would expect to see a diagnosis of cancer of the:

    a. Bladder

    b. Breast

    c. Ovary

    d. Uterus

8. The coder notes that the physician has ordered potassium replacement for the patient. The coder might expect to see a diagnosis of:

    a. Hypokalemia

    b. Hyponatremia

    c. Hyperkalemia

    d. Hypernatremia

9. Where might a coder find information on whether a particular medication has been administered to the patient?

    a. Physician's orders

    b. Nurse's notes

    c. Problem list

    d. Medical history

10. When the physician describes "deep full-thickness burns," he is referring to which degree of burn?

    a. 1st

    b. 2nd

    c. 3rd

    d. 4th

## Domain II   *Diagnosis and Procedure Coding*

11. The physician orders a chest x-ray for a patient who presents with fever, productive cough, and shortness of breath. The physician indicates in the progress notes: Rule out pneumonia. What code(s) should the coder report for the visit when the results have not yet been received?

    a. Pneumonia

    b. Fever, cough, shortness of breath

    c. Cough, shortness of breath

    d. Pneumonia, cough, shortness of breath

12. A series of terms in parentheses sometimes directly following a main term or subterm in ICD-10-CM refers to:

    a. Carryover lines

    b. Exclusion notes

    c. Nonessential modifiers

    d. Eponyms

13. This symbol is used in the Tabular List after an incomplete term that needs one or more of the modifiers that follow:

    a. Brace

    b. Colon

    c. Section mark

    d. Lozenge

14. This symbol is only found in the Tabular List in ICD-10-CM and encloses synonyms, alternative wording, abbreviations, and explanatory phrases:

    a. Parentheses

    b. Colon

    c. Square brackets

    d. Nonessential modifiers

15. The coding guideline for coding sequelae is:

    a. Only the residual condition or nature of the sequela is coded

    b. The cause of the sequela is sequenced first followed by the residual condition

    c. Only the cause of the sequela is coded

    d. The residual condition is sequenced first, followed by the cause of the sequela

16. Which of the following would be classified to an ICD-10-CM category for bacterial diseases?

    a. Herpes simplex

    b. *Staphylococcus aureus*

    c. Influenza, types A and B

    d. *Candida albicans*

17. According to ICD-10-CM, an elderly primigravida is defined as a woman who gives birth to her first child after the age of:

    a. 30

    b. 35

    c. 38

    d. 40

18. The physician sees a patient in the hospital because an attempted therapeutic abortion resulted in a liveborn infant. In ICD-10-CM, how would the services provided to the mother be coded?

    a. Use the code for a complete or unspecified spontaneous abortion (O03.9)

    b. Use the code for the specific type of abortion along with a code from category Z37 (outcome of delivery)

    c. Use the code for a missed abortion (O02.1) followed by code Z38.00 (liveborn, infant, delivered vaginally)

    d. Use code Z33.2, (Encounter for elective termination of pregnancy) followed by Z37.0 (single live birth)

19. Code O80, normal delivery, is assigned for which of the following scenarios:

    a. Delivery resulting in a stillborn

    b. Delivery without prenatal or postpartum complications

    c. Delivery, full-term—breech presentation

    d. Delivery, premature infant with cephalic presentation

20. ICD-10-CM defines the "newborn period" as birth through the____ day following birth.

    a. 28th

    b. 14th

    c. 60th

    d. 30th

21. "Prolonged pregnancy" is used to demonstrate that a woman is over _____ weeks of gestation.

    a. 41

    b. 39

    c. 40

    d. 42

22. An abnormal communication or opening in the ventricular septum that allows blood to shunt from the left ventricle to the right ventricle defines a condition known as:

    a. Patent ductus arteriosus

    b. Atrial septal defect

    c. Hypoplastic left ventricle syndrome

    d. Ventricular septal defect

23. How would the following be coded? Physician's office visit: Diagnosis of hypoglycemia in infant born to a diabetic mother.

    a. P70.0, Syndrome of infant of mother with gestational diabetes

    b. E08.649, Diabetes mellitus due to underlying condition with hypoglycemia without coma

    c. P70.1, Syndrome of infant of a diabetic mother

    d. E08.9, Diabetes mellitus due to underlying condition without complications

24. Routine encounter for supervision of a normal first pregnancy in the second trimester would be coded as:

    a. Z33.1, Pregnant state, incidental

    b. Z34.02, Encounter for supervision of normal first pregnancy, second trimester

    c. O09.812, Supervision of pregnancy resulting from assisted reproductive technology, second trimester

    d. Z34.82, Encounter for supervision of other normal pregnancy, second trimester

25. A woman is admitted with postpartum perineum prolapse which is secondary to second degree laceration which was sustained during a delivery 10 months ago:

    | N81.89 | Other female genital prolapse |
    |--------|-------------------------------|
    | N81.9 | Female genital prolapse, unspecified |
    | O94 | Sequelae of complications of pregnancy, childbirth, and the puerperium |

    a. N81.89

    b. N81.89, O94

    c. O94

    d. N81.9, O94

26. The patient is admitted at 26 weeks' gestation for advanced testing after an inconclusive amniocentesis. After further examination it was determined that the fetus was developing normally. Which diagnosis would the physician submit for the hospital services?

    a. Z13.79, Encounter for other screening for genetic and chromosomal anomalies

    b. Z31.430, Encounter of female for testing for genetic disease carrier status for procreative management

    c. Z36, Encounter for antenatal screening of mother

    d. Z03.79, Encounter for other suspected maternal and fetal conditions ruled out

27. Which of the following conditions is not considered a type of COPD?

    a. Chronic obstructive bronchitis

    b. Emphysema

    c. Asthma

    d. All are considered types of COPD

28. The depth of a pressure ulcer is identified by stages I–IV. Which stage involves full-thickness skin loss involving damage or necrosis into subcutaneous soft tissues?

    a. Stage I

    b. Stage II

    c. Stage III

    d. Stage IV

29. Which of the following is reported using a neoplasm code?

    a. Mild dysplasia of the cervix

    b. Cervical intraepithelial neoplasia I

    c. Moderate dysplasia of cervix

    d. Cervical intraepithelial neoplasia III

30. The patient is seen in his ophthalmologist's office and diagnosed with chronic angle-closure glaucoma, mild in the right eye and acute angle glaucoma in the left eye. Which diagnosis would the physician submit for these services?

    | | |
    |---|---|
    | H40.212 | Acute angle-closure glaucoma,left eye |
    | H40.2211 | Chronic angle-closure glaucoma, right eye, mild stage |
    | H40.20X1 | Unspecified primary angle-closure glaucoma, mild stage |
    | H40.11X1 | Primary open-angle glaucoma, mild stage |

    a. H40.11X1, H40.2211

    b. H40.212, H40.2211

    c. H40.212, H40.1X11

    d. H40.2211, H40.20X1

31. The 71-year-old patient is seen in the office with secondary diabetes mellitus due to a previous partial pancreatectomy. Which diagnosis would the physician submit for the services?

    | | |
    |---|---|
    | E13.8 | Other specified diabetes mellitus with unspecified complications |
    | E13.9 | Other specified diabetes mellitus without complications |
    | E89.1 | Postprocedural hypoinsulinemia |
    | Z90.411 | Acquired partial absence of pancreas |

    a. E13.8, E89.1

    b. E89.1, Z90.411

    c. E89.1, E13.9, Z90.411

    d. E13.9, E89.1

32. A patient is seen in the ED with severe chest pain and was diagnosed with acute myocardial infarction of the anterolateral wall. He is given tissue plasminogen activator (tPA) and transferred within 4 hours to a cardiac specialty hospital. Which diagnosis would the physician submit for the hospital services at the specialty hospital?

> I21.09    ST elevation (STEMI) myocardial infarction involving other coronary artery of anterior wall
>
> I22.0    Subsequent ST elevation (STEMI) myocardial infarction of anterior wall
>
> Z92.82    Status post administration of tPA in a different facility within the last 24 hours prior to admission to current facility

    a. I21.09, Z92.82

    b. I22.0

    c. Z92.82

    d. I22.0, Z92.82

33. Which diagnosis would the physician submit for the hospital services performed at the first hospital?

> I21.09    ST elevation (STEMI) myocardial infarction involving other coronary artery of anterior wall
>
> I22.0    Subsequent ST elevation (STEMI) myocardial infarction of anterior wall
>
> R07.89    Other chest pain
>
> Z92.82    Status post administration of tPA in a different facility within the last 24 hours prior to admission to current facility

    a. Z92.82

    b. I21.09

    c. I22.0

    d. R07.89

34. Anemia caused by a failure of the bone marrow to produce enough red blood cells is referred to as:

    a. Iron deficiency anemia

    b. Sickle cell anemia

    c. Acute blood loss anemia

    d. Aplastic anemia

35. _____ is associated with congenital accessory atrial conduction pathway, physical or psychological stress, hypoxia, hypokalemia, caffeine or marijuana use, stimulant use and digitalis toxicity.

    a. Atrial flutter

    b. Paroxysmal supraventricular tachycardia

    c. Sick sinus syndrome

    d. Wolff-Parkinson-White syndrome

36. The patient was seen in the outpatient wound care clinic for treatment of a decubitus ulcer of the sacrum. Upon examination, the physician listed the diagnosis as unstageable decubitus ulcer of the sacrum. How would this encounter be coded?

| | |
|---|---|
| L89.100 | Pressure ulcer of unspecified part of back, unstageable |
| L89.109 | Pressure ulcer, unspecified part of back, unspecified stage |
| L89.150 | Pressure ulcer of sacral region, unstageable |
| L89.159 | Pressure ulcer of sacral region, unspecified stage |

   a. L89.100

   b. L89.159

   c. L89.150

   d. L89.109

37. The 20-year-old patient was seen in the emergency room with complaints that the physician thought was a urinary tract infection. After a urine culture was done, the physician's diagnosis was confirmed as: Urinary tract infection due to Shiga toxin-producing *E. coli* O157. How would this diagnosis be coded?

| | |
|---|---|
| N39.0 | Urinary tract infection, site not specified |
| P39.3 | Neonatal urinary tract infection |
| B96.21 | Shiga toxin-producing Escherichia coli [E. coli] (STEC) O157 as the cause of diseases classified elsewhere |
| B96.22 | Other specified Shiga toxin-producing Escherichia coli [E. coli] (STEC) as the cause of diseases classified elsewhere |
| B96.23 | Unspecified Shiga toxin-producing Escherichia coli [E. coli] (STEC) as the cause of diseases classified elsewhere |

   a. N39.0, B96.21

   b. P39.3, B96.22

   c. N39.0, B96.23

   d. P39.3, B96.21

38. Which is the correct way to code an encounter for a patient diagnosed with a basal cell carcinoma of the ear and external auditory canal?

| | |
|---|---|
| C43.8 | Malignant melanoma of overlapping sites of skin |
| C43.9 | Maligant melanoma of skin, unspecified |
| C44.201 | Unspecified malignant neoplasm of skin of unspecified ear and external auricular canal |
| C44.211 | Basal cell carcinoma of skin of unspecified ear and external auricular canal |

   a. C44.201

   b. C43.8

   c. C43.9

   d. C44.211

39. A Pap smear of the cervix cannot be interpreted because the sample was inadequate. What type of code should be assigned?

    a. Code that designates abnormal smear

    b. Code that designates satisfactory smear but lacking transformation zone

    c. Code for other abnormal Pap smear

    d. Code for unsatisfactory cytology smear

40. What type of fracture occurs when the bone breaks and the ends of the bone are pushed into each other?

    a. Greenstick

    b. Impacted

    c. Pathological

    d. Transverse

41. Which of the following terms does not indicate the severity of an asthma attack?

    a. Moderate persistent

    b. Acute exacerbation

    c. Mild persistent

    d. Mild intermittent

42. Non-healing burns are coded as:

    a. Infected burns

    b. Chemical burns

    c. Acute burns

    d. Sunburn

43. According to the CPT guidelines, when is it appropriate to code an evaluation and management (E/M) visit based on time?

    a. When the evaluation and management elements for the minimal level have not been met

    b. When counseling and/or coordination of care are more than 50% of the visit

    c. When the time spent with the patient exceeds the time listed as typically spent with the patient for that code

    d. When the medical decision making is high and the history and examination are not well-documented

44. The patient presents for an initial insertion of a dual chamber pacemaker. How is this procedure coded?

> | 33206 | Insertion of new or replacement of permanent pacemaker with transvenous electrode(s); atrial |
> | 33208 | Atrial and ventricular |
> | 33216 | Insertion of a single transvenous electrode; permanent pacemaker or implantable defibrillator |
> | 33217 | Insertion of 2 transvenous electrodes, permanent pacemaker or implantable defibrillator |

    a. 33206

    b. 33206, 33216

    c. 33208

    d. 33208, 33217

45. A costovertebral approach is used for a posterolateral decompression of the spinal cord. The chest surgeon opens and closes the operative site and the neurosurgeon completes the decompression procedure. Which modifier is applied to the chest surgeon's services?

    a. −54, Surgical care only

    b. −62, Two surgeons

    c. −66, Surgical team

    d. −80, Assistant surgeon

46. When the CPT Index and Tabular do not contain a code that describes an adequately documented procedure that was performed by the physician, what action should the coder take?

    a. Assign the code that most closely describes the procedure performed by the physician

    b. Query the physician to determine what the code assignment should be

    c. Assign the unlisted code from the corresponding anatomical section

    d. Assign the code that describes a more complex procedure and attach a −52 modifier

47. The physician completes a percutaneous transluminal coronary angioplasty on a patient with 90% acute blockage of two sites (proximal and mid) left anterior descending artery. A drug-eluting stent is used as each site. How is this service coded?

    a. 92920, 92928

    b. 92928

    c. 92928, 92929

    d. 92943

48. When coding an E/M code, what modifier would be acceptable for use?

    a. −LT, Left side

    b. −32, Mandated services

    c. −51, Multiple procedures

    d. −59, Distinct procedural service

49. The patient undergoes a TRAM flap reconstruction of the breast. How is this service coded?

    a. 19361, Breast reconstruction with latissimus dorsi flap, without prosthetic implant

    b. 19364, Breast reconstruction with free flap

    c. 19366, Breast reconstruction with other technique

    d. 19367, Breast reconstruction with transverse rectus abdominis myocutaneous flap, single pedicle, including closure of donor site

50. The patient is taken to the operating room by the neurosurgeon for repair of a depressed skull fracture following a motorcycle accident where he was an unhelmeted driver. Two large fragments of skull, one 7 cm and one 6 cm, have pierced the dura. The fragments are removed from the brain along with road contaminant, and the dura is repaired. How are the services of the neurosurgeon coded?

    a. 62000, Elevation of depressed skull fracture; simple, extradural

    b. 62005, Elevation of depressed skull fracture; compound or comminuted, extradural

    c. 62010, Elevation of depressed skull fracture; with repair of dura and/or debridement of brain

    d. 62141, Cranioplasty for skull defect; larger than 5 cm in diameter

51. The coder is coding an arthrodesis of the intercarpal joint, and the CPT Index has an entry that reads: Arthrodesis, Interphalangeal Joint 26860–26863. What action should the coder take?

    a. Code the first listed code in the series.

    b. Code the last listed code in the series.

    c. Look up codes 26860–26863, and code all the codes.

    d. Look up codes 26860–26863, and pick the best code.

52. When a patient is seen in the office and then admitted as an inpatient and discharged from the hospital all on the same calendar date, what series of codes should the coder use to code these services?

    a. Office and Other Outpatient Services and Hospital Discharge Services

    b. Observation or Inpatient Care Services (including Admission and Discharge Services)

    c. Office and Other Outpatient Services, Initial Hospital Care, and Hospital Discharge Services

    d. Initial Hospital Care and Hospital Discharge Services

53. The patient undergoes a secondary procedure to relieve pressure in the eye. The physician excises a portion of the trabecular meshwork to relieve the pressure. How is this service coded?

    a. 65850, Trabeculotomy ab externo

    b. 65855, Trabeculoplasty by laser surgery, one or more sessions (defined treatment series)

    c. 66170, Fistulization of sclera for glaucoma; trabeculectomy ab externo in absence of previous surgery

    d. 66172, Fistulization of sclera for glaucoma; trabeculectomy ab externo with scarring from previous ocular surgery or trauma

54. The patient lives in an assisted living facility that does not have nursing care. The caregiver calls the patient's physician to see the patient due to severe combativeness during meals. The physician provides an expanded problem-focused history and examination and uses moderate level medical decision making. What code would the physician use to describe these services?

    a. 99213, Office and other outpatient visit for an established patient with expanded problem-focused history and examination and low medical decision making

    b. 99308, Subsequent nursing facility care, per day, with expanded problem-focused history and examination and low medical decision making

    c. 99335, Domiciliary or rest home visit for an established patient with expanded problem-focused history and examination and low medical decision making

    d. 99348, Home visit for an established patient with expanded problem-focused history and examination and low medical decision making

55. A patient with severe cardiac disease undergoes a cardiectomy and transplantation of a replacement heart system. How is this service coded?

    a. 33935, Heart-lung transplant with recipient cardiectomy-pneumonectomy

    b. 33945, Heart transplant, with or without recipient cardiectomy

    c. 0051T, Implantation of a total replacement heart system (artificial heart) with recipient cardiectomy

    d. 0052T, Replacement or repair of thoracic unit of a total replacement heart system (artificial heart)

56. A patient steps on a piece of glass, driving it deep into the plantar surface of the foot. What code does the coder assign for the removal of this glass?

    a. 20525, Removal of foreign body in muscle or tendon sheath; deep or complicated

    b. 28190, Removal of foreign body, foot; subcutaneous

    c. 28192, Removal of foreign body, foot; deep

    d. 28193, Removal of foreign body, foot; complicated

57. When a Medicare patient receives an injection of IM penicillin G benzathine, 100,000 units only, what is the appropriate code assignment?

| | |
|---|---|
| 96372 | Therapeutic, prophylactic or diagnostic injection (specify substance or drug); subcutaneous or intramuscular |
| 96374 | Therapeutic, prophylactic or diagnostic injection (specify substance or drug); intravenous push, single or initial substance/drug |
| J0558 | Injection, penicillin G benzathine, and penicillin G procaine 100,000 units |
| J0561 | Injection, penicillin G benzathine, 100,000 units |

    a. 96372

    b. J0558

    c. 96374

    d. 96372, J0561

58. The patient is taken to the endoscopy suite, where the endoscope is passed into the esophagus but does not continue past the diaphragm into the stomach. Based on this documentation, what CPT code would be selected to represent this procedure?

    a. 43200, Esophagoscopy, rigid or flexible; diagnostic, with or without collection of specimen(s) by brushing or washing (separate procedure)

    b. 43231, Esophagoscopy, rigid or flexible; with endoscopic ultrasound examination

    c. 43235, Esophagogastroduodenoscopy, flexible, transoral; diagnostic, including collection of specimen(s) by brushing or washing, when performed (separate procedure)

    d. 43260, Endoscopic retrograde cholangiopancreatography (ERCP); diagnostic, including collection of specimen(s) by brushing or washing, when performed (separate procedure)

59. The physician places a needle into the patient's back using intraoperative fluoroscopy guidance. The physician then injects local anesthetic and steroids into the epidural space bilaterally at the L4 and L5 level of the spine. What is the correct procedure coding for this case?

    | | |
    |---|---|
    | 64483 | Injection, anesthetic agent and/or steroid, transforaminal epidural, with imaging guidance (fluoroscopy or CT); lumbar or sacral, single level |
    | 64484 | Injection, anesthetic agent and/or steroid, transforaminal epidural, with imaging guidance (fluoroscopy or CT); lumbar or sacral, each additional level (List separately in addition to code for primary procedure.) |
    | 0230T | Injection(s), anesthetic agent and/or steroid, transforaminal epidural, with ultrasound guidance, lumbar or sacral, single level |
    | 0231T | Injection(s), anesthetic agent and/or steroid, transforaminal epidural, with ultrasound guidance, lumbar or sacral, each additional level (List separately in addition to code for primary procedure.) |
    | −50 | Bilateral |

    a. 0230T, 0231T

    b. 0230T–50, 0231T–50

    c. 64483, 64484

    d. 64483–50, 64484–50

60. The patient receives a partial living donor liver transplant. To correctly code this case, what additional information is required?

    a. Whether the patient is related to the donor

    b. How many segments were involved in the procedure

    c. Whether a recipient hepatectomy was performed

    d. The approach used to perform the procedure

61. The physician directly accesses an arteriovenous shunt using ultrasound guidance to visualize the puncture site. The shunt is completely imaged and evaluated for blockage. How is the procedure coded?

    a. 36147, 76937

    b. 36147, 75791, 76937

    c. 36215, 75710

    d. 36818, 76937

62. The surgeon asks if the surgical preparation codes (15002–15005) are appropriate for use with the restorative procedure that was performed. Which of the following is a true statement?

    a. Codes 15002–15005 are used when the wound will be healed by secondary intention

    b. Codes 15002–15005 are the same as the debridement codes but are used with the skin graft codes

    c. Codes 15002–15005 are to be used with autograft, flap or skin substitute graft

    d. Codes 15002–15005 are not used with wounds to be treated by negative pressure wound therapy

63. The patient undergoes a flexible bronchoscopy and thermoplasty is performed in the right, middle bronchus for asthmatic constriction. How is this procedure coded?

    a. 31641, Bronchoscopy, rigid or flexible, including fluoroscopic guidance, when performed; with destruction of tumor or relief of stenosis by any method other than excision (eg, Laser therapy, cryotherapy)

    b. 31660, Bronchoscopy, rigid or flexible, including fluoroscopic guidance, when performed; with bronchial thermoplasty, 1 lobe

    c. 31899, Unlisted procedure, trachea, bronchi

    d. 32999, Unlisted procedure, lungs and pleura

64. The patient had lung lesions in the upper and lower left lobes. They were removed by wedge resection with margins using a thoracoscopic approach. What is the correct code assignment for this case?

    a. 32505, 32506

    b. 32607, 32608

    c. 32666, 32667

    d. 32670

65. A 78-year-old male has a stage 3 pressure ulcer on the sacrum. The ulcer is excised and closed with myocutaneous flaps, transferred from the left and right buttocks. How is this service coded?

    a. 15934, 15734

    b. 15934, 15738

    c. 15936, 15734, 15734-59

    d. 15936, 15756, 15756-59

66. The surgeon repairs the extensor digitorum communis and extensor indices proprius of the second digit. The collateral ligament of the second MCP joint was also repaired. What is the correct code assignment for this case?

    a. 26433, 26433, 26540

    b. 26455, 26455, 26541

    c. 26418, 26418, 26545

    d. 26418, 26418, 26540

67. The physician injects the left facet joint nerves of L1 and L2 with a destructive agent, using fluoroscopy guidance. What is the correct code assignment for this case?

   a. 64635, 64636

   b. 64493, 64494

   c. 0216T, 0217T

   d. 64493, 64494, 77003

68. Tests performed: Gas dilution for lung volumes, airway resistance by impulse oscillometry and carbon monoxide diffusing capacity. How are these tests coded?

   a. 94726

   b. 94726, 94729

   c. 94727, 94728, 94729

   d. 94747, 94728

69. The cardiac surgeon performs a coronary artery bypass ×3, grafting the left internal mammary artery to the left anterior descending artery and the greater saphenous vein to the obtuse marginal and circumflex arteries. The surgeon performed a video endoscopic harvesting of the right greater saphenous vein. The surgeon also performs a transmyocardial laser revascularization of the left atrial apex through thoracotomy. What is the correct code assignment for this case?

   a. 33140, 33511, 33533

   b. 33141, 33508, 33518, 33533

   c. 33141, 33508, 33519

   d. 33140, 33512

70. **In-office Chemotherapy Administration**

   The patient is a 73-year-old woman who arrives today for her scheduled chemotherapy treatment. She is being treated for metastatic papillary serous low malignant potential cancer to lungs and brain.

   What diagnosis codes are reported for this encounter?

   a. C34.90, C79.31, C79.60

   b. C56.9, C78.00, C79.31, Z51.11

   c. C56.9, C78.00, C79.31

   d. Z51.11, C56.9, C78.00, C79.31

71. **In-Office Chemotherapy Administration**

    The patient is a 73-year-old woman who arrives today for her scheduled chemotherapy treatment. All injections are sequential.

    **Treatment today:**

    Carboplatin infusion, 50 mg
        Start time 1:30 p.m., End time 2:05 p.m.
    Paclitaxel infusion, 25 mg
        Start time 2:06 p.m., End time 3:10 p.m.
     Ondansetron infusion, 1 mg
        Start time 3:12 p.m., End time 3:32 p.m.

    a.  96365, 96366, 96372, J2405, J9045, J9267 x 25

    b.  96413, 96417, 96368, J2405, J9045, J9267

    c.  96413, 96417, 96367

    d.  96413, 96417, 96367, J2405, J9045, J9267 x 25

72. The patient is admitted to the hospital for elective cholecystectomy for acute cholecystitis and cholelithiasis. Prior to the administration of anesthesia, the patient develops tachycardia and the surgery is cancelled. Which of the following would be used to report this encounter?

    a.  K80.19, R00.0, Z53.09

    b.  K80.00, R00.0, Z53.09

    c.  K80.00, Z53.09

    d.  K80.00, R00.0, Z53.01

73. The patient has previously diagnosed benign prostatic hypertrophy with urinary retention and presents for a TURP. The final diagnosis shows foci of adenocarcinoma. Which of the following codes would be used to report this encounter?

    a.  D07.5, N40.1, R33.8

    b.  C61, N40.0, R33.8

    c.  C61, N40.1, R33.8

    d.  D07.5, N40.1, R33.9

## Domain III   *Regulatory Guidelines and Reporting Requirements for Outpatient Services*

74. The patient is seen by the physician and noted to have a chief complaint of shortness of breath. In the progress notes, the physician diagnoses asthma and recommends that the patient present to the emergency room of XYZ Hospital immediately. The physician further documents that the patient has severe wheezing and no obvious relief with bronchodilators. What should the coder do when preparing the bill?

    a.  Code asthma

    b.  Code asthma with status asthmaticus

    c.  Code asthma with acute exacerbation

    d.  Query the physician for more detail about the asthma

75. A patient diagnosed with breast cancer who is currently being treated is admitted to the hospital for the management of her chemotherapy-induced anemia. Which of the following would be reported as the first listed diagnosis?

    a. Malignant neoplasm of breast (female), unspecified

    b. Anemia, unspecified

    c. Antineoplastic chemotherapy induced anemia

    d. Anemia in neoplastic disease

76. How often must an Advanced Beneficiary Notice be signed when multiple instances of the same questionable service are provided?

    a. On an annual basis

    b. The first time the questionable service is provided

    c. On a monthly basis

    d. At the time each questionable service is provided

77. What is the purpose of "linking" on a physician claim?

    a. Show how many times a service was provided

    b. Explain medical necessity of a procedure

    c. Group related surgical procedures together

    d. Show the day a procedure was performed

78. The specific legislation that provides a limitation on certain referrals of designated health services to facilities in which the provider has a financial interest refers to:

    a. Balanced Budget Act of 1997

    b. Health Information Portability and Accountability Act

    c. Wired for Health Care Quality Act

    d. Stark Legislation

79. The patient is seen in the outpatient department of the hospital with a productive chronic cough and the record states "questionable lung cancer." What should be coded as the patient's diagnosis?

    a. Cough

    b. Observation without need for future medical care

    c. Diagnosis of unknown etiology

    d. Lung cancer

80. A Medicare patient with no symptoms or history has a diagnostic endoscopy of the entire colon, from the rectum to the cecum and no issues were found. How is this coded?

    a. G0105, Colorectal cancer screening; colonoscopy on individual at high risk

    b. G0121, Colorectal cancer screening; colonoscopy on individual not meeting criteria for high risk

    c. 45330, Sigmoidoscopy, flexible; diagnostic, including collection of specimen(s) by brushing or washing, when performed (separate procedure)

    d. 45378, Colonoscopy, flexible; diagnostic, including collection of specimen(s) by brushing or washing, when performed (separate procedure)

81. A coding manager reviewed the following information before the claim was submitted. What change would be required to ensure proper payment?

| Patient Name | CPT Code | Description | ICD-10-CM Code | Description |
|---|---|---|---|---|
| John Doe | 30300 | Removal of foreign body, intranasal; office type procedure | H44.701 | Unspecified retained (old) intraocular foreign body, nonmagnetic, right eye |

   a. A modifier is required on the CPT code.

   b. The diagnosis must be correctly linked to the procedure.

   c. The diagnosis code requires greater specificity.

   d. Additional CPT code(s) are required.

82. Which of the following is the *least* effective way to select an audit sample?

   a. Random sample of records for all physicians in a group

   b. All services provided on a randomly selected day

   c. Records selected by the physician for review

   d. All rejected claims during a specific time period

83. A physician asks how he has been paid for four patients for whom he performed a posterior cervical three-level laminectomy within the past year. Upon review of these claims and the coding, what does the coding manager learn?

| | |
|---|---|
| 63045 | Laminectomy, facetectomy and foraminotomy (unilateral or bilateral with decompression of spinal cord, cauda equina and/or nerve root[s], [for example, spinal or lateral recess stenosis]), single vertebral segment; cervical |
| 63048 | each additional segment, cervical, thoracic, or lumbar (List separately in addition to code for primary procedure.) |

| | CPT Codes | Diagnosis | Description |
|---|---|---|---|
| Patient 1 | 63045 | M50.30 | Degeneration of cervical intervertebral disc |
| Patient 2 | 63045 | M50.20 | Displacement of cervical intervertebral disc without myelopathy |
| Patient 3 | 63045 63048 | M50.20 | Displacement of cervical intervertebral disc without myelopathy |
| Patient 4 | 63045 63048 | M50.30 | Degeneration of cervical intervertebral disc |

   a. CPT coding accuracy needs improvement.

   b. ICD-10-CM coding accuracy needs improvement.

   c. The physician misidentified patients who received this surgery.

   d. All of the cases were coded correctly.

84. After reviewing this Production Report for June, what action should the coding manager take?

| Production Report for Dr. Lyndon, Dermatology 6/1/XX to 6/30/XX | | | | |
|---|---|---|---|---|
| CPT Code | Frequency | % | Charges | Payments |
| 99212 | 156 | 46.2% | $5,772.00 | $4,040.40 |
| 99213 | 147 | 43.6% | $7,350.00 | $5,945.00 |
| 99214 | 10 | 2.9% | $730.00 | $511.00 |
| 99215 | 24 | 7.1% | $2,712.00 | $2,316.40 |
| 99243 | 56 | 65.1% | $7,000.00 | $5,900.00 |
| 99244 | 27 | 31.3% | $4,050.00 | $3,894.00 |
| 99245 | 3 | 3.4% | $600.00 | $492.00 |

    a. Educate Dr. Lyndon about the appropriate use of new patient codes.

    b. Educate Dr. Lyndon on the correct percentages of consultation codes.

    c. Determine why there were so few visits for the month.

    d. Investigate why the charges were not paid in full.

## Domain V  *Information and Communication Technologies*

85. A physician needs a software application that will allow him to computerize his office budget, looking at various categories of expenses such as personnel, office expense, and office supplies and watching patterns of expenditures. What tool would he likely install?

    a. Word-processing software

    b. Database software

    c. Spreadsheet software

    d. Database management software

86. The physician is concerned about using the Internet to transmit billing data. The coder assures the physician that the data is protected using:

    a. Encryption

    b. Encoding

    c. Functional interoperability

    d. Interface engines

87. A physician's office can improve their co-pay collections and increase revenue by using an electronic health record to assist them in:

    a. Benefits/eligibility checking

    b. Charge capture

    c. Scheduling

    d. Pharmacy benefits

88. Which of the following activities would be in violation of AHIMA's Code of Ethics?

    a. Coding an intentionally inappropriate level of service

    b. Following established coding policies and procedures

    c. Protecting the confidentiality of patients' written and electronic records

    d. Taking remedial action when there is direct knowledge of a colleague's incompetence or impairment

89. The patient has received copies of records from her health record which she requested earlier. In her request she specifically asked for the discharge summary, the operative report, and the pathology report. The records that she received did not include the pathology report. The enclosed letter said that the other document was not enclosed because of the minimum necessary rule. What should the director tell the patient when she calls?

    a. The correct documents were sent. The patient can file a complaint with the hospital.

    b. The pathology report was not included in the designated record set so it was not sent

    c. The minimum necessary rule only allows access to dictated reports that have been transcribed

    d. Everything she requested should have actually been sent since the patient is an exception to the minimum necessary rule

90. Which of the following deals specifically with the confidentiality of substance abuse records?

    a. Freedom of Information Act

    b. Public Health Service Act

    c. Balanced Budget Act of 1997

    d. HIPAA

91. The patient has an appointment with a urologist for an initial visit. When must the patient be given the Notice of Privacy Practices?

    a. At the first visit

    b. When the patient receives his pre-appointment information

    c. Within 2 days after the first appointment

    d. At the second visit to the physician

92. Which of these is "the result of effective data protection measures?"

    a. System security

    b. Data security

    c. Encryption

    d. Integrity

## Domain VII *Compliance*

93. Which of the following organizations does not make up the Cooperating Parties for the approval of ICD-10-CM Coding Guidelines?

    a. American Medical Association (AMA)

    b. American Health Information Management Association (AHIMA)

    c. Centers for Medicare and Medicaid Services (CMS)

    d. National Center for Health Statistics (NCHS)

94. One part of a physician's office compliance plan is to respond appropriately to detected violations. Which of the following steps would be a first step of a corrective action plan if the office manager notices that the practice of "unbundling" is commonplace among the coders?

    a. Issue oral warnings to all employees in the department

    b. Refund overpayments from a third-party payer due to this practice

    c. Post the new ICD-10-CM codes each year on the departmental bulletin board

    d. Establish an open-door policy between the physician, the compliance officer, and the employees

95. Which of the following is not a risk area that the Office of the Inspector General has identified for physician practices?

    a. Billing for noncovered services as if they are covered

    b. Billing for a more expensive service than the one actually performed

    c. Developing, coordinating, and participating in coding training programs

    d. Coding/charging one or two middle levels of service codes exclusively

96. Which of the following is an example of abuse?

    a. Billing for services not provided

    b. Selling or sharing patients' Medicare numbers

    c. Performing occasional services considered by the carrier to be medically unnecessary

    d. Unbundling or exploding charges

# Multiple Choice Exam 2 Answers

| | | | |
|---|---|---|---|
| 1. | 25. | 49. | 73. |
| 2. | 26. | 50. | 74. |
| 3. | 27. | 51. | 75. |
| 4. | 28. | 52. | 76. |
| 5. | 29. | 53. | 77. |
| 6. | 30. | 54. | 78. |
| 7. | 31. | 55. | 79. |
| 8. | 32. | 56. | 80. |
| 9. | 33. | 57. | 81. |
| 10. | 34. | 58. | 82. |
| 11. | 35. | 59. | 83. |
| 12. | 36. | 60. | 84. |
| 13. | 37. | 61. | 85. |
| 14. | 38. | 62. | 86. |
| 15. | 39. | 63. | 87. |
| 16. | 40. | 64. | 88. |
| 17. | 41. | 65. | 89. |
| 18. | 42. | 66. | 90. |
| 19. | 43. | 67. | 91. |
| 20. | 44. | 68. | 92. |
| 21. | 45. | 69. | 93. |
| 22. | 46. | 70. | 94. |
| 23. | 47. | 71. | 95. |
| 24. | 48. | 72. | 96. |

# EXAM 2 MEDICAL CASES

## EXAM 2—CASE 1

*Please code for the services of the physician.*

**DATE OF SERVICE:** 12/29/20XX

**CHIEF COMPLAINT:** Flu symptoms, cough

**HISTORY OF PRESENT ILLNESS:** The patient is an 18-year-old man who is new to my practice and presents to the office today with the following symptoms. Over the past 7 days, he has had diffuse body aches, shortness of breath, cough, productive now, which has changed from initially dry to a greenish-yellow phlegm. He has had some nausea and emesis ×2 today. There has been no diarrhea. He had been taking fluids but decreased appetite. No severe headache, no sore throat, no ear pain. Similar symptoms are in other family members. He presents here with mother for further care and treatment. Approximately 2 days ago, he felt weak and had a brief syncopal episode.

**PAST MEDICAL HISTORY:** Unremarkable

**MEDICATIONS:**

Wal-Tussin

Excedrin

**ALLERGIES:** SULFA

**SOCIAL HISTORY:** He is tobacco dependent as he smokes continuously approximately two packs per day. Dr. X was his primary care provider in the past. He is here with mother.

**REVIEW OF SYSTEMS:** See HPI, all other systems reviewed and otherwise negative.

**PHYSICAL EXAMINATION:**

**VITAL SIGNS:** Temperature 100.3, blood pressure 130/68, pulse 106, respirations 20, saturation 97% on room air

**GENERAL:** Awake, alert, nontoxic-appearing male

**HEENT:** There are well-healed eschars to his right nose and right maxilla region. Pupils are equal and round. Extraocular muscles intact. Tympanic membranes are unremarkable. Mucous membranes are moist. Posterior oropharynx is clear.

**NECK:** Supple. No rigidity.

**CHEST:** Some slight crackles in the right base

**CARDIOVASCULAR:** S1 and S2 normal. Heart tones are crisp. No murmur.

**ABDOMEN:** Soft, nontender throughout, normoactive bowel tones

**EXTREMITIES:** Warm, dry, and well perfused. No clubbing, cyanosis, or edema.

**NEUROLOGICAL:** Nonfocal. His chest x-ray demonstrated an early right middle lobe infiltrate. His white blood cell count was 11.3 with a left shift, 10% bands, 69 segs. His basic chemistry demonstrated a bicarb of 19.2, glucose of 105. The patient was given 500 mg of Levaquin IV push under my direct supervision after a sputum and blood cultures ×2. The patient was feeling improved. His temperature did go up to 102 while here, and he was given 1 g of Tylenol orally.

## EXAM 2—CASE 1 (*continued*)

**DIAGNOSIS:** Right middle lobe pneumonia

**DISCHARGE INSTRUCTIONS:**

1. Levaquin 500 mg p.o. q.d. a total of 10 days
2. Clear liquids. Advance as tolerated.
3. Phenergan 25 mg per rectum q. 6h. nausea
4. Tylenol 1 g q. 6h. p.r.n.
5. Recommend smoke cessation classes for documented tobacco use disorder

**HISTORY:** Comprehensive

**EXAMINATION:** Comprehensive

**MEDICAL DECISION MAKING:** Moderate

*Enter two diagnosis codes and four procedure codes.*

**DX1**

**DX2**

**PR1**

**PR2**

**PR3**

**PR4**

## EXAM 2—CASE 2

*Please code for the services of the physician.*

**OFFICE VISIT**

**CHIEF COMPLAINT:** Diarrhea and nausea

**HISTORY OF PRESENT ILLNESS:** This is a 70-year-old Caucasian male, established patient, who presents today to the office with complaints of diarrhea, and nausea present over the last 6 weeks that have increased gradually in frequency. Currently, he's having diarrhea that's 3 times a day. It's watery at times, sometimes soft. He thinks that things are worsening. The color of the stool is tan or brown. He has no black or tarry stools. He notes no bright red blood per rectum. He does admit to lethargy.

Upon questioning, he does admit to being on an antibiotic recently, approximately 6 weeks ago. Before his symptoms started, he had been put on Z-Pak for some sinus symptoms, and he did notice that his symptoms started after being on the Z-Pak.

He was started on Prilosec several weeks ago for some irritation due to Fosamax and he has been on Prilosec since then.

In addition, he relates today that he was scratched by some dogs and according to our chart, hasn't had a tetanus shot since 1998.

**PAST MEDICAL HISTORY:**

Numerous medical issues, in particular:

1. Cardiac issues
2. Hypertension
3. Hypercholesterolemia

**CURRENT MEDICATIONS:**

1. Aspirin
2. Calcium
3. Ticlid
4. Zocor
5. Prilosec

**SOCIAL HISTORY:** He denies alcohol or tobacco.

**REVIEW OF SYSTEMS:** Negative for chest pain or shortness of breath. He does admit to increased flatulence and abdominal pain, only after eating, which resolves after the flatulence resolves.

**PHYSICAL EXAMINATION:**

**VITAL SIGNS:**

**BLOOD PRESSURE:** 120/54.

**PULSE:** 56.

**TEMPERATURE:** 98.1.

**WEIGHT:** 135

## EXAM 2—CASE 2 (*continued*)

**GENERAL:** He is in no acute distress. Able to give a good history. He's alert and oriented without evidence of severe lethargy or fatigue.

**HEART:** Regular rate and rhythm. No murmurs, gallops, or rubs or heaves.

**LUNGS:** Clear to auscultation

**ABDOMEN:** Soft and nontender. No organomegaly. Hyperactive bowel sounds. No skin changes.

**EXTREMITIES:** Without cyanosis, clubbing, or edema

**SKIN:** No abnormalities, except for several abrasions and excoriations on his anterior arms due to dogs scratching at him today.

**ASSESSMENT AND PLAN:**

1. I gave him a Td shot today. The abrasions are somewhat deep and have some debris. I cleansed the one on the right forearm and rebandaged it.

2. With regard to his significant diarrhea, I do want to rule out C. Difficile, so will send off a stool for C. Difficile blood count toxin. Also will send off a culture to rule out *Salmonella, Shigella*, or enteric Campylobacter, and I've also asked him to stop the Prilosec right now to see if his symptoms improve off Prilosec as this may be an offending agent as well.

3. All questions were answered. He will return the stool sample in the morning.

**HISTORY:** Detailed

**EXAMINATION:** Detailed

**MEDICAL DECISION MAKING:** Moderate

---

*Enter four diagnosis codes and three procedure codes.*

**DX1**

**DX2**

**DX3**

**DX4**

**PR1**

**PR2**

**PR3**

## EXAM 2—CASE 3

*Please code for the services of the physician.*

**DATE OF ADMISSION:** 01/15/20XX

**DATE OF CONSULTATION:** 01/15/20XX

**REQUESTED BY:** Dr. Y

**CHIEF COMPLAINT:** Not feeling good and constipation

**CONSULT SERVICE:** Endocrinology

**HISTORY OF PRESENT ILLNESS:** The patient is a 4-year-old boy who was taken to the emergency room by his parents because he had constipation, and he was subsequently admitted as an inpatient. He has had no stools for 5 days. He also began vomiting the morning of admission. He has had decreased food intake over the past 5 days. He has had polyuria and polydipsia for the past 2 months, also bedwetting for 1 to 2 months. He has had a 7-lb weight loss. He had not been complaining of abdominal pain, no complaints of blurred vision, no complaints of headache.

In the emergency room, by mom's report, he was given an enema. They also elected to do some labs. He was found to have a blood sugar level over 400 and a pH of 7.10. He was admitted to the pediatric intensive care unit.

**PAST MEDICAL HISTORY:** He was the product of a normal pregnancy. Birth weight 8 lb 10 oz. He has had no hospitalizations. He has no known drug allergies.

**FAMILY HISTORY:** Negative for type 1 diabetes. There is type 2 diabetes only in a maternal great-grandmother. There is a maternal grandmother with rheumatoid arthritis, thyroid problems, cardiovascular disease (had CABG in mid-40s), and dyslipidemia. Mom is not aware of any issues regarding health on the maternal grandfather's side of the family, but admittedly does not know much about her father's history. His father is Filipino/Samoan ethnicity, knows of no diabetes in the family and no major health problems. The patient has a 2-year-old brother who is healthy. Mom is 35 weeks pregnant. She has had no gestational diabetes. Father had some cold symptoms, and the patient developed cold symptoms also in the past week.

**SOCIAL HISTORY:** The patient lives with his parents and sibling.

**REVIEW OF SYMPTOMS:** Negative for fever or fatigue. There has been a 5 to 7-lb weight loss as mentioned above. Nasal discharge as mentioned above, no complaints of sore throat, mild cough, no chest pain, decreased appetite, vomiting as mentioned above and constipation as mentioned above, polyuria, polydipsia, nocturia, no dysuria, no weakness, no headaches. Regarding mood changes, Mom has noted that he has seemed to have more behavioral issues upon eating sugar. Mom does believe his skin and lips to be dry for the past few weeks.

**PHYSICAL EXAMINATION:** The patient is an alert, smiling boy in no distress. Weight 25.1 kg, temperature 36.7, pulse 119, respiratory rate 18, blood pressure 99/79.

**HEENT:** Conjunctivae normal. Pupils reactive. Glimpses of his fundi normal. Oral mucosa moist. Breath not fruity in odor. No oropharyngeal exudate.

**NECK:** Supple with no thyroid enlargement

**LUNGS:** Clear, no wheezing

**CARDIAC:** Normal rhythm, no murmur

## EXAM 2—CASE 3 (*continued*)

**ABDOMEN:** Soft, nontender, normal bowel sounds

**GENITALIA:** He had normal prepubertal genitalia. Testes descended bilaterally.

**SKIN:** Notable for 2 small café-au-lait spots on his trunk, slightly doughy texture of his skin

**NEUROLOGIC:** Sensation was grossly intact. He had normal speech.

**LABORATORY STUDIES:** On admission, venous pH 7.10, blood glucose 449, sodium 144, potassium 4.3, chloride 110, CO2 less than 5, BUN 7, creatinine 0.6, calcium 11.2, magnesium 2.2, phosphorus 4.2. CBC was remarkable for a white blood cell count of 13.5, 63 polys, 22 lymphocytes, 10 monocytes, hematocrit 46.3. Hemoglobin A1c pending at the time of this dictation.

**IMPRESSION:** This is a 4-year-old with new-onset type 1 diabetes, presenting in severe diabetic ketoacidosis (DKA). His DKA is resolving. DKA management as per diabetes clinical pathway, he is currently on an insulin infusion at 0.1 units per kg/hour and D10 fluids. Blood glucose checked q2h, electrolytes q4h at present. He will be transitioned to subcutaneous insulin later in the day, starting at 1 unit per kg per day. In view of the family situation, with Mom's upcoming delivery, likely NPH and Humalog insulin will be a bit easier for this family. Diabetes education will begin today with diabetes nurse educator, and later in the week with a nutritionist and social worker.

Regarding constipation, we will continue to follow this. Also, of note is the fact that on his initial studies he had 2+ protein as well as ketonuria. Would recheck urinalysis later during his hospital stay. Patient to be transferred from unit and will be on the Endocrine Service.

**HISTORY:** Comprehensive

**EXAMINATION:** Comprehensive

**MEDICAL DECISION MAKING:** High

*Enter two diagnosis codes and one procedure code.*

---

**DX1**

**DX2**

**PR1**

## EXAM 2—CASE 4

*Please code for the services of the physician.*

**CHIEF COMPLAINT:** Persistent vaginal bleeding, follow-up to spontaneous AB

**HISTORY OF PRESENT ILLNESS:** The patient is a 30-year-old woman who presents to the emergency room with the chief complaint of persistent vaginal bleeding and cramping. The patient was seen here on January 22. At that time, she reported being 8 weeks pregnant. She had a complete evaluation that included a beta hCG of 514, an ultrasound that showed no contents within the uterus. She was thought to have had a complete spontaneous AB. She states that she has had persistent cramping and bleeding and also is interested in the results of her follow-up beta hCG. This is the patient's second pregnancy. She has had a previous spontaneous AB. Past medical history is also significant for anxiety, depression, and anemia.

**CURRENT MEDICATIONS:**

1. Clonazepam

2. Trazodone

3. Amitriptyline

4. Vitamin B$_{12}$

She is taking nothing until she knows for sure whether or not she is pregnant.

**ALLERGIES:** She states she is allergic to SULFA.

**SOCIAL HISTORY:** She is an occasional smoker.

**FAMILY HISTORY:** Noncontributory

**REVIEW OF SYSTEMS:** There is no history of headache, nosebleed, syncope, seizure, cough or cold symptoms, vomiting, diarrhea, other joint aches or pains, or rash.

**PHYSICAL EXAMINATION:**

**VITAL SIGNS:** Blood pressure 104/79, pulse rate 81, respiratory rate 16, temperature 96.8. O$_2$ sat remains at 100%.

**GENERAL:** The patient is awake, alert, somewhat flat affect, no acute distress.

**HEENT:** Skull is atraumatic. Pupils are reactive. Fundi are normal. TMs are clear. There were no oral lesions.

**NECK:** Supple without adenopathy

**LUNGS:** Clear

**HEART:** Tones are normal

**ABDOMEN:** Soft. Completely nontender.

**PELVIC:** Examination performed by me showed normal genitalia, normal mucosa, a nulliparous os. The os was closed. Uterine size was consistent with a nonpregnant uterus. There was no bleeding present at all and no adnexal tenderness.

**EXTREMITIES:** No cyanosis, clubbing, or edema

## EXAM 2—CASE 4 (*continued*)

**NEUROLOGICAL:** The patient is intact.

The patient was thought to have a complete spontaneous AB. Hemoglobin and hematocrit are 13 and 39 demonstrating no evidence of anemia. Beta hCG that was 514 on January 22 is now 35. Urinalysis did reveal a UTI. Patient was started on Urimar. She was assured that she has had a complete AB and should expect light bleeding and cramping over the next week and will follow up for any further complications. She was sent home in stable condition.

**DIAGNOSIS:** Prior spontaneous AB, complete; UTI

**HISTORY:** Detailed

**EXAMINATION:** Comprehensive

**MEDICAL DECISION MAKING:** Moderate

---

*Enter one diagnosis code and one procedure code.*

**DX1**

**PR1**

## EXAM 2—CASE 5

*Please code for the services of the surgeon.*

**DATE OF PROCEDURE:** 10/30/20XX

**PREOPERATIVE DIAGNOSIS:** Traumatic left quadriceps tendon rupture

**POSTOPERATIVE DIAGNOSIS:** Traumatic left quadriceps tendon rupture

**PROCEDURE:** Repair of left quadriceps tendon rupture

**ANESTHESIA:** Spinal

**COMPLICATIONS:** None

**DRAINS:** None

**ESTIMATED BLOOD LOSS:** 50 cc to 100 cc

**PROCEDURE:** The patient was brought to the operating room and after the instillation of a satisfactory spinal anesthesia, the left lower extremity was appropriately prepared and draped in the usual sterile fashion. A midline incision was made and centered over the patella and carried down to the quadriceps mechanism. Medial and lateral dissection was carried out to expose the retinaculum, which was torn approximately 2 cm laterally and medially. There was a direct avulsion of the quadriceps tendon off the patella with a small fleck of osteophytic bone. The quadriceps tendon was freshened. Also the bony surface of the patella was debrided of soft tissue and hematoma and fibrous tissue. Once this was repaired, three holes, center, mid lateral, and mid medial were marked. Following this, a #5 Ethibond and #2 fiberwire were placed in the quadriceps mechanism both medially and laterally, beginning in the midportion with a Krackow suture. Following this, three drill holes were made longitudinally from superior to inferior through the patella and a suture passer was used to retrieve the ends of the suture. When these were secured, the quad tendon was brought down into the patellar bed. Following this, #2 Ethibond retinacular sutures were added from the superolateral and superomedial junction of the patella laterally and medially. These were then tightened. As they were tightened, the sutures in the patella were securely tightened as well. The retinacular sutures were then tightened. Supplemental 2-0 Vicryl anteriorly into the quad tendon and patellar soft tissue and retinaculum was then accomplished. This knee could be flexed to about 30 degrees before there was significant tension on this quadriceps tendon. Therefore, we will be holding him in extension. Following this, a thorough Waterpik irrigation was accomplished. The subcutaneous was closed with interrupted 2-0 Vicryl, and the skin closed with skin clips. A sterile dressing and a knee immobilizer were placed. The patient was taken to the recovery room in satisfactory condition.

*Enter one diagnosis code and one procedure code.*

**DX1** [                                        ]

**PR1** [                                        ]

## EXAM 2—CASE 6

*Please code for the services of the surgeon.*

**DATE OF OPERATION:** 01/30/20XX

**PREOPERATIVE DIAGNOSIS:** Multiple myeloma with pending stem cell transplant

**POSTOPERATIVE DIAGNOSIS:** Multiple myeloma with pending stem cell transplant

**PROCEDURE:** Placement of tunneled central venous NeoStar catheter via the right internal jugular vein with ultrasound and fluoroscopic assistance.

**ANESTHESIA:** Local with MAC

**ESTIMATED BLOOD LOSS:** Minimal

**FLUIDS:** 750 mL of crystalloid

**DRAINS:** None

**SPECIMENS:** None

**COMPLICATIONS:** None

**INDICATIONS:** This patient is a 47-year-old man with a diagnosis of multiple myeloma. Stem cell transplantation is pending, and the patient is in need of a central venous catheter suitable for pheresis.

**PROCEDURE:** After obtaining informed consent, the patient was brought to the operating room and placed supine on the operating table. The skin of the anterior chest and neck was shaved, prepared, and draped in the standard sterile fashion. Using ultrasound guidance by Dr. X, a needle with syringe was advanced into the internal jugular vein with good blood return. A larger introducer needle was then advanced parallel to the previous needle under ultrasound guidance and placed into the right internal jugular vein with good blood return. A guidewire was advanced through the introducer needle under fluoroscopic guidance. The needle was then removed, leaving the guidewire in place. A 5-mm incision was made at the site of the wire exiting the skin with a #11 blade scalpel. It should be noted that the skin of the right neck was anesthetized with 1% lidocaine for analgesia. At this point, a suitable location in the right chest was chosen for the catheter exit site.

This area, as well as the subcutaneous tract, was anesthetized with 1% lidocaine. A 5-mm skin incision was made at the anticipated catheter exit site with a #11 blade scalpel. A tunneler device was then used to create the subcutaneous tunnel, bringing the tunneler in a cephalad fashion and out through the previous skin incision in the neck.

At this point, a dilator was passed over the guidewire under fluoroscopy to dilate the tract. This was done serially. An introducer peel-away catheter was threaded over the guidewire, and the guidewire was then removed. The previously tunneled NeoStar catheter was then advanced through the peel-away sheath under fluoroscopy. The sheath was removed, and the catheter had a good position in the cavoatrial junction. There was an acute angle in the catheter site as it exited the fascia of the neck. This was corrected by extending the skin incision and creating a nice curve in the catheter without kinks. Again, distal placement was confirmed at the cavoatrial junction under live fluoroscopy. The catheter withdrew blood and flushed easily at all three ports. One thousand units per cc of heparin flush were used to heplock the catheter. The catheter was secured to the skin of the right chest with a 4-0 Prolene suture. A 4-0 Vicryl was then used to reapproximate the skin of the neck incision. Dermabond was applied to the neck incision site, and sterile dressings were applied. The patient tolerated the procedure well and without any complications. A chest x-ray is pending in the recovery room to confirm adequate placement of the catheter and to rule out a pneumothorax.

Enter one diagnosis code and one procedure code.

**DX1**

**PR1**

## EXAM 2—CASE 7

*Please code for the services of the surgeon.*

**DATE OF OPERATION:** 01/05/20XX

**PREOPERATIVE DIAGNOSIS:** Congenital cataract of the right eye

**POSTOPERATIVE DIAGNOSIS:** Congenital cataract of the right eye

**OPERATION:** Cataract extraction with primary posterior capsulotomy and limited anterior vitrectomy with intraocular lens.

**INDICATIONS:** Patient with a congenital cataract of the right eye, needed to have surgical intervention to remove it, which was performed here today.

**ANESTHESIA:** General orotracheal anesthesia

**ESTIMATED BLOOD LOSS:** Negligible

**COMPLICATIONS:** None

**SPECIMENS SENT TO PATHOLOGY:** None

**PROCEDURE IN DETAIL:** The patient was brought back to the operating room, adequately premedicated, and intubated without complications. Directly after induction, the patient had pressures taken in both eyes and was found to have a pressure in the right eye of 16 and in the left eye of 17.

That was within 2 minutes of induction, error rate less than 5%.

Then keratometry readings were performed, three sets of two readings on each eye. On the right eye 44.5 × 46.25. Second reading is 44 × 46.25. The third reading is 44.5 × 46. In the left eye, 44.75 × 45, 44.25 × 45 and 43.75 × 45. Central corneal thickness for the right eye was 593 microns ± 1.5 microns and left eye 562 microns ±1.8 microns. Axial lengths were then measured using I3 ultrasound. For the right eye, the axial length was found to be 20.28 and the left eye 20.44. With the given K's and the axial lengths for the right eye, it was determined that for approximately 2 to 2.5 undercorrection, a 27.5 lens needed to be put in his eye and that was the one that was chosen.

Then the patient was prepared and draped in the usual sterile ophthalmic fashion after he received several mydriatic and cycloplegic drops. He also received one drop of Ciloxan to the right eye every 5 minutes for three drops and then one drop of flurbiprofen to the right eye every 5 minutes × 3. Once the patient was prepared and draped in the usual sterile ophthalmic fashion, a limited lateral peritomy was performed.

Hemostasis was achieved with bipolar cautery and then a keratome was used to enter the eye. Healon GV was placed in the eye to maintain anterior chamber formation.

A super-sharp blade was used to make a paracentesis at 6 o'clock. Then a cystotome was used to make a rent in the anterior capsule. A continuous curvilinear capsulorrhexis was attempted with a capsulorrhexis forceps. However, the cataract was such that it was anterior polar in nature and it was off center. It wasn't directly on the pupillary axis. That anterior polar protrusion made it so that continuing the continuous curvilinear capsulorrhexis was impossible, so a vitrector was placed in the eye. The lens was removed, including the cataract. Then Healon GV was used to inflate the eye again. A rent was made in the posterior capsule, and a limited anterior vitrectomy was performed through that rent. The incision was widened with a 3.2 short cut blade and then a 27.5 diopter SA60AT single piece intraocular lens was injected into the eye, serial number 829167.075, and the lens was rotated to be in place. It was found to be in good position.

## EXAM 2—CASE 7 (*continued*)

The Healon was removed with aspiration of the vitrector. The incision was closed with a double armed 8-0 Vicryl suture, mattress fashion suturing of the incision. It was found to be water tight. Then the conjunctiva was closed with one interrupted 7-0 chromic gut suture. 2.5 cc of dexamethasone was injected over the incision and then 0.4 cc of Kefzol was injected in the inferonasal quadrant.

The patient tolerated the procedure well. He received a drop of Pred Forte in his eye, followed by Betadine, followed by TobraDex. A pressure patch, followed by a shield, was then placed on his eye and held in place with Tegaderm. The patient tolerated the procedure well. He was extubated in the operating room and taken to the recovery room in satisfactory condition.

*Enter one diagnosis code and one procedure code.*

**DX1**

**PR1**

## EXAM 2—CASE 8

*Please code for the services of the physician.*

**DATE OF PROCEDURE:** 11/21/20XX

**PROCEDURE:** 24-hour pH probe

**INDICATIONS:** The patient is a complicated teenager with type 1 diabetes who has had issues with delayed gastric emptying. She is a known diabetic and she does have GI reflux. She is here for full evaluation of that symptom complex and is accompanied by her mother, who has signed an informed consent.

The double-bore pH probe was placed nasally when the patient was under anesthesia. The overall Boix-Ochoa score was 24.5, with normal being less than 16.6. There was no reflux during the night when she was asleep with the exception of one very prolonged episode that lasted 26.3 minutes. The overall reflux score was 6.8% with normal being less than 5.1%.

It would be advisable for her to stay on the medication profile that she is already taking but I do not think she is a candidate for surgery.

*Enter three diagnosis codes and one procedure code.*

**DX1**

**DX2**

**DX3**

**PR1**

# EXAM 3

*For the following questions, choose the best answer. A blank answer sheet for these multiple choice questions can be found on page 103.*

## Domain I   *Health Information Documentation*

1. The coder notes that the physician has prescribed Retrovir for the patient. The coder might find which of the following on the patient's discharge summary?

    a. Otitis media

    b. AIDS

    c. Toxic shock syndrome

    d. Bacteremia

2. What diagnosis would the coder expect to see when a patient with pneumonia has inhaled food, liquid, or oil?

    a. Lobar pneumonia

    b. *Pneumocystis carinii* pneumonia

    c. Interstitial pneumonia

    d. Aspiration pneumonia

3. Where would a coder who needed to locate the histology of a documented breast cancer most likely find this information?

    a. Pathology report

    b. Progress notes

    c. Nurse's notes

    d. Operative report

4. The coder notes that on the patient's laboratory results, the hemoglobin is 7.3 g/dL. The physician orders iron supplements. What should the coder report?

    a. Abnormal laboratory findings

    b. Iron-deficiency anemia

    c. Hemorrhaging

    d. The coder should query the physician to ask him to add an appropriate diagnosis

5. Where would information on treatment given on a particular encounter be found in the health record?

    a. Problem list

    b. Physician's orders

    c. Progress notes

    d. Physical examination

6. The patient's vital signs are part of which type of data in the health record?

   a. Medical history

   b. Physical examination

   c. Demographic data

   d. Physician's orders

7. In the following diagnostic statement, which of the sites is the primary malignancy: "Metastatic carcinoma of the lungs, bone, and brain?"

   a. Lungs

   b. Bone

   c. Brain

   d. Unknown primary

8. The ejection faction measures the amount of blood pumped from the heart with each heartbeat. A normal heart pumps at least _____% of the blood in the left ventricle with each heartbeat.

   a. 50

   b. 55

   c. 60

   d. 70

9. Which of the following is the most common type of coagulation defect?

   a. Hemophilia A

   b. Hemophilia B

   c. Hemophilia C

   d. Christmas disease

## Domain II   *Diagnosis and Procedure Coding*

10. In ICD-10-CM, this symbol is used to enclose synonyms, alternative wordings, abbreviations, and explanatory phrases:

    a. Square brackets

    b. Parentheses

    c. Slanted brackets

    d. Brace

11. The use of this symbol simplifies ICD-10-CM tabular entries and saves printing space by reducing repetitive wording and connects a series of terms on the left or right with a statement on the opposite side. This symbol is a:

    a. Section mark

    b. Lozenge

    c. Colon

    d. Brace

12. In ICD-10-CM, the fifth character subclassification used with categories Z38.0, Z38.3, and Z38.6 indicates whether a baby was:

    a. Born outside the hospital and not hospitalized

    b. Born in hospital and whether or not it was a cesarean delivery

    c. Born at home

    d. Born before admission to hospital

13. Which of the following would be classified to an ICD-10-CM category for viral diseases?

    a. Chlamydia

    b. Streptococcus

    c. Epstein-Barr

    d. *Candida albicans*

14. Symptomatic HIV infection should be coded to which of the following codes?

    a. R75, Inconclusive laboratory evidence of human immunodeficiency virus (HIV)

    b. B20, Human immunodeficiency virus (HIV) disease

    c. Z72.51, High risk heterosexual behavior

    d. Z21, Asymptomatic HIV infection

15. Which of the following conditions would be considered a sequela of an injury/disease?

    a. Scarring following a third-degree burn

    b. Polycystic kidney disease

    c. Medication taken by the wrong person

    d. Pathologic fracture of the vertebra due to osteoporosis

16. A patient is admitted with first-, second-, and third-degree burns of the back. How would this be coded?

    a. Code second-degree burn only

    b. Code all the first-, second-, and third-degree burns

    c. Code first-degree burn only

    d. Code third-degree burn only

17. In ICD-10-CM, burns are classified in Category T31 according to the extent of body surface involved. What principle/rule is involved in estimating this body surface?

    a. Code only any third-degree burns

    b. Code burns as a late effect

    c. Code according to the rule of nines

    d. Code burns as multiple burns

18. According to ICD-10-CM, an adverse effect of a medication taken in conjunction with an alcoholic beverage is to be coded as a(n):

    a. Late effect

    b. Poisoning

    c. Complication

    d. Adverse reaction

19. In ICD-10-CM, which one of the following conditions is a mechanical complication of an internal implant, device, or graft?

    a. Scarring due to presence of breast implants

    b. Inflammation due to indwelling catheter

    c. Pain due to renal dialysis device

    d. Obstruction of heart valve prostheses

20. The diagnosis of "allergic reaction to unknown drug taken as prescribed" would be considered to be a(n):

    a. Adverse effect

    b. Late effect

    c. Poisoning

    d. Misadventure

21. A patient presents to the physician's office after a fall from a chair. The patient is complaining of pain in the right leg, so the physician orders an x-ray. The final impression was simple greenstick fracture, lower-end, physeal of tibia and fibula. How would this be coded?

    a. S89.80A, Other specified injuries of lower leg, initial encounter

    b. S89.101B, Unspecified physeal fracture of lower end of the right tibia, subsequent encounter for fracture with routine healing;
       S89.301B, Unspecified physeal fracture of the lower end of right fibula, subsequent encounter for fracture with routine healing

    c. S89.80XA, Other specified injuries of lower leg, initial encounter

    d. S89.101A, Unspecified physeal fracture of lower end of the right tibia, initial encounter;
       S89.301A, Unspecified physeal fracture of the lower end of right fibula, initial encounter

22. The patient is a 5-year-old girl whose clothes caught fire while she was helping her mother bake cookies at home. She suffered first- and second-degree burns of her abdomen and right forearm. The physician dressed the burns and prescribed antibiotics. Impression: Burns of her abdomen and right forearm. How would this be coded?

    | | |
    |---|---|
    | T21.12XA | Burn of first degree of abdominal wall |
    | T21.22XA | Burn of second degree of abdominal wall |
    | T22.111A | Burn of first degree of right forearm |
    | T22.211A | Burn of second degree of right forearm |
    | T22.10XA | Burn of first degree of shoulder and upper limb, except wrist and hand, unspecified site |
    | T22.20XA | Burn of second degree of shoulder and upper limb, except wrist and hand, unspecified site |

    a. T21.22XA, T22.211A

    b. T21.12XA, T22.111A, T22.211A, T21.22XA

    c. T21.22XA, T22.20XA

    d. T21.12XA, T22.211A, T22.10XA

23. A female patient is seen in the physician's office because of pain in her right lower leg. The leg was also red and swollen. The physician was concerned because the patient was postoperative and after a careful examination, rendered the final impression of: Postoperative cellulitis of right lower leg. How is this coded?

> L03.115    Cellulitis of right lower limb,
> L03.119    Cellulitis of unspecified part of limb
> T81.4XXA   Infection following a procedure

   a. T81.4XXA

   b. L03.115

   c. T81.4XXA, L03.119

   d. T81.4XXA, L03.115

24. Which of the following is considered a type of unstable angina?

   a. Prinzmetal angina

   b. Crescendo angina

   c. Variant angina

   d. Angina pectoris

25. If the physician documents "Counseling, 20 minutes on attention deficit disorder" and wants to assign code 99213, what additional documentation must be made to allow this code assignment?

   a. The nature of the presenting problem

   b. The history component of the documentation

   c. The examination component of the documentation

   d. The length of the entire visit

26. Which type of asthma is caused by an environmental allergen factor?

   a. Chronic obstructive

   b. Cough variant

   c. Intrinsic

   d. Extrinsic

27. The patient was admitted to the hospital for moderate-stage primary low tension open angle glaucoma of the right and left eyes. The right eye was controlled, but the left eye progressed to severe-stage glaucoma. What is the correct diagnosis code for the physician's services?

    | | | |
    |---|---|---|
    | H40.121 | Low tension, open-angle glaucoma, right eye | |
    | H40.122 | Low tension, open-angle glaucoma, left eye | |
    | H40.123 | Low tension, open-angle glaucoma, bilateral | |
    | | 0 | stage unspecified |
    | | 1 | mild |
    | | 2 | moderate |
    | | 3 | severe |
    | | 4 | indeterminate |

    a.  H40.1212, H40.1222

    b.  H40.1212, H40.1223

    c.  H40.1232

    d.  H40.1233

28. The coding manager completes an audit of patients who were listed on the surgery schedule for cervical two-level discectomies. After reviewing this coded data, what education did the manager determine would be beneficial for the coding staff?

    | | |
    |---|---|
    | 63030 | Laminotomy (hemilaminectomy), with decompression of nerve root(s), including partial facetectomy, foraminotomy and/or excision of herniated intervertebral disc; 1 interspace, lumbar |
    | 63035 | each additional interspace, cervical or lumbar (List separately in addition to code for primary procedure.) |

    | Case | CPT Code | Diagnosis | Code Description |
    |---|---|---|---|
    | 1 | 63030 63035 | M50.20 M50.20 | Other cervical disc displacement, unspecified cervical region Other cervical disc displacement, unspecified cervical region |
    | 2 | 63030 63035 | M50.00 M50.00 | Cervical disc disorder with myelopathy, unspecified cervical region Cervical disc disorder with myelopathy, unspecified cervical region |
    | 3 | 63030 63035 | S13.141A S13.141A | Dislocation, fourth cervical vertebra, initial encounter (traumatic) Dislocation, fourth cervical vertebra, initial encounter (traumatic) |

    a.  Linking of diagnoses to procedures

    b.  ICD-10-CM coding for specificity

    c.  The use of add-on codes

    d.  Anatomy of the spinal column

29. The patient is seen by his nephrologist for stage I CKD. The patient had a kidney transplant six years ago. Which diagnosis codes are submitted for this encounter?

> N18.1   Chronic kidney disease, Stage I
> T86.10  Complication of kidney transplant, unspecified
> Z94.0   Kidney transplant status
> Z90.5   Acquired absence of kidney

   a. N18.1, Z94.0, Z90.5

   b. N18.1, T86.10, Z94.0

   c. N18.1, Z94.0

   d. N18.1, T86.10

30. Which of the following groups of External cause codes takes priority over all other groups of External cause codes?

   a. Child and adult abuse External cause codes

   b. Terrorism External cause codes

   c. Cataclysmic events External cause codes

   d. Transport accident External cause codes

31. If the reporting format limits the number of External cause codes that can be used in reporting clinical data, which of the following External cause codes would be reported first?

   a. Place of occurrence External cause codes

   b. Cause/intent External cause codes

   c. External status External cause codes

   d. Activity External cause codes

32. Which of the following conditions causes metabolic alkalosis?

   a. Ketoacidosis

   b. Renal failure

   c. Ingestion of base-depleting drugs

   d. Massive doses of steroids

33. The postpartum period, or puerperium, begins immediately after delivery and continues for ____ weeks.

   a. 4

   b. 5

   c. 6

   d. 8

34. The placental stage of delivery extends from the expulsion of the child until the placenta and membranes are expelled defines which of the following stages of labor?

   a. First stage

   b. Second stage

   c. Third stage

   d. Fourth stage

35. In ICD-10-CM, a young primigravida is defined as:

    a. Second or more pregnancy in a female less than 16 years old at time of delivery

    b. First pregnancy in a female less than 16 years old at time of delivery

    c. First delivery in a female less than 15 years old

    d. Second delivery in a female less than 15 years old

36. A woman who is not currently pregnant but has a history of recurrent pregnancy loss is best described by which of the following code statements?

    a. N96, Recurrent pregnancy loss

    b. O26.2-, Pregnancy care for patient with recurrent pregnancy loss

    c. Z87.51, Personal history of pre-term labor

    d. Z87.59, Personal history of other complication of pregnancy, childbirth, and the puerperium

37. An elderly patient comes to the emergency room complaining of left upper arm pain. The physician orders an x-ray and questions the patient about a possible injury. The patient states that she did not fall or hurt her arm in any way. It simply hurt when she woke up. After reviewing the x-ray report, the physician notices a fracture of the humerus. Considering other conditions that the patient has, his final diagnosis is pathological fracture of the humerus. How would this case be coded?

    a. M84.422A, Pathological fracture, left humerus, initial encounter for fracture

    b. M84.522A, Pathological fracture in neoplastic disease, left humerus, initial encounter for fracture

    c. M80.022A, Age-related osteoporosis with recurrent pathological fracture, left humerus, initial encounter for fracture

    d. S42.302A, Unspecified fracture of shaft of humerus, left humerus, initial encounter for fracture

38. Full-thickness skin loss involving damage or necrosis into subcutaneous soft tissues describes stage _____ of decubitus ulcer.

    a. I

    b. II

    c. III

    d. IV

39. Which of the following statements indicates an adverse effect?

    a. Aspirin (over-the-counter) overdose resulting in a coma, suicide attempt.

    b. Patient mixed Diuril and alcoholic beverage, which resulted in syncope, described as an accident.

    c. A woman is admitted for an intentional overdose of marijuana and cocaine.

    d. Atrial tachycardia due to digitalis glycosides toxicity. Patient took the medication as prescribed.

40. Which of the following conditions would be considered a perinatal condition rather than a congenital anomaly?

    a. Cleft lip and cleft palate

    b. Erb's palsy

    c. Patent ductus arteriosus

    d. Tetralogy of Fallot

41. What diagnoses and procedures should be reported for recurrent left inguinal hernia with laparoscopic repair?

| | |
|---|---|
| K40.91 | Unilateral inguinal hernia, without obstruction or gangrene, recurrent |
| K40.30 | Unilateral inguinal hernia, with obstruction, without gangrene, not specified as recurrent |
| K40.31 | Unilateral inguinal hernia, with obstruction, without gangrene, recurrent |
| 49520 | Repair recurrent inguinal hernia, any age, reducible |
| 49521 | Repair recurrent inguinal hernia, any age, reducible, incarcerated or strangulated |
| 49651 | Laparoscopy, surgical, repair recurrent inguinal hernia |

   a. K40.91, 49520

   b. K40.31, 49521

   c. K40.91, 49651

   d. K40.30, 49520

42. Status migrainosus is defined as headache with a duration greater than at least _____ hours.

   a. 72

   b. 84

   c. 96

   d. 100

43. What is the proper code assignment when the documentation states simple wound repair of three arm lacerations at 1.5 cm, 3.0 cm, and 4.0 cm and intermediate wound repair of two hand lacerations at 1.5 cm and 2.0 cm?

| | |
|---|---|
| 12001 | Simple repair of superficial wounds of scalp, neck, axillae, external genitalia, trunk and/or extremities (including hands and feet); 2.5 cm or less |
| 12002 | 2.6 cm to 7.5 cm |
| 12004 | 7.6 cm to 12.5 cm |
| 12005 | 12.6 cm to 20.0 cm |
| 12041 | Repair, intermediate, wounds of neck, hands, feet and/or external genitalia; 2.5 cm or less |
| 12042 | 2.6 cm to 7.5 cm |
| 12044 | 7.6 cm to 12.5 cm |

   a. 12042, 12004

   b. 12044

   c. 12005

   d. 12041, 12041, 12001, 12002, 12002

44. When the physician's office performs a bilateral hand x-ray and the physician interprets the x-ray, what modifier(s) are required on the claim?

> | –26 | Professional component |
> |-----|------------------------|
> | –50 | Bilateral |
> | –51 | Multiple procedure |
> | –LT | Left side |
> | –RT | Right side |
> | –TC | Technical component |

   a. –50

   b. –TC, –51

   c. –LT, –RT

   d. –26, –LT, –RT

45. The physician excises two benign lesions measuring 0.5 cm and 2.0 cm from the patient's shoulder. Each excision site was closed with a simple repair. How should the coder code this service?

   a. Code the excision of a 2.5 cm lesion

   b. Code the excision of a 2.5 cm lesion and a 2.5 cm simple repair

   c. Code the excision of a 0.5 cm lesion and a 2.0 cm lesion

   d. Code the excision of each lesion separately and the simple repairs separately

46. Chemotherapy is provided at the physician's office for a patient with colorectal cancer. The patient receives 5-FU over 38 minutes, followed by oxaliplatin for 42 minutes for chemotherapy and a nonchemotherapy drug, leucovorin, for 5 minutes. How is this infusion service coded?

> | 96365 | Intravenous infusion, for therapy, prophylaxis, or diagnosis (specify substance or drug); initial, up to 1 hour |
> |-------|------|
> | 96374 | Therapeutic, prophylactic or diagnostic injection (specify substance or drug); intravenous push, single or initial substance/drug |
> | 96413 | Chemotherapy administration, intravenous infusion technique; up to 1 hour, single or initial substance/drug |
> | 96415 | each additional hour (List separately in addition to code for primary procedure.) |
> | 96417 | each additional sequential infusion (different substance/drug), up to 1 hour (List separately in addition to code for primary procedure.) |

   a. 96413, 96365

   b. 96413, 96415, 96374

   c. 96413, 96417

   d. 96413, 96417, 96374

47. The patient complains of pain, swelling, and the feeling of warmth in the ankle. The physician aspirates 12 cc of fluid from a cyst in the patient's ankle joint. How is this procedure coded?

    a. 10021, Fine needle aspiration; without imaging guidance

    b. 20605, Arthrocentesis, aspiration and/or injection, intermediate joint of bursa (eg, temporomandibular, acromioclavicular, wrist, elbow or ankle, olecranon bursa); without ultrasound guidance

    c. 20615, Aspiration and injection for treatment of bone cyst

    d. 27604, Incision and drainage, leg or ankle; infected bursa

48. The CPT code book tells coders that a code description has changed from last year by preceding the code with which of the following symbols?

    a. •

    b. ▲

    c. > <

    d. +

49. Prolonged pregnancy is pregnancy that has advanced beyond ___ completed weeks of gestation.

    a. 39

    b. 40

    c. 41

    d. 42

50. Which of the following is excluded from the surgical global?

    a. Consultation to determine the need for procedure

    b. Local, regional, or topical anesthesia administered

    c. The surgical procedure performed

    d. Routine postoperative follow-up care

51. The pathologist does a gross and microscopic examination on three surgical specimens from a bronchoscopy procedure. Specimens submitted were biopsies of lung, bronchus, and trachea. The pathologist is not employed by the hospital. What is the correct code assignment for the services of the pathologist?

| | |
|---|---|
| 88300 | Level I—Surgical pathology, gross examination only |
| 88305 | Level IV—Surgical pathology, gross and microscopic examination |
| –26 | Professional component |
| –TC | Technical component |

    a. 88300, 88305

    b. 88305–26

    c. 88305–26 ×3

    d. 88300–TC, 88300–TC, 88305–TC

52. The patient (not covered by Medicare) is sent to a dermatologist by her primary care physician for diagnosis of a suspicious rash. A detailed history and examination are done, a biopsy is taken, and medication is prescribed. The findings are sent back to the primary care physician. How is this E/M service coded?

    a. 99203, Office or other outpatient visit for the evaluation and management of a new patient, which requires these three key components of detailed history, detailed examination, and medical decision making of low complexity.

    b. 99214, Office or other outpatient visit for the evaluation and management of an established patient, which requires at least two of these three key components of detailed history, detailed examination, and medical decision making of moderate complexity.

    c. 99243, Office consultation for a new or established patient, which requires these three key components of detailed history, detailed examination, and medical decision making of low complexity.

    d. 99254, Inpatient consultation for a new or established patient, which requires three key components of comprehensive history, comprehensive examination, and medical decision making of moderate complexity.

53. A portion of a patient's kidney is removed using an incisional technique. How is this service coded?

    a. 50045, Nephrotomy, with exploration

    b. 50240, Nephrectomy, partial

    c. 50340, Recipient nephrectomy (separate procedure)

    d. 50543, Laparoscopy, surgical; partial nephrectomy

54. The patient has a misaligned phalangeal shaft fracture demonstrated on a two-view x-ray, performed and read by the physician in the office. The physician manipulates the finger into alignment and places a rigid finger splint. How are these services coded?

    | | |
    |---|---|
    | 26720 | Closed treatment of phalangeal shaft fracture, proximal or middle phalanx, finger or thumb; without manipulation, each |
    | 26725 | with manipulation, with or without skin or skeletal traction, each |
    | 26727 | Percutaneous skeletal fixation of unstable phalangeal shaft fracture, proximal or middle phalanx, finger or thumb, with manipulation, each |
    | 73120 | Radiologic examination, hand; 2 views |
    | 73140 | Radiologic examination, finger(s), minimum of 2 views |

    a. 26720, 73120

    b. 26725, 73120

    c. 26725, 73140

    d. 26727, 73140

55. The patient undergoes a revision tympanoplasty without ossicular chain reconstruction and a mastoidectomy. How is this service coded?

    a. 69631

    b. 69631, 69502

    c. 69635

    d. 69641

56. A 36-year-old male patient is taken to the operating room, and a central venous catheter is tunneled through the subclavian vein and terminated in the superior vena cava. How is this catheter insertion coded?

    a. 36557

    b. 36558

    c. 36569

    d. 36571

57. To correctly code a total thyroidectomy, what vital piece of information must be documented to support code assignment?

    a. Whether parathyroid glands are excised

    b. Whether a surgical drain was placed

    c. Reason for thyroidectomy

    d. Surgical approach

58. The patient has a blocked right iliac artery that cannot be opened. Therefore, the patient undergoes a left femoral bypass to the right with a Gore-Tex prosthetic graft. The right femoral artery still does not show adequate back bleeding. A thromboendarterectomy is performed on the right common femoral artery. Adequate blood flow is achieved, and the anastomosis is completed. What is the correct coding for this procedure?

    | 34201 | Embolectomy/thrombectomy, without or without catheter; femoropopliteal, aortoiliac artery, by leg incision |
    |---|---|
    | 35371 | Thromboendarterectomy, including patch graft, if performed, common femoral |
    | 35558 | Bypass graft, with vein; femoral-femoral |
    | 35621 | Bypass graft, with other than vein; axillary-femoral |
    | 35661 | Bypass graft, with other than vein; femoral-femoral |

    a. 34201, 35558

    b. 34201, 35621

    c. 35371, 35558

    d. 35371, 35661

59. Which of the following codes is assigned to report electronic analysis, reprogramming, and refill of implanted intrathecal pump, performed by a pump technician under the general supervision of a physician?

    a. 62369, Electronic analysis of programmable, implanted pump for intrathecal or epidural drug infusion (includes evaluation of reservoir status, alarm status, drug prescription status; with reprogramming and refill)

    b. 62370, Electronic analysis of programmable, implanted pump for intrathecal or epidural drug infusion (includes evaluation of reservoir status, alarm status, drug prescription status); with reprogramming and refill (requiring physician's skill)

    c. 95990, Refilling and maintenance of implantable pump or reservoir for drug delivery, spinal (intrathecal), or brain (intraventricular), includes electronic analysis of pump, when performed

    d. 95991, Refilling and maintenance of implantable pump or reservoir for drug delivery, spinal (intrathecal), or brain (intraventricular), includes electronic analysis of pump, when performed; requiring physician's skill

60. Which of the following describes the service coded with CPT code 32669?

    a. Removal of one segment of the lung using a thoracotomy approach

    b. Removal of one lobe of the lung using a thoracotomy approach

    c. Removal of one segment of the lung using a thoracoscopic approach

    d. Removal of one lobe of the lung using a thoracoscopic approach

61. The patient had a tear in the lateral posterior horn of the right meniscus and a complete tear of the anterior cruciate ligament. The surgeon performs an open repair of the meniscus using arrow tacks and reconstructs the anterior cruciate ligament using a patellar tendon graft. How is this service coded?

    | 27403 | Arthrotomy with meniscus repair, knee |
    |-------|----------------------------------------|
    | 27407 | Repair, primary torn ligament and/or capsule, knee; cruciate |
    | 27428 | Ligamentous reconstruction (augmentation), knee; intra-articular (open) |
    | 29882 | Arthroscopy, knee, surgical; with meniscus repair (medical OR lateral) |
    | 29888 | Arthroscopically aided anterior cruciate ligament repair/augmentation or reconstruction |

    a. 27403, 27407

    b. 27403, 27428

    c. 29882, 27407

    d. 29882, 29888

62. Which of the following is a true statement about the molecular pathology codes described in CPT?

    a. Tests in this section are quantitative unless otherwise noted

    b. These tests are used to detect histocompatibility antigens

    c. There are three tiers of test codes found in this section

    d. Results for tests in this section are reported using the Bethesda System

63. The patient has undergone previous prostate surgery and is having trouble voiding completely. The physician performs an internal measurement of the distance between the bladder neck and the external sphincter, deploying a temporary urethral stent. What is the correct code assignment for this procedure?

    a. 52282

    b. 52332

    c. 53855

    d. 53899

64. The patient has a tethered thoracic spinal cord requiring posterior single level laminectomy and lysis of the adhesions. What is the correct code assignment for this procedure?

    a. 63200

    b. 63266

    c. 63271

    d. 63277

65. The surgeon performs a posterior lumbar interbody fusion using synthetic cages at two levels (L4-5 and L5-S1). The discs are removed to prepare the interspaces and posterior segmental instrumentation is placed. Morselized bone is used, which is obtained from the patient's iliac crest. What is the correct code assignment for this case?

    a. 22612, 22614, 22840, 29031

    b. 22630, 22632, 22842, 22851, 22851, 20937

    c. 22633, 22634, 22842, 22851, 20938

    d. 22558, 22585, 22840, 22851, 22851, 29037

66. The patient is admitted with shortness of breath and cough and is diagnosed with MRSA *Staphylococcal aureus* pneumonia. The physician also documents a MRSA colonization. Which of the following would be reported?

    a. J15.212, Z22.322

    b. J15.212

    c. J15.212, Z22.322, R06.02, R05

    d. J15.212, R06.02, R05

67. The 26-year-old diabetic female patient is admitted with ketoacidosis. She recently had wisdom teeth removal with a subsequent abscess of the nearby tooth. This appears to be the source of the poorly controlled Type 1 diabetes mellitus. The patient was re-hydrated due to dehydration and was given IV antibiotics for the abscess. Which of the following codes would be reported?

    a. E11.65, K04.7, E86.0

    b. E10.10, E87.2, E10.65, K04.7, E86.0

    c. E10.10, E10.65, K04.7, E86.0

    d. E11.65, E87.2, K04.7, E86.0

68. The patient is a 47-year-old post right kidney transplant patient seen for an annual kidney ultrasound. The US reveals a huge mass, and the patient is prepped for surgery. The diseased kidney is removed, and the pathology report reveals the diagnosis of renal cell carcinoma in a transplanted kidney. The attending physician concurs, and the patient receives an initial dose of chemotherapy prior to discharge. Which of the following codes would be reported?

    a. C80.2, C64.1

    b. T86.19, C80.2, C64.1

    c. T86.19, C80.2

    d. Z51.11, T86.9, C80.2, C64.1

69. The patient is seen in the wound clinic for treatment of decubitus ulcers. The physician documents the final diagnoses as: Ulcer of left heel, stage 1; ulcer of right heel, stage 2. Which of the following codes would be reported?

    a. L89.621, L89.612

    b. L89.621

    c. L97.421, L97.412

    d. L89.622, L89.611

70. The 93-year-old female patient is admitted with confusion, tachycardia, fever, and tachypnea. The blood cultures were negative, but the physician documents the following final diagnoses: severe sepsis, septic shock, and respiratory failure. Which of the following codes would be reported?

    a. A41.9, R65.21, J96.00, R41.0, R50.9, R00.0, R06.82

    b. A41.89, R65.21, J96.00

    c. R65.21, J96.00

    d. A41.9, R65.21, J96.00

71. A new patient is seen for a cough. The physician completes a detailed history and a comprehensive exam and uses moderate medical decision making in evaluating the patient. An albuterol 2.5 mg and Atrovent 0.5 mg nebulizer treatment was given, and MDI teaching was performed. What is the correct code assignment for this case?

    a. 99202, 94640, J7611, J7644

    b. 99203, 94640, J7611, J7644

    c. 99204, 94640, 94664, J7620

    d. 99203, 94640, 94664, J7620

72. The patient undergoes a CT of the abdomen with and without contrast, a CT of the pelvis with and without contrast, and an MRI of the pelvis with contrast. What is the correct code assignment for this case?

    a. 74178, 72196

    b. 72194, 74170

    c. 72196, 74183

    d. 72194, 74170, 72196

## Domain III   *Regulatory Guidelines and Reporting Requirements for Outpatient Services*

73. A physician sees a patient for congestive heart failure. The patient is known to have a hiatal hernia and arthritis. The congestive heart failure is evaluated, blood pressure recorded, and medications adjusted for the congestive heart failure and the hypertension. What conditions are reportable?

    a. Congestive heart failure

    b. Congestive heart failure; hypertension

    c. Congestive heart failure; hypertension; arthritis

    d. Congestive heart failure; hypertension; arthritis; hiatal hernia

74. A patient is evaluated by his family practitioner for acute chest pain. The physician documents as the final diagnosis chest pain due to probable gastric ulcer and a history of cholecystectomy. What should the coder report?

    a. Chest pain; gastric ulcer

    b. Gastric ulcer

    c. Chest pain

    d. Chest pain; history of cholecystectomy

75. A Medicare patient with a family history of colon cancer and a personal history of colon polyps undergoes an examination of the entire colon and the terminal ileum. What is the correct coding assignment for this procedure?

    a. G0104, Colorectal cancer screening, flexible sigmoidoscopy

    b. G0105, Colorectal cancer screening, colonoscopy on individual at high risk

    c. 45300, Sigmoidoscopy, flexible; diagnostic, with or without collection of specimen(s) by brushing or washing

    d. 45378, Colonoscopy, flexible; diagnostic, including collection of specimen(s) by brushing or washing, when performed (separate procedure)

76. The following coding was reviewed by the coding manager before the claims were submitted. What change would the coding manager request to help ensure payment?

| Case | CPT Code(s) | Description | Diagnosis | Description |
|------|-------------|-------------|-----------|-------------|
| 1 | 90713 | Polio vaccine | Z23 | Influenza vaccine |
| 2 | 82465<br>73030 | Cholesterol<br>Shoulder x-ray | M25.512<br>E78.0 | Shoulder pain, left<br>Hypercholesterolemia, pure |

    a. Modifiers should be placed on the CPT codes

    b. Code the diagnoses codes to a greater level of specificity

    c. Additional CPT codes are required to describe the service

    d. Link the diagnoses codes correctly to the procedures

77. The following is a summary of visits for John Smith on November 2:

    > 9:30 a.m.   Seen by Dr. X for asthma, requiring nebulizer treatment and medication
    >
    > 3:30 p.m.   Seen by Dr. X again for worsening asthma, requiring another nebulizer treatment and more medication

    To help ensure payment, which of the following modifiers should be reported by Dr. X for the services provided at 3:30 p.m.?

    a. −51, Multiple procedures

    b. −58, Staged or related procedure or service by the same physician during the postoperative period

    c. −76, Repeat procedure by same physician

    d. −77, Repeat procedure by another physician

78. A coder uses local coverage determinations (LCDs) from Medicare to identify:

    a. What procedures require prior approval before payment is made by the third party

    b. What CPT codes justify the necessity of a test or service

    c. What is the reimbursement for a specific procedure

    d. What ICD-10-CM codes justify the medical necessity of a test or service

## Domain IV  *Data Quality and Management*

79. What is a claim called that contains all required data elements needed to process and pay the claim quickly?

    a. Open

    b. Clean

    c. Closed

    d. Final

80. The amount that a nonparticipating (nonPAR) physician who does not accept assignment can bill a Medicare beneficiary is called the:

    a. NonPAR value

    b. Contractual limit

    c. Limiting charge

    d. Nonassigned charge

81. After reviewing the following hospital charges for Dr. Peters for patient #213429, the coder should:

    Patient #213429

    Date of Admission: 8/12/20XX

    Date of Discharge: 8/15/20XX

| Date of Service | CPT Code | Code Description | Diagnosis | Charge |
|-----------------|----------|------------------|-----------|--------|
| 8/12/20XX | 99255 | Consultation | G40.309 | $247.00 |
| 8/13/20XX | 99221 | Initial hospital | I10 | $167.00 |
| 8/14/20XX | 99221 | Initial hospital | G40.309 | $167.00 |
| 8/15/20XX | 99238 | Hospital discharge | I10 | $105.00 |

    a. Question that a different diagnosis was used on some days

    b. Bill the codes exactly as the physician submitted them

    c. Notice that the two daily visits are coded incorrectly

    d. Request the records from the hospital to verify the services

82. A 60-year-old woman calls the office saying that she was billed for a "male" shot, saying "I always get the same thing." The claim for that date shows 1 unit of J1071 was billed, with diagnoses of Z79.890 and N95.2. The encounter form for the visit states "Estrogen therapy." What error does the coding manager suspect?

| | |
|---|---|
| J1050 | Injection, medroxyprogesterone acetate (conjugated estrogen), 1 mg |
| J1071 | Injection, testosterone cypionate, 1 mg |
| Z79.890 | Hormone replacement therapy |
| N95.2 | Postmenopausal atrophic vaginitis |

   a. The coder chose a code for the wrong medication.

   b. The coder chose a code for the wrong dosage of medication.

   c. The coder assumed that estradiol was administered at that visit.

   d. The coder reported an incorrect diagnosis code for the service.

## Domain V  *Information and Communication Technologies*

83. Which of the following would be considered an advantage of using e-mail for transmission of data?

   a. Employers and online services retain the right to archive messages transmitted through their systems.

   b. E-mail may be discoverable for legal purposes.

   c. E-mail can be used to clarify treatment instructions or medication administration.

   d. E-mail can be printed, circulated, forwarded, and stored in numerous paper and electronic files.

84. The physician asks that a computerized record be kept of all his patients with basic demographic and encounter data compiled. What software application would be used?

   a. Word processing

   b. Database

   c. Spreadsheet

   d. Process tracking

85. Which of the following software applications would be used to aid in the coding function in a physician's office?

   a. Grouper

   b. Encoder

   c. Pricer

   d. Diagnosis calculator

86. A physician asks that his total patient encounters be calculated by month, by quarter, and by year. The physician would also like a monthly average. What software application should be used?

    a. Word processing

    b. Database

    c. Spreadsheet

    d. Process tracking

## Domain VI  *Privacy, Confidentiality, Legal, and Ethical Issues*

87. The head of the surgery department asks to see a patient's medical record. This physician is not listed as her surgeon in the record. What do you do?

    a. Give the physician the medical record as he requested

    b. Inform the physician that because he is not listed as the patient's surgeon, he must obtain the appropriate authorization signed by the patient in order to review the record

    c. Inform the physician that you are unable to provide the chart because he is not listed as the patient's attending physician

    d. Inform the physician that you are too busy to retrieve the patient's chart

88. A child was examined and treated for child abuse in the emergency department at the hospital. As a result, the child has been taken into protective custody by the Office of Child Protection because of suspected child abuse by the parents. The father requests copies of the designated record set for the visit. He has a copy of the child's birth certificate listing him as the father, and he possesses a picture ID. Do you release a copy of the emergency department record?

    a. Yes, after he has completed a legitimate release of information authorization.

    b. Decline to release the information and contact the hospital's attorney.

    c. Contact the Office of Child Protection for permission to release the record.

    d. Refer the matter to the hospital administrator and follow the administration's instructions after he meets with the father.

89. The "minimum necessary rule" refers to which of the following:

    a. Copying all billing and medical records as requested by the patient

    b. Releasing copies of the entire medical record for all disclosure requests

    c. Disclosing personal health information is held to the smallest amount of information necessary to accomplish the intended purpose of the use or disclosure

    d. Requesting personal health information by public officials who have a right to the information as dictated by state law

90. Although the HIPAA Privacy Rule allows patients access to personal health information about themselves, which of the following cannot be disclosed to patients?

    a. Interpretation of x-rays by the radiologist

    b. Billing records

    c. Progress notes written by the attending physician

    d. Psychotherapy notes

## Domain VII *Compliance*

91. The term that refers to the degree to which the same results are achieved each time a record is coded during a coding audit is:

    a. Validity

    b. Completeness

    c. Reliability

    d. Timeliness

92. The term used to describe private citizens who may bring suit on behalf of themselves and the government against fraudulent healthcare providers is:

    a. Defendants

    b. *Qui tam* plaintiffs

    c. *Res ipsa loquitur*

    d. *Res gestae*

93. _____legislation prohibits physicians from referring Medicare patients to a clinical lab in which he or an immediate family member has a financial interest.

    a. Kennedy-Kasselbaum

    b. Stark

    c. Fist

    d. Delay

94. This federal agency develops an annual healthcare "work plan":

    a. IRS

    b. FBI

    c. DEA

    d. OIG

95. Which of the following would be considered healthcare abuse?

    a. Falsifying a patient's diagnosis to justify tests or procedures

    b. Accepting kickbacks

    c. Inadvertently sending in a claim twice

    d. Intentional upcoding

96. There are some activities that are not subject to prosecution and protect the organization from civil or criminal penalties in relation to the Federal Anti-Kickback Statute. These exceptions are called:

    a. *Qui Tam* actions

    b. Fraud Enforcement and Recovery Act of 2009

    c. Safe Harbor

    d. Sherman Anti-trust Act

# Multiple Choice Exam 3 Answers

| | | | |
|---|---|---|---|
| 1. | 25. | 49. | 73. |
| 2. | 26. | 50. | 74. |
| 3. | 27. | 51. | 75. |
| 4. | 28. | 52. | 76. |
| 5. | 29. | 53. | 77. |
| 6. | 30. | 54. | 78. |
| 7. | 31. | 55. | 79. |
| 8. | 32. | 56. | 80. |
| 9. | 33. | 57. | 81. |
| 10. | 34. | 58. | 82. |
| 11. | 35. | 59. | 83. |
| 12. | 36. | 60. | 84. |
| 13. | 37. | 61. | 85. |
| 14. | 38. | 62. | 86. |
| 15. | 39. | 63. | 87. |
| 16. | 40. | 64. | 88. |
| 17. | 41. | 65. | 89. |
| 18. | 42. | 66. | 90. |
| 19. | 43. | 67. | 91. |
| 20. | 44. | 68. | 92. |
| 21. | 45. | 69. | 93. |
| 22. | 46. | 70. | 94. |
| 23. | 47. | 71. | 95. |
| 24. | 48. | 72. | 96. |

# EXAM 3 MEDICAL CASES

## EXAM 3—CASE 1

*Please code for the services of the physician.*

**CHIEF COMPLAINT:** Nosebleed

**HISTORY OF PRESENT ILLNESS:** The patient is a 69-year-old man who presents to the emergency department with spontaneous onset of a nosebleed at approximately midnight. The patient was awakened by a sensation in his throat that he thought was posterior nasal discharge, and subsequently he discovered that in fact his nose was bleeding. He was unable to achieve hemostasis at home, and so presents to the emergency department. He denies prior problems with nosebleeds. He further denies any history of coagulopathy and is not on any medications that should cause anticoagulation.

**PAST MEDICAL HISTORY:**

1. Hypertension
2. Depression with anxiety
3. Gastroesophageal reflux disease

**PAST SURGICAL HISTORY:**

1. Status post appendectomy
2. Status post perforated viscus
3. Status post laminectomy

**CURRENT MEDICATIONS:**

1. Rabeprazole
2. Inderal
3. Amitriptyline
4. Alprazolam

**ALLERGIES:**

1. OPIOID analgesics
2. TORADOL

**SOCIAL HISTORY:** The patient is married. Lives independently with his spouse. His primary physician is Dr. X. He does not use tobacco and denies excessive ethanol use.

**FAMILY HISTORY:** Negative for any coagulopathy

**REVIEW OF SYSTEMS:** Negative, other than those items in the HPI

**PHYSICAL EXAMINATION:**

**VITAL SIGNS:** Blood pressure 132/72, pulse 84, respiration 16, temperature is 97.8

**GENERAL:** The patient is awake and alert. He is nontoxic and otherwise in no acute distress.

**HEENT:** Sclerae were anicteric. The palpebral conjunctivae are pink. TMs are clear bilaterally. The oropharynx demonstrated some posterior sanguinous drainage but otherwise was clear.

**NECK:** Supple

**LUNGS:** Breath sounds clear and symmetric

## EXAM 3—CASE 1 (*continued*)

**CARDIAC:** Regular S1, S2. No murmur or gallop appreciated.

**ABDOMEN:** Soft, nontender, without hepatosplenomegaly or mass

**EXTREMITIES:** No deformities, clubbing, or edema. Pulses full and symmetric throughout.

**SKIN:** Warm and dry. No jaundice, pallor, or cyanosis noted. No skin rashes present.

**NEUROLOGIC:** The patient is alert and fully oriented. Pupils equal, round, and reactive to light. The remainder of the examination is nonfocal.

**EMERGENCY DEPARTMENT COURSE:** A nasal clip was placed and left in place for approximately 15 minutes. Reevaluation of the patient at that time revealed moderate bleeding in the right nasal passage, but the left passage was clear. The right side was subsequently packed with cotton pledgets soaked with Parkes solution. After leaving these in place for approximately 15 minutes, the bleeding was well controlled. There was, however, a single bleeding point of an exposed vessel, which was identified. This was cauterized successfully, with good hemostasis achieved. The patient's nasal passages were subsequently swabbed with antibiotic ointment. He was observed for an additional 20–30 minutes, and his bleeding remained well controlled. He was subsequently discharged home in good condition.

**DISCHARGE INSTRUCTIONS:**

1. He was advised to avoid any aspirin and to avoid blowing his nose for 2 days.

2. He was advised to continue using Neosporin or a similar antibiotic ointment to the right nasal passage three times per day.

3. He was recommended to follow up either with an ENT physician of his choice or Dr. X in 3 to 5 days. The patient was subsequently discharged home in good condition.

**EMERGENCY DEPARTMENT DIAGNOSIS:** Epistaxis

**HISTORY:** Comprehensive

**EXAMINATION:** Comprehensive

**MEDICAL DECISION MAKING:** Low

---

*Enter one diagnosis code and two procedure codes.*

**DX1**

**PR1**

**PR2**

## EXAM 3—CASE 2

*Please code for the services of the physician.*

**REQUESTING PHYSICIAN:** Dr. Z, Primary Care

**HISTORY:** This is a very pleasant 63-year-old white man with multiple past medical history who is seen initially with the chief complaint of altered mental status at the nursing home. An infectious disease consult has been obtained for a possible urinary tract infection and sepsis.

**SOCIAL HISTORY:** The patient is a nursing home resident here.

**MEDICATIONS:** Avonex and Norvasc

**ALLERGIES:** None

**REVIEW OF SYSTEMS:** Pertinent for altered mental status

**PHYSICAL EXAMINATION:**

**VITAL SIGNS:** The patient is currently afebrile. Blood pressure 152/94.

**GENERAL:** The patient is in no distress. Alert, awake, and oriented times two.

**CARDIOVASCULAR:** Regular rate and rhythm. Positive S1 and S2. No murmurs.

**LUNGS:** Clear to auscultation. No wheezes or crackles.

**ABDOMEN:** Bowel sounds positive. Nontender.

**EXTREMITIES:** Good pulses. No edema.

**LABORATORY DATA:** Urinalysis positive for pyuria. Urine culture with gram-negative, anaerobic *Providencia stuartii*.

**ASSESSMENT:**

1. Sepsis due to *Providencia stuartii*
2. Urinary tract infection

**RECOMMENDATIONS:**

1. Recommend starting the patient on Rocephin.
2. Check blood cultures times two sets.

Thank you for recommending this consultation. Please fax a copy to Dr. Z's office.

**HISTORY:** Detailed

**EXAMINATION:** Detailed

**MEDICAL DECISION MAKING:** Moderate

*Enter three diagnosis codes and one procedure code.*

**DX1**

**DX2**

**DX3**

**PR1**

## EXAM 3—CASE 3

*Please code for the services of the physician.*

**SERVICE:** Trauma service

**HPI:** This patient arrived at the emergency department on 10/07/20XX at approximately 19:00. The patient is a 25-year-old Hispanic woman who is status post pedestrian versus motor vehicle collision. The patient reports a questionable loss of consciousness prior to arrival. Upon arrival the patient's prehospital blood pressure was noted to be 130/90 with prehospital heart rate of 126. The patient was in severe pain, complaining of pain mostly over the left anterior chest wall and of the left leg, and was admitted to trauma service. Upon questioning the patient denied allergies.

**PAST MEDICAL HISTORY:** Normal

**MEDICATIONS:** None

**PAST SURGICAL HISTORY:** Significant for removal of the gallbladder

**FAMILY HISTORY:** Normal

**SOCIAL HISTORY:** Occasional use of alcohol, approximately 2 to 3 drinks per week, but the patient denied use of tobacco or illicit drugs.

**REVIEW OF SYSTEMS:** No fever or fatigue; no systemic complaints. The patient's dermatologic review of systems was negative. She reports no rashes or any outstanding skin conditions. The patient's ear, nose, and throat review of systems was also unremarkable. The patient's cardiovascular, pulmonary, and gastrointestinal systems were all unremarkable with no specific complaints toward chest pain, shortness of breath, or change in bowel habits. Additionally, the patient's musculoskeletal review of systems was normal without prior history of musculoskeletal disease or weakness. The patient's genitourinary review of systems was normal with no complaints of dysuria, abnormal genitalia, burning, or itching. Psychiatric and neurologic review of systems was also unremarkable. The patient's skin was unremarkable historically but upon presentation the patient did complain of a rash and abrasion secondary to her trauma.

**PRIMARY SURVEY:** Clear airway that required no intervention. The patient arrived in C spine immobilization in a hard collar and backboard. The patient was found to be breathing spontaneously and unlabored.

Skin was warm, normal in color, without signs of external hemorrhage. The patient's carotid, femoral, radial, and dorsalis pedis pulses were all palpable and 2+ positive.

The patient was found to be alert, GCS approximately 14 with the only abnormality of the eyes not opening spontaneously and only to voice. Pupils were found to be reactive, 4-2, and symmetric. The patient's Glasgow coma scale upon initial evaluation in the trauma bay was that of GCS 14 and the patient's total trauma score was 12. The patient had a CT scan of the head, chest, abdomen, and pelvis, as well as reconstructed views of the cervical, thoracic, and lumbar spines performed. These scans were reviewed with the doctor in the radiology department. The CT of the head was negative, with no obvious skull deformity or fracture, and no intracranial bleeding. Her chest revealed several abnormalities including a pulmonary contusion of the left upper lobe, hemopneumothorax, and depressed rib fractures at left ribs 2, 3, 4, 5, and 6. The rib fractures at 4 and 5 were comminuted. Rib 6 was severely displaced and crushed inward. However, upon evaluation of the CT scan there was no evidence or indication of thoracic vascular injury. CT scan of the abdomen was unremarkable. The patient's CT scan of the pelvis revealed left pubic rami fracture. The patient's cervical, thoracic, and lumbar spine images were reconstructed using the CT scan. These images revealed C spine, T spine, and L spine that were essentially without abnormality. The patient's point of care laboratory results included a hemoglobin of 14.1, sodium 143, potassium 3.6, chlorine 102, BUN 12, base excess of 2, pH 7.38, PO2 37, PCO2 45, lactate 1.9.

**SECONDARY SURVEY:** HEENT: The patient's pupils were equally round and reactive to light bilaterally, going from 4 mm to 2 mm with direct light stimulation. The patient's gaze was normal with tympanic membranes on the right and left clear. The oropharynx was found to be clear but tender at the chin. Gag reflex was intact and inclusion was normal. Neck revealed collapsed veins with trachea midline. There was no tenderness or

## EXAM 3—CASE 3 (*continued*)

crepitance in the neck. The chest revealed some external bilateral upper chest abrasions. The chest wall was seen to be symmetric; however, breath sounds were found to be abnormal with decreased breath sounds, particularly in the left chest. Heart sounds were regular rate and rhythm without murmurs, rubs, or gallops. The patient was not found to have crepitance of the chest wall. However, there was severe tenderness to palpation at the left anterior chest wall. Abdomen revealed no external trauma to the abdomen, no tenderness to palpation, obese yet normal contour to the abdomen. Abdomen was dull to percussion. Pelvis stable and nontender by examination. Genitourinary revealed no blood at the meatus and the urine pregnancy test was negative. Rectal revealed normal sphincter tone with brown stool. Spine revealed a nontender cervical, thoracic, and lumbar spine. There was no evidence of step-off deformity at any of these levels. Neuro revealed motor strength 5+/5+ in both right and left upper and lower extremities. Additionally sensory examination revealed no deficits. Vascular exam revealed 2+ radial pulses bilaterally. Additionally femoral, posterior tibial, and dorsalis pulses were all 2+ bilaterally.

**ASSESSMENT:** 25-year-old female involved in a pedestrian versus motor vehicle trauma. The patient suffered multiple injuries. The patient suffered rib fractures from ribs 2 to 6 on the left side. Ribs 4 and 5 on the left side were found to have the comminuted fractures with resultant hemopneumothorax and pulmonary contusion.

Rib 6 was also a severely displaced rib fracture with displacement into the thoracic cavity. Reconstructed images of the cervical, thoracic, and lumbar spines were negative. C spine showed questionable transverse fracture at level T4.

**PLAN:**

1. Watch respiratory status due to pulmonary insult. The patient is to receive IPPV treatments in the TICU.

2. Orthopedic consultation for the suprapubic ramus fracture.

**ADDENDUM**

**REVISION TO ADMISSION H&P DICTATION:** The patient had no evidence of fracture abnormality on her C spine on reconstructed images. Repeat, there was no abnormality on C spine, which was negative. This was cleared radiographically.

**HISTORY:** Comprehensive

**EXAMINATION:** Comprehensive

**MEDICAL DECISION MAKING:** High

---

*Enter four diagnosis codes and one procedure code.*

**DX1**

**DX2**

**DX3**

**DX4**

**PR1**

## EXAM 3—CASE 4

*Please code for the services of the surgeon.*

**ADMISSION DATE:** 11/16/20XX

**SURGERY DATE:** 11/16/20XX

**PREOPERATIVE DIAGNOSIS:** Right renal calculi

**POSTOPERATIVE DIAGNOSIS:** Right renal calculi

**PROCEDURE:** Right percutaneous nephrolithotomy, placement of percutaneous nephrostomy tube, and placement of right double J ureteral stent, as well as nephroscopy

**SURGEON:**

**ASSISTANT:** None

**ESTIMATED BLOOD LOSS:** 75 mL

**SPECIMENS REMOVED:** Multiple renal calculi

**FINDINGS:** Very hard renal calculus with satellite calculi requiring flexible nephroscopy, laser lithotripsy, as well as an upper pole calyceal diverticulum with a narrow neck

**COMPLICATIONS:** None

The patient is a 33-year-old man with significant history of nephrolithiasis. He is status post right-sided pyeloplasty, as well as a prior percutaneous nephrolithotomy. He had a stone recurrence early in the year and wanted to wait to have this taken care of despite the risks of progressive renal damage. We reviewed the treatment options, and he chose percutaneous nephrolithotomy despite the risks. These included, but are not limited to, bleeding, infection, renal damage, renal damage to the point of requiring dialysis or nephrectomy, bleeding requiring transfusion with associated risks such as HIV and hepatitis, MID, DVT, stroke, death, and pneumothorax. The patient understood and consented. On the date of the operation, a percutaneous access was obtained onto the ureter by interventional radiology. The patient was brought to the operating room and placed in supine position. General anesthesia was induced. He was then placed in the prone position and padded in the appropriate pressure points. The patient was then prepared and draped in the standard fashion. An implant guidewire was then placed down the patient's catheter into the bladder under fluoroscopic guidance. The tract was noted to be dense due to his prior surgery, but it was dilated up to 12-French sequentially with the implants dilators. A two-wire introducer was then placed on the ureter, and a second wire was placed into the patient's bladder. The nephroscopy dilating balloon was then placed under fluoroscopic guidance into the patient's renal pelvis. The balloon was insufflated to 18 atmospheres of pressure. The nephroscope sheath was placed over the balloon into the renal pelvis.

The balloon was desufflated and removed leaving a safety guidewire and a working guidewire. The stones were immediately identified. Using the ultrasonic laser lithotrite, a large satellite fragment was identified and attempted to be broken up. This ultrasonic laser lithotrite was used until it had actually broken. This was removed, and we attempted to get another one while we incorporated the use of a laser fiber with a 500-micron fiber at settings of 1 joule and 10 Hz. The stone was then carefully lithotripped, so as to not create large fragments. Once the ultrasonic lithotrite was replaced, the laser was removed. The stone was then fragmented into large pieces. A number of pieces approximately 0.5 cm were then removed with grasping forceps. These were sent off the table as a specimen. Smaller specimens were then lithotripped until they were aspirated through the ultrasonic lithotrite. The nephroscope was

## EXAM 3—CASE 4 (*continued*)

removed. The flexible nephroscopy identified a large stone in the upper pole calyx. Of note, an additional stone was noted under fluoroscopic guidance in the upper pole and it was noted to be in a diverticulum with a small tract. The diverticulum was dilated with the flexible nephroscope. The stone was, however, intraparenchymal. During the course of this, the stone in the satellite calyx in the upper pole had fallen into the renal pelvis. The flexible nephroscope was removed, and the rigid nephroscope was placed. The stone was crushed using the ultrasonic lithotrite and grasped and removed as well with the large grasping forceps. The collecting system was examined for small fragments, and each one was grasped under fluoroscopic guidance. The entire kidney was noted to be cleaned of stones after the procedure. Using the guidewire, a double J 6-French × 26 cm stent was placed down the ureter into the bladder and noted to curl. It was then curled into the renal pelvis. A 10-French percutaneous nephroscopy tube was then placed in the renal pelvis into the upper pole, as to be away from the stent. The nephroscope sheath was removed. The percutaneous nephrostomy was locked into place, and a nephrostogram was performed confirming the correct placement of both the double J ureteral stent and the percutaneous nephrostomy tube. The skin was then sutured closed using 2-0 silk and secured to the suture with the percutaneous nephrostomy tube. All tubes were then placed to gravity drainage. The patient was placed back in the supine position, awakened from anesthesia, and taken to the recovery room in stable condition.

*Enter one diagnosis code and one procedure code.*

**DX1**

**PR1**

## EXAM 3—CASE 5

*Please code for the services of the surgeon.*

**PREOPERATIVE DIAGNOSIS:** Conn's syndrome with abnormal aldosterone secretion from the left adrenal gland

**POSTOPERATIVE DIAGNOSIS:** Conn's syndrome with abnormal aldosterone secretion from the left adrenal gland

**OPERATION PERFORMED:** Laparoscopic left adrenalectomy

**ATTENDING SURGEON:**

**ANESTHESIA:** General

**ESTIMATED BLOOD LOSS:** Less than 20 cc

**FLUID REPLACEMENT:** 1,000 cc lactated Ringer's solution

**URINE OUTPUT:** 175 cc

**SPECIMENS:** Left adrenal gland

**INDICATIONS FOR PROCEDURE:** This 46-year-old African-American woman has hypertension and hypokalemia. Her medications include Norvasc and potassium supplement. Workup revealed hyperaldosteronism that, after adrenal vein sampling, appeared to localize specifically to the left adrenal gland with markedly elevated levels of aldosterone. After the risks and benefits of the procedure and possible complications were explained, the patient elected to undergo laparoscopic left adrenalectomy.

**DESCRIPTION OF PROCEDURE:** The patient was brought to the operative suite and positioned on the operating room table in the right lateral decubitus position with the left side up. She was adequately padded and taped in position. She was then prepared and draped in the usual sterile fashion. Initial access to the abdomen was obtained using a direct cut-down technique below the left ribs. Insertion of a blunt cannula was undertaken and the abdomen was insufflated under direct visualization. There appeared to be limited working space in the abdomen due to the patient's central obesity and a large amount of intra-abdominal fat. In addition, the patient had a very large fatty liver that was clear over to the left abdomen. Under direct visualization, we placed a more medial 5.0-mm trocar in the left hypochondrium and in addition, two 5.0-mm trocars in the left hypochondrium more lateral to our initial access site.

We proceeded to mobilize the left colon from the left sidewall using harmonic shears, and we adequately mobilized the colon out of the way. We then proceeded to roll the colon mesentery medially where we could identify Gerota's fascia.

We then followed Gerota's fascia superiorly and rolled the inferior pole of the spleen medially and superiorly, rolling the spleen off its left lateral attachments. This allowed us to identify the area of the adrenal gland. We then proceeded to open up Gerota's fascia gently using an L-hook cautery and identified the adrenal gland in place, which appeared to be somewhat long and flat in appearance.

After Gerota's fascia was completely opened to expose the adrenal gland in its entirety, meticulous dissection was carried out inferiorly and medially, where we identified a solitary left adrenal vein, which we triply clipped and divided. Further L-hook cautery was then used to dissect the gland from the underlying fat. This was done with excellent hemostasis. Additional small blood vessels were clipped and divided, and further dissection enabled identification of the left phrenic vein, which again was triply clipped and divided. We then further dissected the adrenal gland off its bed using L-hook cautery with excellent hemostasis. We then placed the gland into an impermeable entrapment sac and removed it through the initial access site, passing it off the field. Inspection of the adrenal bed revealed it to have

## EXAM 3—CASE 5 (*continued*)

good hemostasis. We irrigated with warm normal saline and aspirated back. There was no evidence of bleeding. We then proceeded to close our initial access trocar site with 0 Vicryl suture on a suture-passer using a figure-of-8 technique. The rest of the abdomen was inspected. We replaced the left colon back into the left upper abdomen. There was no injury to the colon throughout the entire procedure. The patient tolerated the procedure well.

We removed our instruments under direct visualization, desufflating the abdomen completely. There was no bleeding from the trocar sites. The patient's bed was unflexed, and the fascial suture was tied. The skin and fascia were anesthetized with 0.25% Marcaine plain. The skin was closed with 4-0 Monocryl subcuticular stitch. Steri-Strips were applied. Sterile dressing was applied. The patient was transferred to the recovery room in stable and satisfactory condition.

*Enter three diagnosis codes and one procedure code.*

**DX1**

**DX2**

**DX3**

**PR1**

## EXAM 3—CASE 6

*Please code for the services of the surgeon.*

**PREOPERATIVE DIAGNOSIS:** Intraductal carcinoma in situ of the right breast

**POSTOPERATIVE DIAGNOSIS:** Intraductal carcinoma in situ of the right breast

**PROCEDURE:**

Right needle-localized lumpectomy

Axillary sampling

**ANESTHESIA:** General endotracheal

**ESTIMATED BLOOD LOSS:** Minimal

**FLUIDS:** 1,000 cc

**DISPOSITION:** To recovery room

**INDICATIONS:** The patient is a 71-year-old woman who was noted to have abnormal calcifications at roughly the 6 o'clock position of the areola. These were biopsied and found to be intraductal carcinoma in situ. She was inclined to proceed with needle-localized lumpectomy. The risks of bleeding, infection, poor wound healing, and unappealing cosmetics were discussed. The possibility we could find invasive carcinoma was also discussed. The need for postoperative radiation therapy was also discussed. She was well aware of the possibility of positive margins that would lead to further surgery or a mastectomy.

**PROCEDURE:** The patient was initially taken to the Center for Breast Diagnosis, where Dr. X placed a needle at the inferior aspect of the breast.

The patient was then taken to the operating room. General anesthesia was administered. SCDs were placed. A curvilinear incision was made on the inferior aspect of the areola. This was taken down to the subcutaneous tissue. Flaps were raised in each direction for approximately 2 cm and taken down to the chest wall. A long stitch was placed medially, a short stitch superiorly.

The specimen was then removed. The cavity was then thoroughly irrigated; ¼% Marcaine was used for local anesthesia. A sampling of axillary lymph nodes were removed.

The subcutaneous tissue was then approximated using 3-0 Monocryl. The skin was approximated using 4-0 Monocryl in a running subcuticular fashion. A sterile dressing was then applied.

The patient tolerated the procedure well and was taken to the recovery room. The operative findings were discussed with her husband and daughter.

---

*Enter one diagnosis code and one procedure code.*

**DX1**

**PR1**

## EXAM 3—CASE 7

*Please code for the services of the surgeon.*

**DATE OF OPERATION:** 10/26/20XX

**PREOPERATIVE DIAGNOSIS:** Hypertrophic pyloric stenosis

**POSTOPERATIVE DIAGNOSES:** Hypertrophic pyloric stenosis; thrombosed accessory spleen

**OPERATION:**

1. Laparoscopic pyloromyotomy
2. Excision of thrombosed accessory spleen

**ANESTHESIA:** General

**INDICATIONS FOR SURGERY:** Patient is a 4-week-old boy with a 1-week history of progressively projectile vomiting. Patient was brought to the emergency department, where he underwent ultrasound evaluation. Ultrasound findings revealed a pyloric channel of 15 mm in length with a wall thickness of 3.8 mm, consistent with hypertrophic pyloric stenosis. Electrolytes were found to be within reasonable range. Patient is brought to the operating room for pyloromyotomy.

**FINDINGS:** Moderately hypertrophied pylorus. No evidence of mucosal perforation. There was a 1 cm × 2 cm dark purple mass on the omentum, consistent with a thrombosed accessory spleen. This was excised without difficulty and sent for pathologic evaluation.

**PROCEDURE:** After informed consent was obtained, the patient was brought to the operating suite and placed in supine position. After adequate endotracheal anesthesia had been administered, his stomach was decompressed and his bladder was emptied, and his abdomen was prepared and draped in the usual sterile fashion. After infiltration with a local anesthetic, the base of the umbilicus was everted and a vertical 5-mm incision was made. A Veress needle was introduced, and pneumoperitoneum was established to 8 mm Hg pressure at 1 L/minute flow. The Veress needle was then replaced with a radially expandible 5-mm trocar. Laparoscope was introduced and confirmed good placement. Under laparoscopic visualization, stab incisions were made in the right upper quadrant and left upper quadrant. In the right upper quadrant, a pyloric grasper was introduced and in the left upper quadrant, the Arthro blade was introduced. Examination revealed a 1 cm × 2 cm dark purplish mass attached to the omentum near the spleen. This was separate from the spleen. He had a normal-appearing lobulated spleen in the left upper quadrant. This mass was consistent with a thrombosed accessory spleen. Following the stomach distally, the pyloric channel was identified. This was moderately hypertrophied, consistent with the ultrasound diagnosis. While the pylorus was stabilized, the Arthro blade was extruded approximately 2 mm and used to incise the pylorus. The blade was then retracted, and the blunt tip was used to initiate the pyloromyotomy.

This then was replaced with a pyloric spreader, which was used to complete the pyloromyotomy. The mucosa was seen bulging without evidence of mucosal perforation. The pyloromyotomy was extended onto the antrum of the stomach. After there was good bulge of the mucosa, and the superior and inferior edges of the cut pylorus were independently mobile, the duodenum was occluded, and 40 cc of air was inflated into the stomach by the anesthesiologist. This revealed no evidence of a mucosal perforation. The stomach was then decompressed.

The laparoscope was removed and a 5-mm trocar was placed in the right upper quadrant incision site. Laparoscope confirmed good placement. The umbilical trocar was removed, and the umbilical incision was slightly extended to allow placement of an Endo catch bag. Prior to the introduction of the Endo catch bag, the lesion on the omentum was dissected free using electrocautery. There was good hemostasis. The Endo catch bag was then introduced through the umbilical trocar site and was used to retrieve the lesion without spillage or contamination. On palpation, this was soft but solid, consistent with a thrombosed accessory spleen. This was sent for pathologic review.

## EXAM 3—CASE 7 (*continued*)

Reexamination of the intraperitoneal cavity revealed good hemostasis. All instruments and trocars were removed, and the pneumoperitoneum was deflated. The fascia of the right upper quadrant trocar site and the umbilical trocar site were closed with 2-0 Vicryl in figure-of-8 stitch fashion. The umbilical skin incision was closed with 5-0 plain gut in interrupted stitch fashion. The other upper quadrant incisions were closed with Monocryl in subcuticular running stitch fashion. All incisions were cleaned and infiltrated with a local anesthetic. The umbilical trocar site was dressed with sterile gauze and Tegaderm. The other incisions were dressed with Steri-Strips. The patient tolerated the procedure well, was extubated, and then returned to the recovery room in stable condition.

**PATHOLOGY REPORT—EXAM 3 CASE 9**

**CLINICAL INFORMATION**

**PROCEDURE:** Laparoscopic pyloromyotomy

**PREOPERATIVE DIAGNOSIS:** Pyloric stenosis (thrombosed accessory spleen)

**CLINICAL HISTORY:** Not given

**GROSS DESCRIPTION:**

Received fresh for routine examination designated R/O ACCESSORY SPLEEN is a 0.6 g, 1.1 cm × 1.0 cm × 0.5 cm, red-brown nodule with external smooth, glistening surface. The specimen is bisected and submitted entirely in one cassette.

**MICROSCOPIC DESCRIPTION:**

Sections through the accessory spleen revealed subcapsular markedly congested splenic sinusoids with minimal periarteriolar lymphocytic aggregates. Centrally the splenic tissue displays marked congestion and hemorrhage with loss of the sinusoidal pattern. Instead the parenchyma is largely replaced by capillaries with an intervening loose fibrin meshwork. At the periphery the hilum of the accessory spleen contains an extensive neutrophilic infiltrate. Scattered calcified nodules are noted within the splenic parenchyma.

**DIAGNOSIS:**

ABDOMINAL NODULE, EXCISION: ACCESSORY SPLEEN WITH CONGESTION AND HEMORRHAGE

---

*Enter two diagnosis codes and two procedure codes.*

---

**DX1**

**DX2**

**PR1**

**PR2**

## EXAM 3—CASE 8

*Please code for the services of the surgeon.*

**PREOPERATIVE DIAGNOSIS:** Intraocular foreign body, left eye

**POSTOPERATIVE DIAGNOSIS:** Intraocular foreign body, left eye

**PROCEDURE:** Pars plana vitrectomy. Removal of intraocular foreign body.

**ANESTHESIA:** General endotracheal tube

**PROCEDURE IN DETAIL:** After induction of general anesthesia the patient was prepared and draped in a sterile fashion and a lid speculum placed. A free port pars plana vitrectomy was initiated, and anterior vitrectomy of the anterior vitreous was done. This was followed by examination of the posterior pole. The view was significantly obstructed due to a significant corneal scar through the center of the cornea. We cautiously cleaned the vitreous until we were confident that the retina was not detached and we did a 360° removal of the posterior hyaloid and a very opaque vitreous. We identified an intraocular foreign body that was nonmetallic because it did not rise when we used the intraocular magnet. After this we placed some Perfluoron to protect the macular area, although there was some swelling of the macula and a small hemorrhage of the retina in the macular area, but it did not appear that any retinal hole, tear, or detachment was present. We grabbed the foreign body with forceps because of its very large size and did approximately a 5-mm wound extending from the temporal sclerotomy in order to remove the large intraocular foreign body. After the foreign body was removed we removed the remaining Perfluoron, examined the peripheral retina, and we did not see obvious tears or detachments. After this, we closed the sclerotomy wounds with 8-0 nylon suture and the conjunctiva with an 8-0 Vicryl suture. After this, we did a subtendon block of anesthesia for comfort, and following this we used a little Tisseel glue on the surface of the cornea and put a bandage contact lens as from previous repair the patient had had corneal glue on the eye that was very rough and uncomfortable. Following this, the eye was patched and shielded with a sterile patch and some Maxitrol ointment was applied to the eye. There were no complications. Specimens sent to pathology. There were no drains or packs. Our plan is to admit the patient overnight and will follow the patient tomorrow.

*Enter one diagnosis code and three procedure codes.*

**DX1**

**PR1**

**PR2**

**PR3**

# EXAM 4

*For the following questions, choose the* best *answer. A blank answer sheet for these multiple choice questions can be found on page 145.*

## Domain I   *Health Information Documentation*

1. Which reference book would be used by the coder to determine which diagnosis from the problem list is treated by a drug prescribed by the physician?

   a. *Taber's Cyclopedic Medical Dictionary*

   b. *Gray's Anatomy*

   c. *Physicians' Desk Reference*

   d. *Medicine—Current Clinical Strategies*

2. What is the name of the formal document prepared by a surgeon at the conclusion of surgery to describe the surgical procedure performed?

   a. Operative report

   b. Tissue report

   c. Pathology report

   d. Anesthesia record

3. On what form would the following be documented, "Chest x-ray, AP and Lateral, to rule out pneumonia"?

   a. Progress notes

   b. Physical examination

   c. Physician's orders

   d. Nursing notes

4. All of the following information is needed to correctly code skin grafts *except:*

   a. Size of the defect

   b. Location of the donor site

   c. Type of graft used

   d. Location of the defect

5. What information is needed to correctly assign a CPT emergency department code?

   a. Whether the patient is new or established to the emergency department physician

   b. How much time the physician spent with the patient

   c. What was the level of history, examination, and medical decision making

   d. Whether the physician is an employee of the hospital

6. A coder has a question about how to use a newly created ICD-10-CM code. What would be the best reference?

    a. *CPT Assistant*

    b. *Coding Clinic*

    c. Local coverage determinations (LCDs)

    d. Correct coding initiatives

7. In which of the following situations would a physician query be required if no diagnosis is documented by the physician?

    a. A routine preoperative chest x-ray on a 95-year-old patient reveals a collapsed vertebral body. The patient is being evaluated for pneumonia

    b. In the absence of a cardiac problem an EKG shows bundle branch block

    c. The lab work shows low potassium level and coder notes that the patient was given oral potassium

    d. The patient is admitted with nausea and vomiting and diagnosed with gastroenteritis. The nausea and vomiting is documented as a final diagnosis

8. A condition that describes a deficiency of red blood cells because of bone marrow failure of production is called:

    a. Iron-deficiency anemia

    b. Sickle-cell anemia

    c. Aplastic anemia

    d. Pancytopenia

## Domain II    *Diagnosis and Procedure Coding*

9. In ICD-10-CM, the name of a disease, condition, or structure usually derived from the name of the person who discovered or described it first, is known as a(n):

    a. Carryover line

    b. Nonessential modifier

    c. Inclusion note

    d. Eponym

10. The symbol in ICD-10-CM's Tabular List used after an incomplete term that needs one or more of the modifiers that follow so that it can be assigned to a given category or code is:

    a. Colon

    b. Section mark

    c. Brace

    d. Lozenge

11. This symbol in ICD-10-CM encloses supplementary words or explanatory information that may be present in the statement of a diagnosis or procedure:

    a. Square brackets

    b. Colon

    c. Parentheses

    d. Brace

12. A symptom, as defined in ICD-10-CM, is the:

    a. Condition established after study to be responsible for a patient's admission to hospital

    b. Subjective evidence of disease reported by the patient to the physician

    c. Objective evidence of a disease as observed by a physician

    d. Type of procedure performed for definite treatment of a patient

13. When coding sepsis and severe sepsis, which code should be sequenced first?

    a. Code for the postprocedural infection

    b. Code for SIRS of a non-infectious origin

    c. Code for the associated organ dysfunction(s)

    d. Code for the systemic infection

14. This elderly female patient was seen today in the physician's office for the administration of her first radiation treatment for glioblastoma multiforme, which was recently diagnosed. The diagnosis was listed as: "Radiotherapy for management of glioblastoma multiforme in her right occipital lobe." How is this coded?

| | | |
|---|---|---|
| Z51.0 | Encounter for antineoplastic radiation therapy |
| Z51.11 | Encounter for antineoplastic chemotherapy |
| C71.4 | Malignant neoplasm of occipital lobe |
| C71.9 | Malignant neoplasm of brain, unspecified |

    a. Z51.0, C71.4

    b. Z51.11, C71.4

    c. Z51.0, C71.9

    d. Z51.11, C71.9

15. A 55-year-old morbidly obese woman with familial hypercholesterolemia was seen in her physician's office for a follow-up visit. She has managed to control her condition with medication and was also counseled at this time to maintain her smoke-free status. An appointment was set up for a return visit in 4 months. What is the correct code assignment for this case?

| | |
|---|---|
| E78.0 | Pure hypercholesterolemia |
| E78.5 | Hyperlipidemia, unspecified |
| E66.9 | Obesity, unspecified |
| E66.01 | Morbid obesity |
| E66.3 | Overweight |

   a. E78.0, E66.9

   b. E78.5, E66.3

   c. E78.0, E66.01

   d. E78.5, E66.9

16. The patient with paranoid alcoholic psychosis is seen in the physician's office for a follow-up visit. Upon questioning, the patient reluctantly admits to experiencing some delusions and to an intake of large amounts of alcohol on a continuous basis. The physician schedules another appointment for the patient in 1 month. How should this be coded?

| | |
|---|---|
| F10.251 | Alcohol dependence with alcohol-induced psychotic disorder with hallucinations |
| F10.229 | Alcohol dependence with intoxication, unspecified |
| F10.250 | Alcohol dependence with alcohol-induced psychotic disorder with delusions |
| F10.129 | Alcohol abuse with intoxication, unspecified |

   a. F10.251

   b. F10.250

   c. F10.229

   d. F10.129

17. A 65-year-old woman was seen in the ophthalmologist's office for an annual eye examination. The patient was known to have chronic narrow-angle glaucoma in her right eye (moderate stage), so the physician has been diligent in checking her left eye for glaucoma also. It was noted that the intraocular pressure in the left eye was now quite high as well, resulting in a diagnosis of acute narrow-angle glaucoma (mild stage) in that eye. How is this coded?

| | |
|---|---|
| H40.2212 | Chronic angle-closure glaucoma, right eye |
| H40.212 | Acute angle-closure glaucoma, left eye |
| H40.20X2 | Unspecified primary angle-closure glaucoma |
| H40.213 | Acute angle-closure glaucoma, bilateral |
| H40.2232 | Chronic angle-closure glaucoma, bilateral |

   a. H40.2212, H40.212

   b. H40.213

   c. H40.2232

   d. H40.20X2

18. An 84-year-old woman is seen in the hematologist's office for pernicious anemia that has been recently diagnosed. This patient is also known to have agammaglobulinemia, a frequent occurrence in patients with pernicious anemia. This patient is also being treated for chronic atrophic gastritis, another condition associated with her anemia. She is being treated with medications for these conditions and will return to the hematologist's office in 2 months. What is the correct code assignment for this case?

| | |
|---|---|
| D80.1 | Nonfamilial hypogammaglobulinemia (agammaglobulinemia) |
| D51.0 | Pernicious anemia |
| D53.9 | Nutritional anemia, unspecified |
| D53.0 | Protein deficiency anemia |
| K29.40 | Chronic atrophic gastritis, without bleeding |
| K29.41 | Chronic atrophic gastritis, with bleeding |
| K29.00 | Acute gastritis, without bleeding |

a. D53.0, D80.1, K29.41

b. D51.0, D80.1, K29.40

c. D53.0, D80.1

d. D53.9, D80.1, K29.00

19. The patient is a 79-year-old man who is being seen in the physician's office for follow-up of his condition and medication renewals. This patient has congestive heart failure resulting from his malignant hypertension, chronic kidney disease, stage III, and type 2 diabetes with polyneuropathy. The patient has been a diabetic for many years. How is this coded?

| | |
|---|---|
| I13.0 | Hypertensive heart and chronic kidney disease with heart failure and stage 1 through stage 4 chronic kidney disease, or unspecified chronic kidney disease |
| I13.10 | Hypertensive heart and chronic kidney disease without heart failure, with stage 1 through stage 4 chronic kidney disease, or unspecified chronic kidney disease |
| I13.11 | Hypertensive heart and chronic kidney disease without heart failure, with stage 5 chronic kidney disease or end stage renal disease |
| I50.9 | Congestive heart failure |
| N17.9 | Acute kidney failure, unspecified |
| N18.3 | Chronic kidney disease, stage 3 |
| E11.42 | Type 2 diabetes mellitus with diabetic polyneuropathy |
| E10.42 | Type 1 diabetes mellitus with diabetic polyneuropathy |

a. I13.0, I50.9, N18.3, E11.42

b. I13.10, I50.9, N18.3, E10.42

c. I13.11, I50.9, N17.9, E11.42

d. I13.0, N18.3, E11.42

20. A 12-year-old girl comes to the physician's office with her grandmother because of the following complaints: fever, discolored nasal discharge, puffy eyes, stuffy nose, and pain in the cheek areas. She was checked by the physician who confirmed all of her complaints and also detected fluid in her sinuses. The physician diagnosed acute sinusitis in the maxillary and frontal sinuses and prescribed antibiotics and Tylenol. How is this coded?

> | | |
> |---|---|
> | J01.80 | Other acute sinusitis (acute sinusitis involving more than one sinus but not pansinusitis) |
> | J01.90 | Unspecified acute sinusitis |
> | J32.0 | Chronic maxillary sinusitis |
> | J32.9 | Unspecified chronic sinusitis |

   a. J32.0, J01.80

   b. J01.90, J32.9

   c. J01.80, J32.0

   d. J01.80

21. The patient is a 57-year-old man who comes to the emergency department with severe abdominal pain. An acute gastric ulcer was identified following testing. There was no sign of malignancy or bleeding. The patient was placed on a special diet and discharged home. Which code is assigned?

   a. K25.7, Chronic gastric ulcer without hemorrhage or perforation

   b. K25.3, Acute gastric ulcer without hemorrhage or perforation

   c. K25.4, Chronic or unspecified gastric ulcer with hemorrhage

   d. K25.0, Acute gastric ulcer with hemorrhage

22. This patient is seen for a follow-up visit because of a possible urinary tract infection. The patient was initially seen in the office about 2 days ago with complaints of urinating frequently, abdominal pressure, and burning on urination. A urinalysis was done, resulting in a diagnosis of acute cystitis due to *Escherichia coli* organism. How is this coded?

> | | |
> |---|---|
> | A49.8 | Other bacterial infection of unspecified site |
> | B96.20 | Unspecified E. coli as cause of diseases classified elsewhere |
> | N30.00 | Acute cystitis without hematuria |
> | N30.10 | Interstitial cystitis (chronic) without hematuria |
> | N30.90 | Cystitis, unspecified, without hematuria |

   a. N30.00, B96.20

   b. N30.00, A49.8

   c. N30.90, B96.20

   d. N30.10, B96.20

23. Which of the following is considered a sequela?

   a. Keloid from a burn

   b. Laceration of the tendon of a finger 2 weeks ago

   c. Cerebral infarction with aphasia

   d. Cellulitis following a paper cut 1 week ago

24. Which of the following diagnoses shows a relationship between the circulatory condition and the hypertension?

    a. Left heart failure with benign hypertension

    b. Chronic coronary insufficiency and hypertension

    c. Acute coronary insufficiency; essential hypertension

    d. Hypertensive cardiomegaly

25. The patient is admitted with mild-stage pseudoexfoliation glaucoma of the right eye and moderate-stage low tension glaucoma of the left eye. What is the correct diagnosis code assignment for the physician's services?

    | H40.141 | Capsular glaucoma with pseudoexfoliation of lens, right eye |
    |---------|-----------------------------------------------------------|
    | H40.122 | Low tension glaucoma of left eye |
    | H40.143 | Capsular glaucoma with pseudoexfoliation of lens, bilateral |
    | | One of the following 7th characters is to be assigned to designate the stage of glaucoma |
    | 0 | stage unspecified |
    | 1 | mild |
    | 2 | moderate |
    | 3 | severe |
    | 4 | indeterminate |

    a. H40.1432

    b. H40.1412, H40.1222

    c. H40.1411, H40.1222

    d. H40.1430

26. In which of the following situations would a code from category G89, Pain, NEC, be appropriate?

    a. The patient is having severe pain due to migraines

    b. The patient is diagnosed with chest pain

    c. The patient with lung cancer seeks medical care for neoplasm-related pain

    d. The patient is seen in the ED with severe generalized abdominal pain

27. How would the diagnoses for the physician services following admission be reported? "The patient is admitted with metastatic carcinoma of the pancreas and omentum."

    | C48.1 | Malignant neoplasm of the omentum |
    |-------|-----------------------------------|
    | C25.8 | Malignant neoplasm of overlapping sites of the pancreas |
    | C25.9 | Malignant neoplasm of pancreas, unspecified |
    | C78.6 | Secondary malignant neoplasm of omentum |
    | C78.89 | Secondary malignant neoplasm of pancreas |
    | C80.1 | Malignant neoplasm, unspecified |

    a. C78.6, C78.89, C80.1

    b. C48.1, C25.9

    c. C78.6, C78.89

    d. C25.8, C25.9, C80.1

28. Which of the following terms describes status asthmaticus?

    a. Exhaustive

    b. Exacerbated

    c. Obstructive

    d. Intractable

29. How would the following ED encounter be coded? "The patient is treated in the ED in a coma due to accidental poisoning due to codeine."

    | | |
    |---|---|
    | T40.2X3 | Poisoning by codeine, assault |
    | R40.20 | Coma |
    | T40.2X1 | Poisoning by codeine, accidental |
    | T40.2X2 | Poisoning by codeine, intentional self harm |
    | T40.2X5 | Adverse effect of codeine |
    | | Seventh character |
    | | A initial encounter |
    | | D subsequent encounter |
    | | S sequela |

    a. T40.2X1A, R40.20

    b. T40.2X3D

    c. T40.2X1A, T40.2X5A

    d. T40.2X2D

30. A cerebral _____ is a bruise of the brain with bleeding into the brain tissue but without disruption of brain continuity.

    a. Concussion

    b. Contusion

    c. Laceration

    d. Subdural hematoma

31. Which of the following conditions is *not* a type of osteoarthritis?

    a. Polyarthritis

    b. Degenerative arthritis

    c. Rheumatoid arthritis

    d. Hypertrophic arthritis

32. The patient visits her OB/GYN physician at 29 weeks for a visit to monitor her benign essential hypertension, which she has had for several years now. How would this visit be coded?

    a. O10.013

    b. O10.013, Z3A.29

    c. I10, O10.013

    d. O16.3, Z3A.29

33. Category Z30, Encounter for contraceptive management, is assigned as the principal diagnosis for admissions or outpatient encounters for the purpose of contraceptive management. Which of the following is *not* included under Category Z30, Encounter for contraceptive management?

    a. Initiation of oral contraceptive management measures

    b. Removal of intrauterine contraceptive device

    c. Encounter for genetic counseling

    d. Sterilization

34. To assign a code from category P55, Hemolytic disease of newborn, what documentation is required?

    a. Statement from mother of newborn stating that she is Rh-negative

    b. Statement of incompatibility on a routine cord blood test

    c. Statement from a nurse that he believes the mother is Rh-negative

    d. Provider confirmation of a diagnosis of isoimmunization or hemolytic disease

35. Angina pectoris sometimes occurs when the patient is at rest, apparently without any stimulation. This type of angina is referred to as:

    a. Prinzmetal angina

    b. Pre-infarction angina

    c. Crescendo angina

    d. Unstable angina

36. All of the following conditions would be considered a sequela of a cerebrovascular disease *except:*

    a. Dysarthria

    b. Alterations of sensations

    c. Dysphagia

    d. History of a TIA

37. Which of the following is considered an internal fixation device?

    a. Cast or splint

    b. Traction

    c. Rods and plates

    d. Steinmann pin

38. Which of the following conditions is not considered a sequela of an injury?

    a. Paralysis of the right wrist due to previous laceration of right radial nerve

    b. Cellulitis in an open wound

    c. Nonunion fracture

    d. Posttraumatic scars due to old burn

39. The excised diameter of a lesion means the measurement of:

    a. The largest lesion dimension

    b. The largest lesion dimension and the measurement of the margin

    c. The largest lesion dimension and the measurement of both margins

    d. Both lesion dimensions added together and the measurement of the margin

**40.** The patient presents to the physician's office with fever and chills and is diagnosed with pneumonia. The physician administers 600 mg of Rocephin, IV over 1 hour and 31 minutes. In addition to the E/M code, how are these services coded?

| | |
|---|---|
| J0696 | Injection, Ceftriaxone sodium (Rocephin), per 250 mg |
| 96365 | Intravenous infusion, for therapy, prophylaxis, or diagnosis (specify substance or drug); initial, up to 1 hour |
| 96366 | each additional hour (List separately in addition to code for primary procedure.) |
| 96374 | Therapeutic, prophylactic or diagnostic injection (specify substance or drug); intravenous push, single or initial substance/drug |

a. 96374, J0696

b. 96365, J0696 ×2

c. 96365, 96366, J0696

d. 96365, 96366, J0696 ×3

**41.** After comparing this patient encounter summary and the progress note, where does the coding manager find that education is needed?

**Progress Note for 5-1-20XX**

| | |
|---|---|
| S | This 10-year-old fell on the playground, cutting his right hand. |
| O | There is a superficial palmar laceration measuring 2.0 cm. |
| A | 2.0 cm palmar laceration, washed with Betadine, anesthetized with 1% lidocaine and closed with one simple stitch of 5-0 nylon. Triple antibiotic ointment applied. |
| P | Suture removal in 1 week. |

**Patient Encounter Summary:**

| Date | CPT Code | Code Description | Diagnosis | Diagnosis Description |
|---|---|---|---|---|
| 5-1-20XX | 13131 | Repair, complex, hand, complex, 1.1 cm to 2.5 cm | S61.411A | Palm laceration, right |
| 5-1-20XX | 99212 | Office visit | S61.411A | Palm laceration, right |

a. A higher level of office visit should have been coded.

b. A −59 modifier should have been added to the office visit.

c. The documentation does not support the codes assigned.

d. The local anesthetic should have been coded.

42. A 67-year-old patient is treated in the office today for a 7.0 cm × 3.0 cm full-thickness venous stasis ulcer of the lower leg. It was debrided previously. A skin graft of Apligraf, a tissue-cultured allogeneic skin substitute, is placed in the entire wound and is sutured in place. How would these physician services be coded?

| | |
|---|---|
| 15220 | Full thickness graft, free, including direct closure of donor site, scalp, arms, and/or legs; 20 sq cm or less |
| 15221 | each additional 20 sq cm, or part thereof (List separately in addition to code for primary procedure.) |
| 15271 | Application of skin substitute graft to trunk, arms, legs, total wound surface area up to 100 sq cm; first 25 sq cm or less wound surface area |
| 15272 | each additional 25 sq cm wound surface area, or part thereof (List separately in addition to code for primary procedure.) |
| 15273 | Application of skin substitute graft to trunk, arms, legs, total wound surface area greater than 100 sq cm; first 100 sq cm wound surface area, or 1% of body area of infants and children |
| Q4100 | Skin substitute, not otherwise specified |
| Q4101 | Skin substitute, Apligraf, per square centimeter |

a. 15220, 15221, Q4100 ×21

b. 15271, Q4101 ×21

c. 15271, 15272, Q4101 ×10

d. 15273, Q4100 ×10

43. When should the coder assign a code for a cast application?

a. When applying a removable splint

b. When revising a cast the patient is now wearing

c. When a fracture treatment has been provided

d. When applying a replacement cast during or after the period of normal follow-up care

44. The patient undergoes a left heart catheterization and a left ventricular angiography using percutaneous femoral access. How is this procedure coded?

a. 93452, Left heart catheterization including intraprocedural injection(s) for left ventriculography, imaging supervision and interpretation, when performed

b. 93453, Combined right and left heart catheterization including intraprocedural injection(s) for left ventriculography, imaging supervision and interpretation, when performed

c. 93458, Catheter placement in coronary artery(s) for coronary angiography, including intraprocedural injection(s) for coronary angiography, imaging supervision and interpretation; with left heart catheterization including intraprocedural injection(s) for left ventriculography, when performed

d. 93460, Catheter placement in coronary artery(s) for coronary angiography, including intraprocedural injection(s) for coronary angiography, imaging supervision and interpretation; with right and left heart catheterization including intraprocedural injection(s) for left ventriculography, when performed

45. The patient undergoes an arthroscopic debridement of the articular cartilage and removal of meniscus in the lateral compartment of the right knee. How is this procedure coded?

| 29870 | Arthroscopy, knee, diagnostic, with or without synovial biopsy (separate procedure) |
|---|---|
| 29877 | Arthroscopy, knee, surgical; debridement/shaving of articular cartilage (chondroplasty) |
| 29881 | with meniscectomy (medial OR lateral, including any meniscal shaving) including debridement/shaving of articular cartilage (chondroplasty), same or separate compartment(s), when performed |
| 29882 | with meniscus repair (medial OR lateral) |

   a. 29881

   b. 29877, 29881

   c. 29877, 29882

   d. 29870, 29877, 29881

46. The patient undergoes a proctosigmoidoscopy, a sigmoidoscopy with biopsy, and a colonoscopy during the same operative session. What is the correct coding assignment for these services?

| 45300 | Proctosigmoidoscopy, rigid; diagnostic, with or without collection of specimen(s) by brushing or washing (separate procedure) |
|---|---|
| 45305 | with biopsy, single or multiple |
| 45330 | Sigmoidoscopy, flexible; diagnostic, including collection of specimen(s) by brushing or washing, when performed (separate procedure) |
| 45331 | with biopsy, single or multiple |
| 45378 | Colonscopy, flexible; diagnostic, including collection of specimen(s) by brushing or washing, when performed (separate procedure) |
| 45380 | with biopsy, single or multiple |

   a. 45378

   b. 45380

   c. 45300, 45331, 45378

   d. 45305, 45331, 45380

47. A physician's office performs an x-ray. The radiologist from a nearby hospital reads the x-ray for the physician's office. What modifier is assigned to the services of the physician's office?

   a. –26, Professional component

   b. –52, Reduced services

   c. –Q6, Service furnished by a locum tenens physician

   d. –TC, Technical component

48. The surgeon repairs a fistula between the rectum and the anus by placing a graft of OASIS® into the wound. How is this service coded?

> 46280    Surgical treatment of anal fistula (fistulectomy/fistulotomy); transsphincteric, suprasphincteric, extra sphincteric or multiple, including placement of seton, when performed
>
> 46288    Closure of anal fistula with rectal advancement flap
>
> 46706    Repair of anal fistula with fibrin glue
>
> 46707    Repair of anorectal fistula with plug (eg, porcine small intestine submucosa [SIS])

    a. 46707

    b. 46280

    c. 46288

    d. 46707, 46706

49. When coding repairs of multiple lacerations in CPT, what action should the coder take?

    a. Code only the most complex repair

    b. Code only the least complex repair

    c. Code all the laceration repairs, listing the most complex repair first

    d. Code all the repairs of the same site using the code for the most complex repair

50. If there is a diagnosis of Metastatic carcinoma of the lung, primary site was breast, but a mastectomy was done six years ago, what is the principal diagnosis?

    a. Metastatic carcinoma of the lung

    b. Carcinoma of the breast

    c. History of malignant neoplasm of the breast

    d. Status post mastectomy

51. _____ is the active management of withdrawal symptoms in a patient who is physically dependent on alcohol or drugs.

    a. Intoxification

    b. Detoxification

    c. Therapy

    d. Rehabilitation

52. The patient has an imaging study done of the brain where tomographic pictures are taken and a computer is used to reassemble the images. Images are taken before and after dye is injected. The images are interpreted by the physician. How is this service coded?

> 70450    Computed tomography, head or brain; without contrast material
>
> 70460        with contrast material(s)
>
> 70470        without contrast material, followed by contrast material(s) and further sections
>
> 78607    Brain imaging, tomographic (SPECT)

    a. 70450

    b. 70450, 70460

    c. 70470

    d. 78607

53. The physician provides 115 minutes of critical care to the patient and documents the time in the record. How is this service coded?

> 99291    Critical care, evaluation and management of the critically ill or critically injured patient; first 30 to 74 minutes
>
> 99292        each additional 30 minutes (List separately in addition to code for primary service)

   a. 99291

   b. 99291, 99292

   c. 99291, 99292, 99292

   d. 99291, 99292, 99292, 99292

54. The physician performs a procedure that cannot be described with a regular code in CPT, so an unlisted code is assigned. The physician wants a −22 modifier applied to the code. What is the best action for the coder to take?

   a. Apply the −22 modifier to the unlisted code as requested by the physician

   b. Explain to the physician that modifiers cannot be used on unlisted codes

   c. Submit a different CPT code that describes a lesser procedure and add a −22 modifier

   d. Submit a different CPT code that describes a more extensive procedure and add a −52 modifier

55. The physician replaces atrial and ventricular leads of a pacing cardioverter-defibrillator transvenously. The cardioverter-defibrillator was placed one year ago, and the battery remains intact. How is this coded?

   a. 33212, 33217, 33244

   b. 33215, 33215

   c. 33217, 33244

   d. 33218, 33218

56. The surgeon makes a burr hole in the skull over the cerebrum, based on stereotactic CT guidance, and aspirates a brain abscess via a needle. What is the correct code assignment for this case?

   a. 61140, 61782

   b. 61150, 61781

   c. 61156, 61781

   d. 61320, 61796

57. The surgeon documents the procedure performed as "Fistulization of sclera for glaucoma" and selects code 0123T. To support the use of this code, what necessary documentation is missing?

   a. Method used

   b. Exact location in the eye

   c. Primary versus secondary procedure

   d. Nothing, all necessary documentation is present

58. The surgeon performs a laparoscopic myomectomy with removal of seven intramural myomas weighing 230 grams. What is the correct code assignment for this procedure?

    a. 58140

    b. 58146

    c. 58545

    d. 58546

59. The patient is the victim of blunt force abdominal trauma. The surgeon repairs the ruptured spleen that is salvageable and performs a partial splenectomy. What is the correct code assignment for these procedures?

    a. 38101

    b. 38115

    c. 38120

    d. 38129

60. The physician completes an extracapsular cataract extraction by routine phacoemulsification and insertion of IOL implant. What is the correct code assignment for this case?

    a. 66940, 66985

    b. 66982

    c. 66983

    d. 66984

61. A flexible bronchoscopy is conducted on a patient who is not responding to treatment for pneumonia. Multiple transbronchial biopsies and endobronchial biopsies are performed in the right lower lobe. What is the correct code assignment for these procedures?

    a. 31622, 31625, 31629

    b. 31622, 31625, 31628

    c. 31625, 31628

    d. 31625, 31629

62. The patient was hit in the chest with the steering wheel during a head-on collision. Following a CT scan, the surgeon performed an endoscopy of the chest cavity and removed a blood clot from the pericardium. How is this procedure coded?

    a. 32658

    b. 32661

    c. 39010

    d. 39499

63. A 3-year-old patient is ready to start chemotherapy and requires the placement of a PICC line. What is the correct code assignment for this procedure?

    a. 36555

    b. 36568

    c. 36569

    d. 36570

64. The patient undergoes a colposcopy of the vulva and entire vagina with vulvar biopsies. The physician also performs an endometrial biopsy. What is the correct code assignment for this case?

    a. 57421, 58100

    b. 56821, 57420, 58110

    c. 56820, 56605, 57421, 58110

    d. 57420, 58110

65. The patient received a living, related donor renal transplant with removal of left kidney. Venous, arterial, and ureteral anastomoses were completed. The patient's peritoneal dialysis catheter was also removed. Backbench work was performed by a different surgeon. What is the correct code assignment for this case?

    a. 50365, 49422

    b. 50360, 49422

    c. 50365, 49429

    d. 50340, 50360, 50700, 35221, 49402

66. A 20-year-old college student is seen in the health clinic with fever, malaise, myalgia, and anorexia. The physician documents clinical signs of swelling of both sides of the patient's face. Final diagnosis was listed as infectious parotitis. Which of the following would be reported?

    a. B26.9

    b. B26.9, R50.9, R53.81, R63.0, R59.0

    c. B26.89, R50.9, R53.81, R63.0, R59.0

    d. K11.20

67. A patient presents to the ED with hematuria. The patient admits to taking a combination of Coumadin and over-the-counter Alka-Seltzer for nasal congestion. The physician had not prescribed the Alka-Seltzer. The patient subsequently noticed the blood in her urine. Which of the following would be reported?

    a. T45.511A, T39.011A

    b. T45.515A, T39.015A, R31.9

    c. T45.511A, T39.011A, R31.9

    d. T45.515A, T39.015A, R31.0

68. The patient is a construction worker who fell 2 stories from scaffolding while working on a new building. He struck his head and was unconscious for about 45 minutes. The CT showed an open skull fracture with cerebral laceration and contusion. Patient complains of severe headache and dizziness. Discharge diagnoses included headache and dizziness due to skull fracture, cerebral laceration, and contusion. What codes would be reported for this admission?

    a. S02.91XB, S06.332A, R42, R51, W12.XXXA, Y92.6, Y99.0, Y93.H3

    b. S02.91XB, S06.332A, W12.XXXA, Y92.6, Y99.0, Y93.H3

    c. S02.91XB, S06.332A, W12.XXXA, Y92.6, Y99.9, Y93.H3

    d. S06.332A, W12.XXXA, Y92.6, Y99.0, Y93.H3

69. The patient presents with a history of right breast carcinoma that had previously been treated with right lumpectomy and also radiation therapy. She has been recently diagnosed with BRCA1 genetic mutation. The patient underwent bilateral prophylactic mastectomy. How would the diagnoses in this scenario be coded?

    a. Z40.01, Z15.01, Z92.3, Z80.3

    b. Z40.01, Z15.01, Z85.3

    c. Z40.01, Z15.01

    d. Z40.01, Z15.01, Z92.3, Z85.3

70. A 6-year-old patient is seen for a well child check at her pediatrician's office. A comprehensive history and exam are documented. Free, government-provided vaccines for DTaP, IPV, MMR, and Varicella vaccines are administered after physician counseling was completed. What is the correct CPT code assignment for this case?

    a. 99383, 90460, 90461

    b. 99383, 90471, 90472

    c. 99393, 90460 x4, 90461 x4,

    d. 99393, 90471, 90472 x3

71. The physician performs an anterior interbody cervical three level arthrodesis (C5-T1), anterior cervical segmental instrumentation (C5-T1), and structural allograft bone graft. How is this coded?

    a. 22551, 22552, 22842, 29038

    b. 22554, 22585 x2, 22846, 20931

    c. 22600, 22614 x2, 22846, 29031

    d. 22554 x3, 22842, 20937

## Domain III  *Regulatory Guidelines and Reporting Requirements for Outpatient Services*

72. If a patient has undergone an outpatient echocardiogram and the cardiologist concludes in the report that the patient has mitral regurgitation, the coder should:

    a. Assign a diagnostic code for mitral regurgitation

    b. Query the physician about the diagnosis

    c. Code an abnormal finding of the echocardiogram

    d. No code can be assigned

73. During an ambulatory surgery visit for excision of a malignant melanoma of the right forearm, the attending surgeon listed history of benign breast cyst, history of hypertension currently on Tenormin, and a current hammer toe. Which conditions are to be coded?

    a. Malignant melanoma of forearm, hypertension

    b. Malignant melanoma of the right forearm, benign breast cyst, hypertension and hammer toe

    c. Malignant melanoma of the right forearm, benign breast cyst, and hypertension

    d. Malignant melanoma of the right forearm, benign breast cyst

74. A chest x-ray done to evaluate a chronic cough revealed an asymptomatic compression fracture of a lumbar vertebrae. No further evaluation was undertaken. The coder should:

    a. Not assign a code for an acute condition but assign a code for chronic compression fracture

    b. Assign a code for pathologic lumbar compression fracture

    c. Assign a code for acute traumatic vertebral fracture

    d. Not assign a code for this condition

75. During an outpatient visit the attending physician did not define a problem at the conclusion of an emergency department (ED) visit. The coder should:

    a. Assign a code from the list of conditions in the history that occurred in the past

    b. Assign a code for the reason for the last visit to the ED

    c. Assign codes for abnormal laboratory findings

    d. Assign a code for the chief complaint as the reason for the visit

76. In which HCPCS category would the coder find temporary codes for screening cytopathology to code services provided to patients covered by Medicare?

    a. G0008–G9157

    b. J0120–J9999

    c. P2028–P9615

    d. Q0035–Q9969

77. After completing a quality audit on this patient encounter summary, what action should the coding supervisor take?

    **Patient Encounter Summary**
    Dr. Dunn, Primary Care
    Patient #784309

| Date of Service | CPT Code | Code Description | Diagnosis | Charge |
|---|---|---|---|---|
| 5/1/20XX | 73610 | X-ray, ankle, complete | M25.572 | $76.00 |
| 5/1/20XX | 27816 | Closed treatment trimalleolar ankle fracture without manipulation, left leg | S82.852A | $249.00 |
| 5/1/20XX | Q4038 | Cast supplies, short leg adult fiberglass, left leg | S82.853A | $43.00 |
| 5/1/20XX | 29405 | Cast application, short leg, left leg | S82.852A | $65.00 |

    a. Clarify the fracture treatment with the physician.

    b. Instruct the physician about proper coding of cast applications.

    c. Instruct the physician to add an office visit.

    d. Query the physician about the correct diagnosis.

## Domain IV  *Data Quality and Management*

78. A new physician submits four encounters from his first day in clinic. They were all completed incorrectly because a procedure was performed with an E/M visit. What is the best action for the coder to take to resolve the situation for the future?

    a. Recode the charges and then submit them

    b. Educate the physician about the appropriate use of the –25 modifier and the surgical package reporting guidelines

    c. Ask the office manager to inform the physician that procedures are not performed in the office setting

    d. Refuse to process charges until the physician receives formal training

79. Which of the following is the best source of information on what should be included on a new encounter form?

    a. Office manager's opinion

    b. Physician's request

    c. Report of codes assigned in the past year

    d. CPT book section for the specialty of the physician

80. A 1-year-old patient presents to the pediatrician for a physical, MMR, and varicella vaccinations. After reviewing the following coding in an audit, what audit findings did the coding manager determine?

    Patient: Jane Doe
    DOB: 2-28-2010

| Date of Service | CPT Code | Code Description | Diagnosis | Diagnosis Description |
|---|---|---|---|---|
| 2-28-2011 | 99392 | Periodic comprehensive preventive medicine; early childhood (age 1 through 4 years) | Z00.129 | Encounter for routine child health examination, without abnormal findings |
| 2-28-2011 | 90707 | Measles, mumps and rubella virus vaccine (MMR), live, for subcutaneous use | Z00.129 | Encounter for routine child health examination, without abnormal findings |
| 2-28-2011 | 90716 | Varicella virus vaccine, live, for subcutaneous use | Z00.129 | Encounter for routine child health examination, without abnormal findings |

    a. The CPT code(s) are incorrect.

    b. The ICD-10-CM code(s) are incorrect.

    c. CPT code(s) are missing.

    d. The case is coded correctly.

81. Which report contains a summary of all billing data entered for a physician's practice for one day, listing all vital pieces of data to be included on the billing form?

    a. Claim history

    b. Diagnosis distribution

    c. Charge summary report

    d. Frequency distribution

82. During a recent audit, the coding manager compared an inventory report and the coding report for the same period. The findings included that the practice had purchased 25 wrist splints and had coded 15 wrist splints during the month. The supply is now gone. What action should the coding manager take?

    a. Talk to the physician(s) about the use of supplies

    b. Ask the Office Manager to evaluate why the counts don't match

    c. Reeducate the staff and physician(s) about supply coding

    d. Suggest that splints no longer be provided by the office

83. The patient had a total abdominal hysterectomy with bilateral salpingo-oophorectomy. The coder selected the following codes to report:

    | 58150 | Total abdominal hysterectomy, with/without removal of tubes and ovaries |
    |---|---|
    | 58700 | Salpingectomy, complete or partial, unilateral/bilateral (separate procedure) |

    What error has the coder made by using these codes?

    a. Maximizing

    b. Upcoding

    c. Unbundling

    d. Optimizing

## Domain V  *Information and Communication Technologies*

84. What is the computer-based transmission of data in a standardized format between providers and third-party payers called?

    a. Electronic claims processing

    b. Common language interchange

    c. Computer language interchange

    d. Electronic data interchange

85. A physician would like to post policy statements and employee manuals electronically in order to enable his employees to have updated reference tools with search capabilities. He wants to make certain that the information is available only to his employees. What electronic tool would he use?

    a. Internet

    b. Extranet

    c. Intranet

    d. Virtual private network

86. What term is used to describe the ability of different information systems to communicate with each other?

    a. Encryption

    b. Interoperability

    c. Functional strategy

    d. Integrated delivery

## Domain VI  *Privacy, Confidentiality, Legal, and Ethical Issues*

87. These are used to show who accessed a computer system, when it was accessed, and what operations were performed:

    a. Workstation registers

    b. Monthly purging of computer

    c. Annual employee HIPAA acknowledgment

    d. Audit trails

88. Items, collections, or grouping of information maintained by or for a covered entity to make decisions about an individual refers to the:

    a. Designated Record Set

    b. Uniform Discharge Data Set

    c. Legal health record

    d. Personal health record

89. All of the following statements about legal health records are true, *except*:

    a. They are the business records of the organization

    b. They are the records that will be disclosed upon request

    c. They are records of care in any health setting used for patient care, administrative, or business purposes

    d. All of the above are true

90. The specific legislation that provides for criminal penalties for healthcare professionals who "knowingly and willfully" attempt to defraud any of the healthcare benefit programs and further stipulates that physicians or other providers are accountable for information they "know or should know" is the:

    a. Federal False Claims Act

    b. Health Insurance Portability and Accountability Act

    c. Operation Restore Trust

    d. Balanced Budget Act of 1997

91. The governmental agency that develops an annual "work plan" that delineates the specific target areas that will be monitored in a given year is the:

    a. Federal Bureau of Investigation

    b. Defense Criminal Investigative Service

    c. Office of the Inspector General

    d. US Attorneys' Offices

92. Which of the following is an example of fraud?

    a. Inadvertent filing of duplicate claims

    b. Failure to document medical records adequately

    c. Paying or receiving remuneration or kickbacks for referrals

    d. Failure to comply with a particular agreement

93. A program unveiled by the Office of the Inspector General that expanded and simplified methods for healthcare providers to voluntarily report fraudulent conduct affecting Medicare, Medicaid, and other federal healthcare programs is the:

    a. Provider Self-Disclosure Protocol

    b. Federal False Claims Act

    c. Operation Restore Trust

    d. Health Insurance Portability and Accountability Act

94. The term that refers to the degree to which codes accurately reflect the patient's diagnoses and procedures during a coding audit is:

    a. Reliability

    b. Completeness

    c. Timeliness

    d. Validity

95. The patient asked for and received a copy of the disclosures that were made of his PHI. He did not see his attending physician and was concerned that the doctor did not have the information. What is the patient told?

    a. The organization cannot release that information to the patient

    b. Disclosures used for treatment are not recorded so that is why the doctor's name does not appear on the list

    c. The doctor apparently never asked for the records.

    d. The patient should speak to his doctor as to why the records were not requested

96. Qui tam legislation has been widely used in the application and reinforcement of several pieces of legislation. Which of the following is not legislation where qui tam applies?

    a. Health Insurance Portability and Accountability Act

    b. Civil False Claims Act

    c. Medicare Act

    d. Balanced Budget Act

# Multiple Choice Exam 4 Answers

| | | | |
|---|---|---|---|
| 1. | 25. | 49. | 73. |
| 2. | 26. | 50. | 74. |
| 3. | 27. | 51. | 75. |
| 4. | 28. | 52. | 76. |
| 5. | 29. | 53. | 77. |
| 6. | 30. | 54. | 78. |
| 7. | 31. | 55. | 79. |
| 8. | 32. | 56. | 80. |
| 9. | 33. | 57. | 81. |
| 10. | 34. | 58. | 82. |
| 11. | 35. | 59. | 83. |
| 12. | 36. | 60. | 84. |
| 13. | 37. | 61. | 85. |
| 14. | 38. | 62. | 86. |
| 15. | 39. | 63. | 87. |
| 16. | 40. | 64. | 88. |
| 17. | 41. | 65. | 89. |
| 18. | 42. | 66. | 90. |
| 19. | 43. | 67. | 91. |
| 20. | 44. | 68. | 92. |
| 21. | 45. | 69. | 93. |
| 22. | 46. | 70. | 94. |
| 23. | 47. | 71. | 95. |
| 24. | 48. | 72. | 96. |

# EXAM 4 MEDICAL CASES

## EXAM 4—CASE 1

*Please code for the services of the physician.*

**HISTORY:** Follow-up decompression laminectomy and extension of fusion lumbar spine L2 to sacrum performed 1 year ago. Patient generally doing pretty well with back, has achy back discomfort. Main problem is bilateral lateral hip pain. She has a previous diagnosis of trochanteric bursitis. She also describes triggering of her right middle finger with catching of the finger in flexion. The patient had a right knee replacement several years previously.

**PHYSICAL EXAMINATION:**

**VITAL SIGNS:** Blood pressure 137/77; Pulse 79; Temperature is 98.1

**HEENT:** Normal

**CHEST:** Clear

**HEART:** Normal sinus rhythm, no murmur

**SPINE EXAMINATION:** Reveals well-healed incision lumbar spine with minimal tenderness, no paravertebral spasm. Range of motion 80% of normal.

**HIP EXAMINATION:** Reveals full range of motion of hips bilaterally. There is exquisite tenderness over abductor insertion on greater trochanter.

**HAND EXAMINATION:** Reveals triggering of the right middle finger.

**RADIOGRAPHS:** Previous x-rays of lumbar spine reviewed showing excellent instrumented fusion L2 to sacrum with fusion consolidation. Extensive narrowing of the spine at the T3-T4 region.

**IMPRESSION:**

1. Stenosis in thoracic spinal area
2. Bilateral trochanteric bursitis
3. Right middle trigger finger

**PLAN:**

1. Trochanteric bursa is injected bilateral today under sterile conditions using 5 cc of Kenalog.
2. Right middle finger injected today with improvement with 0.5 cc of Kenalog.
3. Flexeril 10 mg p.o. t.i.d. p.r.n. Renew hydrocodone 5/500 1 p.o. q.6 h p.r.n. pain.
4. Consider surgery on stenosed thoracic region of the spine.
5. Return in 6 months' time for reevaluation.

**HISTORY:** Expanded problem-focused

**EXAMINATION:** Detailed

**MEDICAL DECISION MAKING:** Moderate

*Enter four diagnosis codes and five procedure codes.*

DX1 

DX2 

DX3 

DX4 

PR1 

PR2 

PR3 

PR4 

PR5

## EXAM 4—CASE 2

*Please code for the services of the physician.*

**CONSULT REQUESTED BY:** Dr. A

**HISTORY:** The patient is a 33-year-old woman who has had known gallstones and post-prandial right upper quadrant and epigastric pain for the last 3 years. She describes the pain as intense gas pains. The pain radiates occasionally to her back. She notes that her pain is worse with fatty food. She has tried herbal remedies without success. She has no history of jaundice or pancreatitis. She has had no emergency department visits or hospitalizations for the pain. The pain is worsening, and the patient is sent here for evaluation and definitive diagnosis.

**PAST MEDICAL HISTORY:**

    1. Iron deficiency anemia

**PAST SURGICAL HISTORY:** None

**ALLERGIES:** Penicillin

**MEDICATIONS:**

    1. Multivitamins

    2. Iron 65 mg, two daily

**FAMILY HISTORY:** The patient's paternal grandmother had breast cancer. Her paternal grandfather had colon cancer. Her maternal grandfather had lung cancer. Diabetes and hypertension also run in her family.

**REVIEW OF SYSTEMS:** A 14-point review of systems was completed by the patient today in the office. The patient reports weight gain as well as back pain. She denies any chest pain, shortness of breath, or dysuria. The remaining review of systems is negative.

**SOCIAL HISTORY:** The patient is married. She works as a managed care coordinator. She does not smoke. She drinks alcohol occasionally.

**PHYSICAL EXAMINATION:**

**VITAL SIGNS:** Weight 229.4 pounds; Blood pressure 129/72; Heart rate is 86; Temperature 97.5

**GENERAL:** The patient is a pleasant female in no acute distress. Alert and oriented times three.

**HEENT:** There is no jaundice, thyroid masses, or cervical lymphadenopathy.

**RESPIRATORY:** Lung sounds are clear bilaterally

**HEART:** Regular rate and rhythm

**ABDOMEN:** Soft and nontender. There are no scars or hernias.

**MUSCULOSKELETAL:** Gait, strength, and muscle tone within normal limits

**NEUROLOGIC:** Cranial nerves II-XII are grossly intact

**DATA:** Abdominal ultrasound report shows the gallbladder was markedly contracted with multiple stones. The common bile duct measured 6 mm in diameter.

**LABORATORY:** Laboratory dated 11/22/20XX, bilirubin 0.2, AST 20, ALT 28, alkaline phosphatase 29, amylase 62, lipase 21

## EXAM 4—CASE 2 (*continued*)

**ASSESSMENT/PLAN:** The patient is a 33-year-old otherwise healthy woman with classic symptoms of biliary colic. We had an extensive discussion with the patient in regard to the technical aspects of the laparoscopic cholecystectomy. We discussed the potential complications of the surgery that include but are not limited to: need to convert to open surgery, retained stone, bile duct injury, bleeding, infection, DVT, and pneumonia. All of her questions were answered to her satisfaction. Because of the frequency of her pain, she is eager to proceed with surgery. We have tentatively scheduled her surgery for December 13th. If she develops any questions or concerns, she should call the office.

**HISTORY:** Comprehensive

**EXAMINATION:** Comprehensive

**MEDICAL DECISION MAKING:** Moderate

*Enter one diagnosis code and one procedure code.*

**DX1**

**PR1**

## EXAM 4—CASE 3

*Please code for the services of the physician.*

**BRIEF HISTORY:** This is a 41-year-old white man who was the helmeted driver of a dirt bike going approximately 45 miles per hour when he hit an embankment and fell and landed on his left side. There was no loss of consciousness. He had a prolonged extrication time of approximately 3 hours per report. He is seen as a trauma consult at approximately 11 p.m., and the accident had happened at 15:15 hours. He is hemodynamically stable, complaining of some back pain, left chest pain, left arm and forearm pain, and left foot pain.

**PAST MEDICAL HISTORY:**

1.  Hypertrophic pyloric stenosis as an infant

2.  Multiple feet fractures

3.  Vertebral body fractures

**MEDICATIONS:** None

**PAST SURGICAL HISTORY:**

1.  Left distal radius plating

2.  Pylorotomy as an infant

**ALLERGIES:** No known drug allergies.

**FAMILY HISTORY:** Unknown because the patient is adopted.

**SOCIAL HISTORY:** Positive for ETOH approximately one to two drinks per night. Denies any smoking or drugs.

**REVIEW OF SYSTEMS:** Otherwise negative in general, dermatologic, ear, nose, and throat, cardiovascular, pulmonary, gastrointestinal, genitourinary, psychiatric, neurologic, skin. Positive for history of present illness in the musculoskeletal.

**GENERAL:** Airway is clear with no intervention needed. C spine is immobilized in a hard collar. Breathing is spontaneous and unlabored.

**CIRCULATION:** The skin is dry, normal color with no evidence of external hemorrhage.

**PULSES:** Present at the carotid, radial, and femoral pulses, and dorsalis pedis pulses bilaterally.

**DISABILITY:** The patient is alert and oriented ×3. GSC of 15. Pupils equal, round, and reactive to light and accommodation measuring 3 mm in diameter.

**HEENT:** There is not any evidence for any external trauma. Pupils are 3 mm and reactive bilaterally. Gaze is normal. Extraocular movements are intact. Tympanic membranes are clear bilaterally. There is no abnormality of mouth, teeth, or pharynx. Occlusion is normal. No facial bony deformities or crepitus.

**NECK:** Trachea is midline. No jugular venous distention.

**CHEST:** There are some mild abrasions of the left lateral chest wall. He has good movement and chest wall is symmetric bilaterally. Breath sounds are clear to auscultation bilaterally.

**HEART:** Regular rate and rhythm without murmurs, rubs, or gallops. There is no crepitus. There is some mild tenderness to palpation on the left lateral chest wall.

**ABDOMEN:** There are some abrasions in the left lower quadrant of the abdomen; otherwise the abdomen is soft, nontender, and nondistended with good bowel sounds.

**PELVIS:** Stable and nontender

**GENITOURINARY:** There is no blood in the meatus.

**RECTAL:** Examination is deferred.

## EXAM 4—CASE 3 (*continued*)

**SPINE:** Cervical spine is nontender to palpation with no obvious step-offs or deformities and full active range of motion. Thoracic spine is tender at the T8 vertebral body area with no obvious step-offs or deformities. Lumbar spine is nontender to palpation.

**EXTREMITIES:** There is mild tenderness to palpation at the left proximal forearm and left foot approximately at the 4th metatarsal with some mild abrasions over the dorsal aspect of the left forearm. Pulses are present and 3+ of the radial, carotids, femoral, popliteal, posterior tibial and dorsalis pedis pulses bilaterally.

**NEUROLOGIC:** 5/5 strength in range of motion for all four extremities. Sensation is grossly intact.

AP chest reveals central vascular congestion. No pneumothorax or wide mediastinum. AP pelvis revealed no acute fracture or dislocation. Left forearm films revealed a proximal left ulnar fracture that is minimally displaced and evidence of a previously repaired left radius fracture. CT of the head revealed no acute fracture, dislocation, or intracranial bleed. CT of the cervical spine was negative. Multiple left-sided rib fractures and a small hemothorax. CT of the abdomen and pelvis revealed no acute intra-abdominal pathology. Thoracic and lumbar spine reconstruction revealed the T7-8 compression fractures that were old. These were reviewed with Dr. X.

Trauma examination performed in the emergency department was negative in the right upper quadrant and subxiphoid, retropubic area; however, the overall examination was indeterminate because of a poorly visualized perisplenic view.

**LABORATORY EXAMINATIONS:** Obtained and revealed a hemoglobin of 16.1, sodium 144, potassium 3.6, chloride 101, BUN not an applicable base deficit of –1, pH 7.35, $PO_2$-39, $PCO_2$-47, lactate 2.3, glucose 109.

**ASSESSMENT:** A 41-year-old man status post dirt bike accident with multiple left-sided rib fractures, hemothorax, left ulnar fracture that is closed, and chest wall abrasions. His C spine was cleared clinically in the emergency department.

**PLAN:** He was admitted for pain control and observation. Will have a repeat chest x-ray and complete blood count in the morning. Abrasions are cleaned, antibiotic ointment applied, and dressed with bandages. Given a PCA and Toradol for pain. Orthopedics department was consulted, and the patient will need a simple splint for his left ulnar fracture. Pulmonary consult was requested.

**HISTORY:** Comprehensive

**EXAMINATION:** Comprehensive

**MEDICAL DECISION MAKING:** High

*Enter four diagnosis codes and one procedure code.*

**DX1**

**DX2**

**DX3**

**DX4**

**PR1**

## EXAM 4—CASE 4

*Please code for the services of the physician.*

**REASON FOR VISIT:** Patient comes in today for monitoring of his chronic obstructive pulmonary disease, but he is apparently having a flare up that he thinks just started within the last day or so. There has been no fever or chills. He has had cough, but the sputum has been fairly clear. There is no chest pain, but it does feel tight. He has been more dyspneic, particularly with attempts to come to the office today. He's not had any trouble with edema. Patient has long standing CLL.

**MEDICATIONS:**

1. Oxygen, 3 L/minute via nasal cannula continuously
2. Advair, 250/50, one inhalation q 12 h
3. Combivent, 2 puffs four times daily and as needed
4. Zyrtec, 10 mg daily, as needed
5. Prednisone, 5 mg daily
6. Norvasc, 10 mg daily
7. Tylenol No. 3 as needed

**PHYSICAL EXAMINATION:**

**GENERAL:** Pleasant, slightly cushingoid, elderly, white man in no distress, but he is definitely more tachypneic and labored with his speech than usual.

**WEIGHT:** 128

**BLOOD PRESSURE:** 170/80.

**PULSE:** 88 and regular

**RESPIRATIONS:** 16 to 18.

**NOSE:** Nasal mucosa and turbinates clear

**MOUTH:** Clear

**PHARYNX:** Clear

**NECK:** Supple. No cervical or supraclavicular adenopathy.

**LUNGS:** Bilateral wheezes with poor air movement and prolonged expiratory phase; air movement is not as good as usual.

**CARDIAC:** Normal S1 and S2; I don't detect an S3

**ABDOMEN:** No tenderness

**EXTREMITIES:** No cyanosis, clubbing, or edema

**LABORATORY:** Oxygen saturation at rest on 3 L of oxygen with a conserver device is 96%. CBC today from laboratory is WNL.

## EXAM 4—CASE 4 (*continued*)

**ASSESSMENT/PLAN:**

1. COPD/chronic bronchitis, now with acute exacerbation. Treat with prednisone, 40 mg daily for 3 days then taper by 10 mg every third day; also treat empirically with Levaquin, 750 mg daily for 5 days.

2. Questionable asbestosis based on chest radiographic abnormalities, currently receiving disability compensation.

3. Chronic lymphocytic B-cell leukemia; in remission, will monitor again at next visit.

4. Anxiety disorder.

**HISTORY:** Detailed

**EXAMINATION:** Detailed

**MEDICAL DECISION MAKING:** Moderate

---

*Enter two diagnosis codes and one procedure code.*

**DX1**

**DX2**

**PR1**

## EXAM 4—CASE 5

*Please code for the services of the surgeon.*

**PREOPERATIVE DIAGNOSIS:** Right carotid stenosis

**POSTOPERATIVE DIAGNOSIS:** Right carotid stenosis

**PROCEDURE:** Right carotid endarterectomy

**INDICATION:** This patient is a 53-year-old man who was recently hospitalized. During the course of his workup, he was noted to have a right carotid stenosis. This was asymptomatic. Angiography confirmed the finding, and it appeared to be approximately 80% stenosis in the right internal carotid artery. The opposite carotid artery is in good condition. The patient was carefully advised about the risks, benefits, and alternatives for asymptomatic carotid stenosis, including the magnitude of reduction of stroke risk in comparison with the actual stroke risk without surgery. The patient understood that this is a purely prophylactic procedure that could cause stroke as a risk and other complications such as tongue paralysis, lower right lip paralysis, numbness in the neck, bleeding, infection, paralysis, and death. He understands the above and requested that surgery be performed.

**OPERATIVE COURSE:** After general endotracheal anesthesia, the patient was placed in the supine position. The right anterior neck areas were then prepared and draped in the usual fashion. An incision, which was running anterior to the border of the sternocleidomastoid muscles, was made using a #10 blade. Hemostasis was achieved using Bovie, which was used to transverse the platysma. Self-retaining retractors were placed. The plane anterior to the sternocleidomastoid muscle was then developed, using sharp and blunt dissection. Careful hemostasis was employed using bipolar cautery. The carotid sheath was then entered and the carotid and internal jugular veins were dissected out. The Henley retractor was placed. The carotid, was dissected distally. There was no obvious common facial vein in the vicinity of the carotid bifurcation, which was, as predicted, highly placed. This necessitated careful and deliberate dissection distally, so as to preserve the hypoglossal nerve. This required division of the digastric muscle, using cautery. Great care was taken to identify and preserve the hypoglossal nerve. The need for careful preservation of this was attended to throughout the entire procedure. A small vein that was a tributary to the internal jugular vein was ligated and divided in this area as well.

A Rummel tourniquet was placed around the common carotid artery. 0 silk ties were placed around the internal and external carotid artery, and a 0 silk tie Potts ligature was placed around the first branch of the external carotid artery. There was no typically placed superior thyroid artery in this patient. It was unclear which branch of the external artery was thus represented as the first proximal branch that was identified. The carotid sinus nerves were infiltrated using 1% lidocaine in the area, and the bifurcation was extensively dissected out to allow for placement of these sutures around the vessels. A Hemovac drain was placed lateral to the carotid artery, and this was connected to suction. The patient was given 80 units/kg bolus of heparin. The internal, common, and external carotid arteries were test occluded, and there was no change in the EEG. The artery was then opened using a #11 blade. This was extended using Potts scissors. The plaque was shelled out in the usual fashion using #4 Penfield. The plaque was amputated proximally in the usual fashion by dividing it with a #11 blade after elevation using a right-angle clamp. The plaque was then removed from the external carotid artery using a standard eversion technique. The plaque was then dissected free at the internal carotid artery distally. An excellent break point was noted, and there did not appear to be any need for any intimal tack-up stitches placed.

## EXAM 4—CASE 5 (*continued*)

The arteriotomy bed was then carefully inspected, and all flaky material was removed in standard fashion. The arteriotomy was then closed using running 6-0 Prolene suture. Prior to placement of the final sutures, internal/external carotid arteries were back-bled and heparinized saline was employed to remove any potential bubbles. The external and common were then unclamped, allowing perfusion out this route. The internal was subsequently unclamped, after it had been clamped for a total of 30 minutes. There was no change in the EEG or somatosensory of a potential monitoring during that time or at any other time during the operation. There appeared to be no worthy leakage from the arteriotomy site. The arteries were then inspected at great length with a Doppler to ensure an adequate signal. Thus, satisfied, we proceeded to close. The Hemovac drain was left in place. Great care was taken to ensure excellent hemostasis. In light of this rather atypical amount of ooze present, a partial reversal of the heparin was given by the anesthesiologist. The platysma was then closed using interrupted 2-0 Vicryl sutures. The skin was closed using a running 4-0 Monocryl suture. Steri-Strips and a dressing were applied. The patient was then extubated and taken to the recovery room in stable condition, moving all four extremities well.

*Enter one diagnosis code and one procedure code.*

**DX1** 

**PR1**

## EXAM 4—CASE 6

*Please code for the services of the surgeon.*

**DATE OF OPERATION:** 11/01/20XX

**PREOPERATIVE DIAGNOSIS:** Left orbital pseudotumor

**POSTOPERATIVE DIAGNOSIS:** Left orbital pseudotumor

**OPERATION:** Anterior orbitotomy with a biopsy of lacrimal gland, left orbit

**ANESTHESIA:** General

**SURGICAL INDICATIONS:** The patient is a 10-year-old boy with a 2-year history of chronic inflammation of the left orbit including swelling of the medial and lateral recti muscles and the ipsilateral lacrimal gland and Tenon's capsule. Previous diagnostic studies included a normal CBC, C-reactive protein (less than 0.1), and C-ANCA and P-ANCA, which were negative suggesting there was no underlying vasculitis. Because of continued chronic inflammation for which he will probably need oral steroids, pretreatment biopsy of involved tissue was recommended. Brief review of the CT scan revealed that there was considerable enlargement of the lacrimal gland in the left orbit, therefore, biopsy of this tissue was recommended.

**SURGICAL PROCEDURE:** The child was brought to the operating room after adequate preoperative medications. He was induced with face mask anesthesia at which time an intravenous line was inserted, cardiac monitor, blood pressure cuff, EKG leads, and pulse oximeter were attached. The child was then intubated and maintained with an appropriate combination and mixture of anesthetic gases and oxygen compatible with general surgery. His face was prepared and draped in the usual sterile fashion.

Inspection of the left eyelid revealed that there was no crease. There was proptosis of the ipsilateral globe with fullness of the left upper eyelid. There seemed to be a previous scar in the left upper eyelid. Therefore the decision was made to position the anterior orbitotomy on the previous left upper eyelid scar. Therefore approximately a 2-cm area was demarcated with a marking pen in the superotemporal aspect of the upper eyelid above the area where the eyelid crease would normally be. The subcutaneous tissue was infiltrated with 1% Xylocaine with epinephrine. A #67 Beaver blade was used to incise the eyelid skin and superficial orbicularis. Prior to doing this, the eyelid was put on stretch by putting a 6-0 silk through the lash line and pulling the upper eyelid taut. Then the eyelid skin was tented up with small muscle hooks. The orbicularis muscle was incised centrally and then the incision in the orbicularis was extended to the medial and lateral margins of the skin incision. Hemostasis was obtained with bipolar cautery. The sharp dissection was continued posteriorly to the level of the orbital septum. The area of the orbital septum just at its junction with the lateral orbital rim was exposed using Ragnell retractors. The orbital septum was then incised and retracted. One could immediately see the orbital portion of the lacrimal gland prolapsed through the wound. The pseudocapsule of the lacrimal gland was separated on the posterior aspect of the gland. A small amount of tissue was tented up on a forceps and excised using the #67 Beaver blade. The tissue was immediately sent to the histopathology laboratory as a fresh specimen for appropriate histopathology and immunohistochemistry as indicated. Hemostasis was obtained with digital pressure and topical application of Avitene.

Once hemostasis was obtained, the wound was closed in a two-layered approach. First a deep subcutaneous and orbicularis muscle was closed with 5-0 Vicryl, and then the skin was closed with several interrupted 6-0 plain. Topical ointment was placed on the wound. The child was then weaned from general anesthesia, extubated, and brought to the recovery room in good health without complications.

## EXAM 4—CASE 6 (*continued*)

**PATHOLOGY REPORT—EXAM 4 CASE 10**

**CLINICAL INFORMATION**

**PROCEDURE:** Biopsy left orbital lesion

**PREOPERATIVE DIAGNOSIS:** Left orbital lesion

**CLINICAL HISTORY:** 10-year-old boy with chronic orbital inflammation (eye muscles, lacrimal gland) for 2 years

**GROSS DESCRIPTION:**

Received fresh designated LEFT LACRIMAL GLAND is a single, unoriented, irregular tan-pink portion of soft tissue measuring $0.8 \times 0.6 \times 0.1$ cm, which is submitted entirely, intact, in one cassette.

**MICROSCOPIC DESCRIPTION:**

H&E-stained sections reveal a portion of lacrimal tissue, with well-organized lobules of glands separated by fibromuscular tissue bands. Occasional ducts are seen within the fibromuscular tissue. Scattered collections of lymphocytes, plasma cells, and eosinophils are present between the exocrine glands and in foci within the intervening fibrous bands. There is no evidence of a neoplastic process.

**DIAGNOSIS:** LEFT LACRIMAL GLAND, BIOPSY; LACRIMAL GLAND TISSUE WITH AT MOST MILDLY INCREASED INTERSTITIAL LYMPHOCYTES AND PLASMA CELLS (SEE COMMENT)

**COMMENT:** Normal lacrimal gland tissue contains scattered interstitial lymphocytes and plasma cells. The number of lymphocytes and plasma cells present in this biopsy are, at most, mildly increased. An infiltrative or neoplastic cell population is not identified.

---

*Enter one diagnosis code and one procedure code.*

**DX1**

**PR1**

## EXAM 4—CASE 7

*Please code for the services of the surgeon.*

**SERVICE:** Abdominal transplant

**PREOPERATIVE DIAGNOSES:** Persistent rejection and failed renal allograft with allograft nephropathy resulting in end-stage renal disease

**POSTOPERATIVE DIAGNOSES:** Persistent rejection and failed renal allograft with allograft nephropathy resulting in end-stage renal disease

**OPERATIONS AND PROCEDURES:** Transplant nephrectomy

**ANESTHESIA:** General endotracheal

**INDICATIONS FOR THE OPERATION:** The patient is a 25-year-old woman who underwent a kidney transplant that subsequently failed due to persistent rejection. She has met end-stage criteria and is now being dialyzed. However, she continues to suffer persistent rejection despite triple immunosuppression. For this reason, she presents to the OR for elective-nephrectomy to take care of the above issues and also get her off of immunosuppression.

**PROCEDURE:** The patient was identified and brought to the operating room, placed in the supine position, and administered general endotracheal anesthetic. Her abdomen was shaved, prepared, and draped in a sterile fashion. She was explored through her previous right hockey stick incision. This was carried through the layers of the abdominal wall with care to avoid entrance into the peritoneal cavity. The kidney transplant was identified. The capsule was separated freeing the kidney circumferentially down to its vascular pedicle. Large vascular clamps were placed both from a superior and inferior position and crossclamped. The femoral artery pulse was checked and found to be 2+. The kidney was then amputated off its vascular pedicle above the clamps, and vessels were secured with two rows of running 3-0 Prolene. Cross-clamps were removed, and hemostasis was noted with no significant blood loss. The femoral artery was checked again, and it still had a 2+ pulse. Sutures were secured. Hemostasis was noted. The retroperitoneum was irrigated. Again, hemostasis was noted. A JP drain was placed subfascially through a right lower quadrant stab incision and secured to the skin with 2-0 nylon. The fascia was then closed in one layer using looped #1 PDS. The subcutaneous tissue was closed with 3-0 Vicryl, and the skin was closed with staples. A sterile dressing was applied, and the patient was extubated and transported to the recovery room in stable condition, having tolerated the procedure well.

**ESTIMATED BLOOD LOSS:** Less than 100 cc

Needle, sponge, and instrument counts correct.

**SPECIMENS:** Transplanted kidney

The patient received 250 cc of 5% albumin and 100 cc of normal saline.

---

*Enter three diagnosis codes and one procedure code.*

**DX1**

**DX2**

**DX3**

**PR1**

## EXAM 4—CASE 8

*Please code for the services of the physician.*

**REASON FOR VISIT:** Left leg pain

**HISTORY OF PRESENT ILLNESS:** This is an 80-year-old diabetic resident at Nursing Manor. Patient has had this open wound in her left lower leg being dressed by nursing home staff twice a week. It has continued to get smaller, although for the past 5 days, she started having pain in the left leg that will start at the open wound and shoot all the way up to her hip. She has no fever or chills. Blood sugars are checking "normal" running around 114–120.

**PHYSICAL EXAMINATION:** Weight: 202; Blood pressure: 130/58

This is an 80-year-old in no acute distress.

**EXTREMITIES:** Examination of her left leg shows no new swelling. There is some mild erythema around the open wound with some yellow exudate.

**IMPRESSION:**

1. Cellulitis, left leg

2. Diabetic peripheral vascular disease

**PLAN:** The patient was given 1 g of Rocephin IV push today in the office. Continue the dressings per Nursing Manor staff nurses. She may continue her pain medicine as needed. Recheck as needed.

**HISTORY:** Expanded problem

**EXAMINATION:** Expanded problem

**MEDICAL DECISION MAKING:** Moderate

*Enter two diagnosis codes and six procedure codes.*

**DX1**

**DX2**

**PR1**

**PR2**

**PR3**

**PR4**

**PR5**

**PR6**

# ANSWER KEY

## Introduction: Additional Practice Cases

### *Practice Case 1*

| DX1 | Q30.8 | Other congenital malformation of nose |
|-----|-------|----------------------------------------|
| PR1 | 15260 | Full-thickness graft, 20 sq cm or less |
| PR2 | 21235 | Graft, ear cartilage, autogenous to nose or ear |

### *Practice Case 2*

| DX1 | M24.151 | Other articular cartilage disorders, right hip |
|-----|---------|------------------------------------------------|
| PR1 | 29862 | Arthroscopy, hip, with resection of labrum |

### *Practice Case 3*

| DX1 | R10.84 | Generalized abdominal pain |
|-----|--------|-----------------------------|
| PR1 | 45380 | Colonoscopy, flexible with biopsy, single or multiple |
| PR2 | 43239 | EGD with biopsy, single or multiple |

### *Practice Case 4*

| DX1 | J96.00 | Acute respiratory failure |
|-----|--------|----------------------------|
| DX2 | I62.9 | Nontraumatic intracranial hemorrhage, unspecified |
| PR1 | 31600 | Tracheostomy, planned |

### *Practice Case 5*

| DX1 | C50.911 | Malignant neoplasm of unspecified site of right female breast |
|-----|---------|---------------------------------------------------------------|
| DX2 | Z92.21 | Personal history of antineoplastic chemotherapy |
| PR1 | 19307 | Mastectomy, modified radical |

### *Practice Case 6*

| DX1 | J96.00 | Acute respiratory failure, unspecified whether with hypoxia or hypercapnia |
|-----|--------|----------------------------------------------------------------------------|
| DX2 | S27.329A | Contusion of lung, unspecified, initial encounter |
| DX3 | B96.3 | Haemophilus influenzae |
| DX4 | B37.1 | Pulmonary candidasis |
| PR1 | 99291 | Critical care, 1st hour |

## Practice Case 7

| DX1 | E06.3 | Autoimmune thyroiditis |
|---|---|---|
| PR1 | 60220 | Total thyroid lobectomy, unilateral; with or without isthmusectomy |

## Practice Case 8

| DX1 | N18.6 | End-stage renal disease |
|---|---|---|
| DX2 | Z99.2 | Dependence on renal dialysis |
| PR1 | 36818 | Arteriovenous anastomosis, open; by upper arm cephalic vein transposition |

## Practice Case 9

| DX1 | G40.901 | Epilepsy, unspecified, not intractable, with status epilepticus |
|---|---|---|
| DX2 | C34.90 | Malignant neoplasm of unspecified part of unspecified bronchus or lung |
| DX3 | C79.9 | Secondary malignant neoplasm of unspecified site |
| PR1 | 95816 | Electroencephalogram, awake and drowsy |

## Practice Case 10

| DX1 | H49.10 | Fourth [trochlear] nerve palsy, unspecified eye |
|---|---|---|
| PR1 | 70553 | MRI, brain, with and without contrast |

## Practice Case 11

| DX1 | S61.212A | Laceration of finger, right index finger, initial encounter |
|---|---|---|
| PR1 | 99213 | Office and outpatient E/M, established |
| PR2 | 12001 | Wound repair, finger, 1.0 cm |

## Practice Case 12

| DX1 | N39.0 | Urinary tract infection |
|---|---|---|
| DX2 | F20.9 | Schizophrenia |
| PR1 | 99202 | Office and outpatient E/M, new |
| PR2 | 81025 | Pregnancy test |
| PR3 | 81001 | Urinalysis, automated with microscopy |

## *Practice Case 13*

| DX1 | Q17.0 | Skin tag |
|-----|-------|----------|
| DX2 | Q18.1 | Preauricular sinus |
| PR1 | 11442 | Excision, benign lesion, excised diameter 1.1 cm to 2 cm |
| PR2 | 11200 | Removal of skin tags |
| PR3 | 12051 | Repair, intermediate wound, of face, ears, eyelids, nose, lips, and/or mucous membranes, 2.5 cm or less |

## *Practice Case 14*

| DX1 | R00.2 | Palpitations |
|-----|-------|--------------|
| DX2 | Z98.89 | History of surgery to heart and great vessels |
| DX3 | Z87.74 | History of congenital malformation |
| PR1 | 93224 | Electrocardiographic monitoring for 24 hrs, total service |

## *Practice Case 15*

| DX1 | 021.1 | Hyperemesis gravidarum with electrolyte imbalance |
|-----|-------|---------------------------------------------------|
| PR1 | 80048 | Basic metabolic panel |
| PR2 | 85025 | CBC with automated differential |
| PR3 | 36415 | Venipuncture |

## *Practice Case 16*

| DX1 | G45.9 | Transient ischemic attack |
|-----|-------|---------------------------|
| DX2 | I34.1 | Mitral valve prolapse |
| PR1 | 99285 | Emergency department E/M |
| PR2 | 93010 | EKG interpretation |

## *Practice Case 17*

| DX1 | S42.422A | Fracture supracondylar fracture of humerus, subsequent visit |
|-----|----------|--------------------------------------------------------------|
| DX2 | M08.20 | Still's syndrome |
| PR1 | 99201 | Office and outpatient E/M, new |
| PR2 | 20670 | Hardware removal, superficial |

## Practice Case 18

| DX1 | K13.79 | Mucocele (lesion), lower lip |
|---|---|---|
| PR1 | 40812 | Excision of lesion of mucosa and submucosa, vestibule of mouth, with simple repair |

## Practice Case 19

| DX1 | C79.51 | Metastatic disease, femoral neck |
|---|---|---|
| DX2 | C64.9 | Renal cell carcinoma |
| DX3 | M84.552A | Pathologic fracture, femur |
| PR1 | 27236 | Open treatment of femoral fracture |
| PR2 | 27495 | Prophylactic treatment of femur |
| PR3 | 27360 | Partial excision bone, femur |

## Practice Case 20

| DX1 | H71.91 | Middle ear cholesteatoma |
|---|---|---|
| PR1 | 69643 | Tympanoplasty with mastoidectomy |

## Exam 1

1. **b**  The integrated health record is arranged in strict chronological order with different types of information and sources of information mixed together according to the data on the entries. Physicians' offices often use this format (LaTour, Eichenwald Maki, and Oachs 2013, 257).

2. **b**  The condition listed in this question is the only one that is not a complication of labor and delivery. (Cephalic/occipital presentation is a normal fetal presentation at delivery and is not a complication of delivery.) There is also a note in the ICD-10-CM codebook under category code O80 which describes an uncomplicated delivery. All of the other conditions listed here are considered complications (according to the ICD-10-CM codebook) and are to be coded as such (Hazelwood and Venable 2014, 148-150).

3. **c**  Methicillin-resistant *Staphylococcus aureus* is considered as a major source of hospital-acquired infections (Leon-Chisen 2015, 154).

4. **a**  This is one of the prion diseases. Creutzfeldt-Jakob disease is classified in ICD-10-CM at subcategory Z81.0-. Categories A80–A89 classify viral and prion infections of the central nervous system. Two additional websites are: http://www.ninds.nih.gov/disorders/cjd/detail_cjd .htm and http://www.alz.org/dementia/creutzfeldt-jakob-disease-cjd-symptoms.asp.

5. **b**  Hypothyroidism is a condition in which the thyroid gland does not make enough thyroid hormone. Levothyroxine (synthroid) is commonly used to treat this condition. (http://www.nlm .nih.gov/medlineplus/ency/article/000353.htm.)

6. **c**  Klebsiella is the only gram-negative organism listed; all others are gram-positive (Hazelwood and Venable 2014, 16–17).

7. **b**  The codes in the preventive medicine services category of CPT are used to report the preventive medicine E/M of infants, children, adolescents, and adults. They are assigned based on the patient's age (Kuehn 2015, 70).

8. **d**  If the type of diabetes mellitus is not documented in the medical record, the default is type 2 diabetes mellitus. The coder would also want to code the insulin use in addition to the diabetic code selected (Hazelwood and Venable 2014, 46; *ICD-10-CM Official Guidelines for Coding and Reporting 2015*, 1.C.4.a.2).

9. **b**  Clinical data is the most common type of health information and documents the signs, symptoms, diagnoses, impressions, treatments, and outcomes of the care process (LaTour, Eichenwald Maki, and Oachs 2013, 244–245).

10. **c**  Pathology reports are required for cases in which a surgical specimen is removed or expelled during a procedure. Specimens are examined both microscopically and macroscopically (LaTour, Eichenwald Maki, and Oachs 2013, 250).

11. **b**  Extrinsic asthma is caused by environmental allergen factors (Schraffenberger 2015, 270).

12. **b**  A radiologist's findings may be used to clarify an outpatient's diagnosis or reason for services. Based on the fact that the radiologist is a physician, a coder can use a diagnosis from the x-ray (Schraffenberger 2015, 403; *ICD-10-CM Official Guidelines for Coding and Reporting 2015*, IV.K).

13. **a**  The outcome of delivery code (code Z37.0) cannot stand alone (always a secondary code) and must be used with a code describing the delivery. The V00 code is an External Cause of Morbidity code and follows the specific injury code; therefore, it cannot be used alone; and *Y codes* follow the trauma, disease, or injury code and provides detail as to where the situation occurred. Code Z38.00 refers to liveborn infants according to place of birth and type of delivery, and there is a note in the code book that explains that it is to be used as the principal diagnosis code and can therefore stand alone (Hazelwood and Venable 2014, 223; *ICD-10-CM Official Guidelines for Coding and Reporting 2015*, 1.C.16.a.2, 1.20.a.1, and 1.C.21.11).

14. **d**  A fetal death refers to the death of a fetus of a particular weight or gestation, frequently 500 g or more or 22 or more completed weeks of gestation, though the weight and week gestation may vary from state to state (Brodnik, et al. 2012, 382).

15. **d**  The patient experienced an adverse effect (drowsiness) due to sensitivity to the Periactin medication. The Adverse Effect column is selected from the Table of Drugs and Chemicals as the medication was taken as prescribed (Hazelwood and Venable 2014, 197; Optum 2015 *ICD-10-CM for Hospitals*, Table of Drugs and Chemicals; *ICD-10-CM Official Guidelines for Coding and Reporting 2015*, 1.C.19.5.a).

16. **c**  The melanoma is coded to the site of the lesion (Alphabetic Index main term Melanoma, subterm Skin, subterm arm refers the coder to code C43.6-; C43.61 refers to malignant melanoma of right upper limb including shoulder) and the procedure code is determined based on the size of the lesion as well as the margins (Optum 2015 *ICD-10-CM for Hospitals*, Alphabetic Index, main term Melanoma; *CPT Assistant* Fall 1995, 3; May 1996, 11; Nov. 2002, 5; Feb. 2010, 3).

17. **a**  The term "missed abortion" refers to fetal death that occurs prior to the completion of 20 weeks of gestation (Schraffenberger 2015, 322).

18. **c**  A diagnosis of elevated blood pressure reading, without a diagnosis of hypertension, is assigned code R03.0 (Alphabetic Index, main term Elevated, subterms blood pressure, reading, no diagnosis of hypertension) (Schraffenberger 2015, 232; Optum 2015 *ICD-10-CM for Hospitals*, Alphabetic Index, main term Elevated, subterms blood pressure, reading, no diagnosis of hypertension; *ICD-10-CM Official Guidelines for Coding and Reporting 2015*, 1.C.9.a.7).

19. **b**  Infants born to RH-negative mothers often develop hemolytic disease owing to fetal-maternal blood group incompatibility. These conditions are classified to Category P55, hemolytic disease of newborn (Alphabetic Index main term Disease, subterms hemolytic, due to or with, incompatibility, ABO (blood group)) (Leon-Chisen 2015, 370; Optum 2015 *ICD-10-CM for Hospitals*, Alphabetic Index, main term Disease).

20. **a**  The patient had a second-degree laceration (not a third-degree laceration), and the outcome of delivery code is Z37.0 (Leon-Chisen 2015, 336).

21. **a**  In ICD-10-CM, the coding guideline for the sequelae or late effects is to code the residual condition (monoplegia) of the sequela first, followed by the cause of the sequela (poliomyelitis). Per the Coding Guidelines, when a scenario specifies monoplegia of an upper limb and does not identify whether the limb is the dominant or non-dominant side, the default code for the affected left side is non-dominant (Hazelwood and Venable 2014, 5; *ICD-10-CM Official Guidelines for Coding and Reporting 2015*, 1.B.10 and 1.C.6.a).

22. **c**  In some cases symptoms are coded as additional diagnoses when they "represent important problems in medical care." With this question, it would be important to code the coma since it impacts the metastasis to the brain (Hazelwood and Venable 2014, 4; *ICD-10-CM Official Guidelines for Coding and Reporting 2015*, 1.C.18.e and 1.B.6).

23. **a**  When a patient seeks health care for the purpose of contraceptive sterilization, code Z30.2 is assigned as the principal diagnosis (Alphabetic Index main term Contraception, contraceptive with subterm sterilization) (Schraffenberger 2015, 537).

24. **a**  When a patient has bilateral glaucoma and both are documented as being the same type and stage, only one code is reported with the seventh character being the stage (*ICD-10-CM Official Guidelines for Coding and Reporting 2015*, I.C.7.a.2).

25. **c**  The patient who is postmenopausal as a result of natural or age-related menopause and who is asymptomatic is coded using Z78.0 (Alphabetic Index main term State with subterm menopausal refers the coder to Z78.0; the Tabular List for this code states Asymptomatic menopausal state) (Optum 2015 *ICD-10-CM for Hospitals*).

26. **b**  During pregnancy, childbirth, or the puerperium, a patient admitted with a diagnosis of asymptomatic AIDS should receive a principal diagnosis of O98.72 and B20. (Once an individual has confirmed AIDS, code B20 must always be used in future hospital visits.) Code Z37.0 is for the livebirth and Z3A.36 is for the specified (36) weeks of gestation (Schraffenberger 2015, 343; *ICD-10-CM Official Guidelines for Coding and Reporting 2015*, 1.C.a.2.d and 1.C.1.a.2.g).

27. **b**  Metastatic from a specific site implies that the site mentioned is the primary site (Schraffenberger 2015, 144).

28. **a**  To completely describe a pressure ulcer, use as many codes as needed from category L89 to identify the site of the pressure ulcer as well as the stage of the ulcer (*ICD-10-CM Official Guidelines for Coding and Reporting 2015*, I.C.12.a.1).

29. **c**  A poisoning code (for the crack cocaine) is always sequenced first per the ICD-10-CM Coding Guidelines. In all of the other examples, the Acute Respiratory Failure is principal (Schraffenberger 2015, 451; *ICD-10-CM Official Guidelines for Coding and Reporting 2014*, 1.C.10.b and 1.C.19.e.5.b).

30. **d**  When a patient is diagnosed with an infection (such as pneumonia) that is due to MRSA, and that infection has a combination code that includes the causal agent, the appropriate combination code for that infection and its causal organism is assigned. If a patient has a current infection and a MRSA colonization, Z22.322 should also be assigned (Schraffenberger 2015, 117; *ICD-10-CM Official Guidelines for Coding and Reporting 2015*, 1.C.1.e.1).

31. **a**  Coarctation of the aorta is a defect in which the aorta is narrowed somewhere along its length (Schraffenberger 2015, 381).

32. **a**  When a patient is admitted for the purpose of having chemotherapy and develops a complication, such as nausea and vomiting, the principal diagnosis is still the admission for the chemotherapy (Schraffenberger 2015, 149; *ICD-10-CM Official Guidelines for Coding and Reporting 2015*, 1.C.2.e.3).

33. **b**  Down's syndrome (Q90.9), Patau's syndrome (Q91.7), and Edward's syndrome (Q91.3) are classified in chapter 17 Congenital malformations, deformations and chromosomal abnormalities, categories Q90-Q99, Chromosomal abnormalities, not elsewhere classified (Optum 2015 *ICD-10-CM for Hospitals*, categories Q90-Q9; Schraffenberger, 2015, 395).

34. **a**  The Z38.00 code should be used because it was clearly stated that the baby was born vaginally. The fetal alcohol syndrome code should be used instead of the alcohol abuse code because the use of alcohol by the mother was manifested in the infant (Hazelwood and Venable 2014, 158).

35. **a**  Benign prostatic hypertrophy is a rather common disease that is coded in a physician's office, so it is important to recognize the symptoms so that they are not also coded as a diagnostic statement (Hazelwood and Venable 2014, 131).

36. **d**  It is important for the coder to be able to distinguish between the types of complications and what is or is not a mechanical complication. Mechanical complications include breakdowns, displacement, leakage, or other complications. Non-mechanical complications include infection and inflammatory reaction due to cardiac valve prosthesis, other cardiac and vascular implants and grafts, genitourinary prosthetic devices, implants, and grafts, prosthetic device, implant and graft in urinary system, due to internal joint prostheses, internal fixation device, etc. (Hazelwood and Venable 2014, 210–211).

37. **b**  This question refers to coding a subsequent myocardial infarction within a three week time frame of the first infarction. Acute-care treatment extends to a 4-week time period following the first episode of care for this condition in ICD-10-CM (Hazelwood and Venable 2014, 76–77; *ICD-10-CM Official Guidelines for Coding and Reporting 2015,* 1.C.9.e.4).

38. **a**  It is important for the coder to be able to understand what the term *status migrainous* means and the time period is one indicator which helps to define this term. Status migrainous generally refers to a severe migraine attack that lasts for more than 72 hours (Leon-Chisen 2015, 207).

39. **c**  A coder needs to be able to understand all of the terms associated with drug and alcohol abuse, dependence, and treatment. This question simply addresses the definition of detoxification (Schraffenberger 2015, 145).

40. **b**  Personal history in ICD-10-CM means the patient's past medical condition (the malignancy in this case) no longer exists and the patient is not receiving any treatment for the condition (Schraffenberger 2015, 154–155; *ICD-10-CM Official Guidelines for Coding and Reporting 2015*, I.C.21.c.4, I.C.2.d, and I.C.2.m).

41. **c**  Resequencing is indicated with a pound (#) sign (Kuehn 2015, 17).

42. **a**  Emergency department E/M services require all three components to be met or exceeded. The service provided—the ED physician only did a detailed history and a detailed exam—only meets level 99284. The spinal puncture is diagnostic and therefore 62270 (Kuehn 2015, 63–64).

43. **d**  Morselized bone is bone that has been crushed to conform to the area receiving the graft. Read about spine surgery in *The Lumbar Spine* by H. N. Herkowitz, pages 74–76 (Kuehn 2015, 128–129).

44. **c**  Shoulder blade is a synonym of scapula; saucerization means excavation of tissue to form a shallow depression. This returns the shoulder blade to the natural contour as described in this case (*CPT Professional Edition* 2015, 122; *Stedman's* 1595; *Stedman's* 1631).

45. d   Destruction codes are used because the physician curettes the lesions, which is included as a method of destruction. In addition, the lesions are actinic keratoses, which are listed as a form of premalignant lesions that are normally destroyed using this method (Kuehn 2015, 119).

46. a   An indirect laryngoscopy uses a mirror to visualize the larynx. A direct laryngoscopy would use an endoscope. The diagnostic laryngoscopy is included in the endoscopy for removal of the foreign body (Kuehn 2015, 138).

47. a   The coding notes before code 64490 state that bilateral injections should be coded using a –50 modifier. L2–L3 is the second lumbar level injected, therefore 64494 is used in combination with 64493 (*CPT Professional Edition* 2015, 372).

48. c   The *Coder Desk Reference* shows the following for code 33814: "The physician gains access to the mediastinum through an incision through the sternum (median sternotomy). The physician places cardiopulmonary bypass catheters through incisions in the low inferior vena cava, the superior vena cava, and high aorta or femoral artery. The physician stops the heart by infusing cardioplegia solution into the coronary circulation. The physician cross-clamps the aorta and places sump suction in the left atrium to obtain a bloodless surgical field. The physician exposes the aortopulmonary septal defect by cutting through the ascending aorta or main pulmonary artery. The physician closes the defect with a Dacron fabric patch, closes the aortic or pulmonary arterial incision, takes the patient off cardiopulmonary bypass, closes the remaining surgical incisions, and dresses the sternal wound. The physician may leave chest tubes and/or a mediastinal drainage tube in place following the procedure." (OptumInsight 2015a, 338).

49. c   Code 16025 describes the specific work associated with debridement of a burn wound and wound dressing (*CPT Assistant* August 1997, 08(7): 6–7 and October 2012, 22(10): 3–8).

50. b   Code 74262 correctly describes the service listed in this question (*CPT Professional Edition* 2015, 417).

51. c   Tests that are ordered together and performed together that are listed together as a panel must be billed as a panel. If all the tests listed in a panel are not performed, they must be billed individually. In this case, all of the tests listed in the electrolyte panel were performed and must be coded together as 80051 (Kuehn 2015, 238–239).

52. d   The psychotherapy codes are assigned based on time. Each time-based code has a range of times listed in the coding notes. 50 minutes of service qualifies for code 90832 within the range of 38 to 52 minutes. In addition, the pharmacologic management is coded separately as 90863 (Kuehn 2015, 257–258).

53. b   The allergist provides single-dose vials as indicated in CPT code 95144 (Kuehn 2015, 268–269).

54. b   This service requires a 99283 Emergency Department code (due to expanded problem-focused history), the code for the rabies immune globulin, and the administration and rabies vaccine and the vaccine administration (Kuehn 2015, 255–256).

55. b   This question says that the imaging was performed by the radiologist. Therefore, code 10022 cannot be correct because it includes imaging. In addition, the question does not state that the needle biopsy was a fine needle biopsy, which is different. The biopsy is not stated as a wedge biopsy and therefore code 47100 is incorrect. Because code 47000 describes the procedure, the unlisted code of 47399 would not be used (*CPT Assistant*, Fall 1993, 03(3): 11–20 and April 2001, 04(11): 3).

56. b   The primary procedure is an anterior lamellar keratoplasty (65710), and the use of the laser to prepare the recipient site is coded with the add-on Category III code, 0290T (Repka 2011, 18).

57. c   The Category III code describes all of the work necessary to insert the spinous process distraction device, the work described in this question (*CPT Assistant*, July 2007, Volume 17(7): 6–10).

58. c   Each unit of the drug is worth 250 mg. 600 mg is more than 2 units and less than 3 units. Therefore, 3 units are reported (Kuehn 2015, 291).

59. b   The combination code of complex cystometrogram and voiding pressure studies is the only code required. This procedure would be correctly coded by including the –26 modifier to describe the urologist's professional services (Kuehn 2015, 176–177).

60. c   The definition of "new patient" in CPT states that a new patient has not seen a physician from the exact same specialty and subspecialty within the same group practice within the past 3 years. Also, this patient is covered by Medicare and, therefore, consultation codes are not an option for coding purposes (Kuehn 2015, 61–62).

61. c   Ventilating tubes in the ears are placed via a tympanostomy. This procedure code describes a unilateral procedure, and therefore a –50 modifier is required. The tonsillectomy and adenoidectomy are both inherently bilateral procedures, and a –50 modifier is not required on this combination code (*CPT Assistant*, February 1998, 02(8), 11).

62. c   The final closure is coded with 49606, after the repair of the gastroschisis is performed by placing a prosthesis over the protruding intestines (*CPT Assistant*, Winter 1994, 04(4), 12–17).

63. d   There are currently no codes that describe a CABG using a thoracoscopic approach, therefore the unlisted code is assigned (*CPT Professional Edition* 2015, 197–199 and 209).

64. c   The CPT Index directs the coder to 67220–67225 for destruction of a choroid lesion. When evaluating the codes, the coder should select 67220 for photocoagulation of the choroid lesion (*CPT Professional Edition* 2015, 389).

65. c   Code 58262 describes the removal of a 230 g uterus, along with either one or both of the tubes and the ovaries (*CPT Professional Edition* 2015, 338).

66. c   Code 36831 describes the open thrombectomy from an AV fistula (*CPT Assistant*, April 1999, 04(9): 11).

67. b   This procedure is correctly described as code 31290 (*CPT Assistant*, Winter 1993, 04(3): 22–25).

68. d   There is no CPT code that correctly describes the procedure of incision into the bladder neck. Code 52500 describes resection of the bladder neck, but this case involves only cutting into the bladder neck. Therefore, the unlisted code must be assigned (*CPT Professional Edition* 2015, 319).

69. c    32505, 32820, 33330, 33320—Cardiopulmonary bypass was not used on this case. Therefore, code 33300 is coded for the cardiac muscle repair. The inferior vena cava is a great vessel, again repaired without CP bypass, and therefore code 33320 is assigned. Code 32505 describes a therapeutic wedge resection of the lung. The major reconstruction of the chest wall using flaps is coded in addition to the other procedures because of the extensive closure required. The *Coder Desk Reference* describes the following for code 32820: "The physician repairs and reconstructs the chest wall following a major disfiguring injury to the chest (eg, a shotgun blast). Using prosthetic materials, muscle and skin flaps, and possibly skin grafts, the surgeon repairs a large defect(s) in the chest wall. This may require the use of one or more stages to finish the reconstruction" (OptumInsight 2015a, 323).

70. d    60260, 60220, 60512—To correctly code this case, three codes are required. First the left thyroidectomy that removes all the remaining thyroid tissue is coded with 60260. This is not a lobectomy or a traditional thyroidectomy because thyroid tissue has been previously excised. Then, the right lobectomy is coded as 60220 because no prior surgery has been performed on that lobe. The parathyroid glands were spared and autoreplanted, which is coded with 60512 (*CPT Professional Edition* 2015, 347).

71. b    56605, 56606, 56515—To correctly code this case, three codes are required. The patient had two biopsies of the vulva (mons pubis). The first one is coded as 56605, and the second separate lesion is coded as 56606. In addition, the patient had extensive destruction of three lesions of the vulva (labia majora). This is coded as 56515 (*CPT Professional Edition* 2015, 333; *OptumInsight* 2015a, 527).

72. b    38525, 38792—This case requires two codes. The injection procedure for the identification of the sentinel node is coded as 38792, and the excision of the deep axillary node is coded as 38525 (*CPT Professional Edition* 2015, 247; *CPT Assistant*, July 1999, 07(9): 6–7).

73. a    D53.9, K29.70—The signs and symptoms would not be coded as they are integral to the diagnoses of anemia and gastritis (*ICD-10-CM Official Guidelines for Coding and Reporting 2015*, 1.C.18.b).

74. b    C56.9, C79.89, J91.0—The patient had a primary ovarian carcinoma with metastasis throughout the abdominal and pelvic cavities. There is a code first note at J91.0 to code first underlying neoplasm. Carcinomatosis, C80.0, is not to be assigned when the primary and secondary sites are stated. The malignant pleural effusion is also coded (Schraffenberger 2015, 147–148; *ICD-10-CM Official Guidelines for Coding and Reporting 2015*, 1.C.2).

75. c    T81.4XXA, B96.20, S82.201E—In this case, there is a wound infection following a surgical procedure. There is note under code T81.4XXA to use additional code to identify the infection and the organism identified was E.coli which was coded as B96.20. The seventh character E was added to the fracture code to indicate routine fracture healing (Schraffenberger 2015, 23–24).

76. d    E09.9, J84.9, K92.1, M06.9, N18.9, T38.0X5A—DM caused by drug use is coded to category E09 (Schraffenberger 2015, 170).

77. c    Dr. Smith receives 80% of the Medicare allowed amount, which is $160. Dr. Jones receives nothing from CMS because he does not accept assignment. The patient receives the benefits (AMA 2013, 78–79, 136–138).

78.  c   Dr. Smith will receive the entire $200 minus $160 from CMS and the remaining 20% or $40 from the patient. Dr. Jones will receive $218.50 from the patient. This amount is the most he can charge under CMS' limiting charge rule. This figure is derived by determining the nonPAR allowed charge, which is 95% of the PAR amount—in this case, that would be $190. The limiting charge = 115% of that amount or $218.50 (AMA 2013, 78–79, 136–138).

79.  c   Medicare typically doesn't cover preventive medicine, but a new benefit was provided in The Medicare Prescription Drug, Improvement, and Modernization Act of 2003 that provides one preventive physical examination, or the "Welcome to Medicare Physical," for new Medicare Part B enrollees within the first 12 months of entitlement (Kuehn 2015, 71–72).

80.  a   Both code 93000 for the EKG performed, interpreted and reported in the office and the code 0180T for the hospital 64-lead EKG interpretation and report are assigned. When referencing Column 1 and Column 2 NCCI edits, the –59 modifier would be applied to the code in Column 2, code 93000 for this case (Kuehn 2015, 323–324).

81.  a   A diagnosis distribution report will show all of the ICD-9-CM codes used during the prior fiscal year and will allow the office manager to identify issues such as missing digits, use of nonspecific codes, and inappropriate to setting usage (Kuehn 2015, 343–344).

82.  b   The characteristics of data quality are listed as follows: accuracy, accessibility, comprehensives, consistency, currency, definition, granularity, integrity, precision, relevancy, and timeliness. Analysis is not listed as a characteristic (Abdelhak 2016, 128–129).

83.  c   Modifier –AI is now required for patients covered by Medicare when reporting Initial Hospital Service codes and this modifier is missing from the code (Kuehn 2015, 59).

84.  c   A line graph is often used to display time trends. The $x$-axis shows a unit of time, and the $y$-axis measures the value of the variable being plotted (LaTour, Eichenwald Maki, and Oachs 2013, 511–512).

85.  c   Computer assistance cannot address the major obstacle facing today's human coder: the lack of accurate, complete clinical documentation (LaTour, Eichenwald Maki, and Oachs 2013, 444–445).

86.  c   Data mapping describes the connections or paths between classifications and vocabularies. Data mining refers to the process of extracting information from a database and then filtering discrete, structured data. Redundancy is the process by which data entered into one server is simultaneously entered into a second server (LaTour, Eichenwald Maki, and Oachs 2013, 185).

87.  d   Computer-assisted coding (CAC) is the use of computer software that automatically generates a set of medical codes for review validation and use based on the documentation provided by the various providers of healthcare (LaTour, Eichenwald Maki, and Oachs 2013, 444–445).

88.  c   The HIPAA Privacy and Security Rules apply to PHI used or disclosed by covered entities. Covered entities are healthcare providers, healthcare clearinghouses, and health plans that conduct the financial and administrative transactions described in the Transaction and Code Sets Rule (TCS). If an individual provider or an organization does not fit within the definitions of a healthcare provider, clearinghouse, or health plan, the rules do not apply (LaTour, Eichenwald Maki, and Oachs 2013, 314–315).

89. **d**  An advance directive is a legal, written document that specifies patient preferences regarding future health care or specifies another person to make medical decisions in the event the patient has an incurable or irreversible condition and is unable to communicate his or her wishes (Abdelhak 2016, 12).

90. **b**  The HIPAA "minimum necessary" principle/standard has to be applied when determining employee access to PHI (LaTour, Eichenwald Maki, and Oachs 2013, 133–134).

91. **b**  HIPAA defers to state laws on matters concerning minors; therefore, consult state laws regarding the rules for appropriate authorization (Brodnik, et al. 2012, 151).

92. **a**  The request may be denied if it is determined that the PHI or the record was accurate and complete as it stands (Brodnik, et al. 2012, 242).

93. **d**  This is not a required element (Brodnik, et al. 2012, 233).

94. **a**  HIM professionals must resist the temptation to overlook inadequate documentation and report codes without appropriate clinical foundation within the record just to speed up claims processing, meet a business requirement, or obtain additional reimbursement (Hazelwood and Venable 2014, 232).

95. **d**  Regardless of whether the patient is an adult or a minor, the law allows a presumption of consent during an emergency situation (Brodnik, et al. 2012 141).

96. **d**  Coding policies should include the following components: AHIMA Code of Ethics, AHIMA Standards of Ethical Coding, Official Coding Guidelines, applicable federal and state regulations, and internal documentation policies requiring the presence of physician documentation to support all coded diagnosis and procedure code assignments (Schraffenberger and Kuehn 2012, 384).

## Exam 1 Case 1

| DX1 | E10.10 | Type 1 diabetes mellitus with ketoacidosis without coma |
|---|---|---|
| DX2 | J45.909 | Unspecified asthma, uncomplicated |
| PR1 | 99476 | Subsequent inpatient pediatric critical care |

## Exam 1 Case 2

| DX1 | C81.10 | Nodular sclerosis classical Hodgkin lymphoma, unspecified site |
|---|---|---|
| PR1 | 38221 | Bone marrow biopsy, needle |

## Exam 1 Case 3

| DX1 | F90.9 | Attention-deficit hyperactivity disorder, unspecified type |
|---|---|---|
| DX2 | F43.22 | Adjustment disorder with anxiety |
| PR1 | 90837 | Psychotherapy, 60 minutes |

## Exam 1 Case 4

| DX1 | M51.16 | Intervertebral disc disorders with radiculopathy, lumbar region |
|-----|--------|------------------------------------------------------------------|
| DX2 | G89.29 | Other chronic pain |
| PR1 | 63650 | Percutaneous implantation of neurostimulator electrode array, epidural |

## Exam 1 Case 5

| DX1 | C61 | Malignant neoplasm of prostate |
|-----|--------|------------------------------------------------------------------|
| DX2 | C77.2 | Secondary and unspecified malignant neoplasm of intra-abdominal lymph nodes |
| PR1 | 54520 | Orchiectomy |

## Exam 1 Case 6

| DX1 | J45.909 | Unspecified asthma, uncomplicated |
|-----|---------|-----------------------------------------------------------------|
| DX2 | M94.0 | Chondrocostal junction syndrome |
| DX3 | K21.9 | Gastro-esophageal reflux disease without esophagitis |
| DX4 | G43.909 | Migraine, unspecified, not intractable, without status migrainosus |
| PR1 | 99285 | Emergency department visit, level 5 |

## Exam 1 Case 7

| DX1 | D49.1 | Neoplasm of unspecified behavior of respiratory system |
|-----|--------|------------------------------------------------------------------|
| PR1 | 31625 | Bronchoscopy, right or flexible, including fluoroscopic guidance, when performed; with bronchial or endobronchial biopsy(s), single or multiple sites |

## Exam 1 Case 8

| DX1 | J18.9 | Pneumonia, unspecified organism |
|-----|--------|------------------------------------------------------------------|
| PR1 | 99239 | Hospital discharge day management; more than 30 minutes |

## Exam 2

1. **a**  For outpatient services (as is the case in this example) the coder may use documentation provided by a pathologist. Therefore, the coder should code the lesion as a basal cell carcinoma (Schraffenberger 2015, 99; *ICD-10-CM Official Guidelines for Coding and Reporting 2015*, IV.K).

2. **d**  Preventive medicine services category codes are assigned based on the age of the patient (Kuehn 2015, 70).

3. **c**  The total size of a removed lesion, including margins, is needed for accurate coding. This information is best provided in the operative report. The pathology report typically provides the specimen size rather than the size of the excised lesion. Because the specimen tends to shrink, this is not an accurate measurement (Kuehn 2015, 112–113; *CPT Professional Edition 2015*, 71–72).

4. **b**  Protonix is used to treat patients with erosive esophagitis associated with GERD. It decreases the accumulation of acid in the stomach. More information on Protonix is available at http://www.drugs.com/protonix.html.

5. **c**  Haldol is used to treat symptoms of schizophrenia. More information on Haldol is available at http://www.drugs.com/cdi/haldol.html.

6. **d**  A colonoscopy is the examination of the entire colon, from the rectum to the cecum, that may include the terminal ileum (*CPT Professional Edition* 2015, 279).

7. **c**  A serous papillary adenocarcinoma usually originates in the ovary (Schraffenberger 2015, 135).

8. **a**  Hypokalemia is defined as decreased levels of potassium in the blood (Chabner 2014, 763).

9. **b**  Medication records are maintained for all patients and include medications given, time, form of administration, dosage, and strength. The records are updated when the patient is given the medication. Nursing personnel complete the medication records (LaTour, Eichenwald Maki, and Oachs 2013, 249).

10. **c**  When a physician refers to "deep" burns he is referring to third degree burns that extend through the skin into the underlying fascia and may damage the tendons and bones (Schraffenberger 2015, 428–429).

11. **b**  The *ICD-10-CM Official Guidelines for Coding and Reporting*, Section IV. Diagnostic Coding and Reporting Guidelines for Outpatient Services indicate that when a physician qualifies a diagnostic statement as "rule out," the condition qualified in that statement should not be coded as if it existed. Rather, the condition should be coded to the highest level of certainty, such as the signs and symptoms the patient exhibits (Kuehn 2014, 30; *ICD-10-CM Official Guidelines for Coding and Reporting 2015*, 1V.H).

12. **c**  A series of terms in parentheses, called nonessential modifiers, sometimes directly follows a main term or subterm (Hazelwood and Venable 2014, 8; *ICD-10-CM Official Guidelines for Coding and Reporting 2015*, 1.A.7).

13. **b**  The colon is used in the Tabular List after an incomplete term that needs one or more of the modifiers that follow (Hazelwood and Venable 2014, 11; *ICD-10-CM Official Guidelines for Coding and Reporting 2015*, 1.A.7).

14. **c**  Square brackets are found only in the Tabular List and enclose synonyms, alternative wordings, abbreviations, and explanatory phrases (Hazelwood and Venable 2014, 11; *ICD-10-CM Official Guidelines for Coding and Reporting 2015*, 1.A.7).

15. **d**  When coding sequelae, the residual condition or nature of the sequela is sequenced first, followed by the cause of the sequela (Hazelwood and Venable 2014, 5; *ICD-10-CM Official Guidelines for Coding and Reporting 2015*, 1.B.10).

16. **b**  The other organisms listed are either viruses or fungi. *Staphylococcus aureus* is the only bacteria in this list (Hazelwood and Venable 2014, 18–20).

17. **b**  In ICD-10-CM, an elderly primigravida is defined as a woman who gives birth to her first child after age 35 (Optum 2015 *ICD-10-CM for Hospitals*, Subcategory O09.5-).

18. **d**  In addition to code Z33.2 (encounter for elective termination), a code for the outcome of delivery category Z37 may be assigned (*ICD-10-CM Official Guidelines for Coding and Reporting 2015*, 1.C.15.q.1).

19. **b**  Category O80, Normal delivery, is assigned when all of the following criteria are met: (1) delivery of a full-term, single, healthy liveborn infant; (2) delivery without prenatal or postpartum complications; or (3) cephalic or occipital presentation with spontaneous, vaginal delivery requiring minimal or no assistance, with or without episiotomy, without fetal manipulation or instrumentation (Hazelwood and Venable, 2014, 142; *ICD-10-CM Official Guidelines for Coding and Reporting 2015*, 1.C.15.n.1).

20. **a**  The perinatal, or newborn, period is defined as beginning before birth and lasting through 28 days after birth. There is also an inclusion note at the beginning of Chapter 16 reminding the coder of this definition (Hazelwood and Venable 2014, 158; *ICD-10-CM Official Guidelines for Coding and Reporting 2015*, 1.C.16).

21. **d**  Prolonged pregnancy is used to demonstrate that a woman is past 42 weeks' gestation. Also, code O48.1 provides an includes note which states that the pregnancy has advanced beyond 42 completed weeks gestation (Hazelwood and Venable 2014, 141; Optum 2015 *ICD-10-CM for Hospitals*, subcategory code O48.1).

22. **d**  A common congenital cardiac defect, ventricular septal defect, is defined as an abnormal communication or opening in the ventricular septum that allows blood to shunt from the left ventricle to the right ventricle (Hazelwood and Venable 2014, 165).

23. **c**  Code P70.1, Syndrome of infant of a diabetic mother, should be assigned when the newborn infant of a diabetic mother manifests features of this condition (Hazelwood and Venable 2014, 158–159).

24. **b**  In ICD-10-CM, Category Z34 includes codes for supervision of a normal pregnancy. Generally, code Z34.02 is for supervision of normal first pregnancy (second trimester) (Hazelwood and Venable 2014, 143).

25. b  The residual condition (ie, the perineum prolapsed) is to be sequenced first per instructional notes at O94 (Hazelwood and Venable 2014, 151; *ICD-10-CM Official Guidelines for Coding and Reporting 2015*, 1.C.15.p).

26. d  Category Z03 codes are used when a person without a diagnosis is suspected of having an abnormal condition; however, test results and exams prove the condition does not exist (*ICD-10-CM Official Guidelines for Coding and Reporting 2015*, 1.C.21.c.6).

27. c  Asthma (J45) is not considered a type of chronic obstructive pulmonary disease unless it is characterized as obstructed or diagnosed in conjunction with COPD (J44) (Optum 2015 ICD-10-CM for Hospitals, 434).

28. c  Stage III is the correct answer because this stage involves full-thickness skin loss involving damage or necrosis into subcutaneous soft tissues (Schraffenberger 2015, 354).

29. d  Cervical intraepithelial neoplasia III or CIN III is classified in subcategory D06 for carcinoma in situ of the cervix. The other conditions are classified in category N87, Dysplasia of cervix uteri. In ICD-10-CM's Alphabetic Index the main term Neoplasia is referenced followed by subterms intraepithelial, cervix, grade III (severe dysplasia) (Optum 2015 *ICD-10-CM for Hospitals* Alphabetic Index, under main term Neoplasia).

30. b  When a patient has bilateral glaucoma and each eye is documented as having a different type or stage and the classification distinguishes laterality, assign the appropriate code for each eye rather than the code for bilateral glaucoma (Schraffenberger 2013, 165; *ICD-10-CM Official Guidelines for Coding and Reporting 2015*, 1.C.7.a.3).

31. c  The postprocedural hypoinsulinemia (E89.1) is the first-listed code followed by the code E13.9, Secondary diabetes, and finally code Z90.411 for acquired partial absence of pancreas (*ICD-10-CM Official Guidelines for Coding and Reporting 2015*, 1.C.4.6.b.i).

32. a  If a patient has received tPA within the 24 hours prior to admission, the claim submitted by the physician at the specialty hospital will include Z92.82. This is a physician claim rather than the coder at hospital #2. The condition requiring the tPA administration, in this case the MI (code I21.09), is coded first. Code I22.0 is not used because this refers to a subsequent infarction. Chest pain is a symptom of a myocardial infarction and would thus not be coded (*ICD-10-CM Official Guidelines for Coding and Reporting 2015*, 1.C.9.e).

33. b  Code only the acute myocardial infarction (code I21.09) at the first hospital encounter since this is when the patient was first diagnosed in the ED. Code I22.0 would not be used because this code refers to a subsequent infarction which the patient did not have in this particular case. Chest pain would not be coded because it is a symptom of an acute myocardical infarction and the infarction is coded instead (Schraffenberger 2015, 236–237).

34. d  It is important for the coder to know the definition of the various types of anemia for correct coding. This scenario defines aplastic anemia (Hazelwood and Venable 2014, 40–41).

35. b  It is important for a coder to know the definition of the various types of cardiac dysrhythmias and their definitions in order to assign the correct code for such a diagnosis (Hazelwood and Venable 2014, 80–81).

36. c ICD-10-CM's Alphabetic Index lists Ulcer as the main term with the subterm decubitus. There is a note which refers the coder to See, Ulcer, pressure, by site. Referring to main term Ulcer again with subterms pressure, sacral region lists the code as L89.159. Code L89.150 refers to an unstageable pressure ulcer of the sacral region (Schraffenberger 2015, 354; *ICD-10-CM Official Guidelines for Coding and Reporting 2015*, 1.C.12.a).

37. a The urinary tract infection was diagnosed on a 20-year-old patient, not a newborn, and the urine culture indicated *Shiga* toxin-producing *E. coli* O157 so neither the "unspecified" nor the "other specified" *E. coli* codes would be appropriate. To locate this code in the Alphabetic Index, look up the main term Infection with subterm urinary (tract) and the code is listed (N39.0). In the Tabular List, there is a note to use additional code to code the infectious agent (Hazelwood and Venable 2014, 19; Optum 2015 *ICD-10-CM for Hospitals*).

38. d Code C44.211 is the correct code. The first step in coding neoplasms is to reference the Alphabetic index under the main term. In this case, the main term "Carcinoma" is referenced followed by subterm "basal cell." A cross reference note directs the coder to Skin, subterms ear, basal cell carcinoma. The Tabular List is consulted to complete the code (Hazelwood and Venable 2014, 31–32; *ICD-10-CM Official Guidelines for Coding and Reporting 2015*, 1.C.2).

39. d There is a specific code that should be assigned— R87.615, Unsatisfactory cytologic smear of cervix (Schraffenberger 2015, 411).

40. b This explanation describes an impacted fracture (Schraffenberger 2015, 418).

41. b It is the intrinsic form of asthma, which is caused by the body's own immunological response (Schraffenberger 2015, 270).

42. c Non-healing burns are coded as acute burns (Schraffenberger 2015, 438; *ICD-10-CM Official Guidelines for Coding and Reporting 2015*, 1.C.19.d.3).

43. b Option B defines when time can be used to select the E/M code (Kuehn 2015, 51).

44. c See Coding Guidelines codes 33202–33249 (*CPT Professional Edition* 2015, 185–187).

45. b This question is the classic description of two surgeons performing one procedure (Kuehn 2015, 300).

46. c Unlisted codes are to be used when there is no other code within CPT that correctly describes the service (*CPT Professional Edition* 2015, 8).

47. b "All PCI procedures performed in all segments (proximal, mid, distal) of a single major coronary artery through the native coronary circulation are reported with one code." The blockage is not total and there is no associated myocardial infarction documented (*CPT Professional Edition* 2015, 574–575).

48. b The only modifier in the list that is eligible for use with an E/M code is the –32 modifier (Kuehn 2015, 54).

49. d *CPT Professional Edition* 2015, Index page 947 instructs the coder to see codes 19367–19369 for the TRAM procedure. In this example, the coder should recognize that Transverse Rectus Abdominis Myocutaneous is the meaning of the abbreviation TRAM.

50. **c**   The documentation includes that the bone fragments pierced the dura; therefore, the two codes describing extradural procedures are not appropriate. Cranioplasty is not described in the documentation. Code 62010 for the elevation of the depressed skull fracture with repair of dura and/or debridement of brain describes the performed procedures (OptumInsight 2015a, 572).

51. **d**   The coder should always reference the codes found in the Tabular before code assignment (Kuehn 2015, 20–21).

52. **b**   This is the definition of the codes used to describe admission and discharge on the same calendar date (*CPT Professional Edition* 2015, 17–18; Kuehn 2015, 60–61).

53. **d**   Secondary procedures are those that are performed following previous surgery. Option D, code 66172, describes that this surgery is done following a previous ocular surgery (Kuehn 2015, 204).

54. **c**   This question defines a domiciliary (Kuehn 2015, 67; *CPT Professional Edition 2015*, 28–29).

55. **c**   A heart system transplant is coded with a category III code because no category I code is available (OptumInsight 2015a, 877).

56. **c**   Documentation does not state the structures where the foreign body was found, only that it was driven deep into the plantar surface of the foot; therefore, the appropriate code is 28192 (OptumInsight 2015a, 262–263).

57. **d**   The codes are differentiated according to the route of administration. For Medicare cases, a Level II HCPCS code (J series) is reported with the identification of the specific substance or drug. In this case, use both 96372 and J0561 (Kuehn 2015, 291).

58. **a**   When the scope is not used to examine the stomach, the procedure is an esophagoscopy (*CPT Assistant*, Spring 1994, 01(4), 1–11; *CPT Professional Edition 2015*, 260).

59. **d**   A coding note at 64484 states that these procedures are unilateral and the –50 modifier should be appended if the procedure is performed bilaterally. The guidance used is fluoroscopy; therefore, the 64483 and 64484 code series should be assigned. 0230T and 0231T are to be assigned when ultrasound guidance is used, based on a coding note in CPT (*CPT Professional Edition* 2015, 372).

60. **c**   The liver transplant codes allow for either a partial or whole, cadaver or living donor transplant. The transplant codes do not require information about the segments involved. The difference between codes 47135 and 47136 is whether a recipient hepatectomy was performed. With an orthotopic transplant, the native liver is removed (hepatectomy). With a heteroptic transplant, the native liver remains in place and the transplanted liver is placed in an ectopic location. The *Coder Desk Reference* describes the following for code 47135: "The physician performs partial or whole liver transplantation to the normal anatomic position of the liver in a patient of any age. The physician makes an abdominal incision. The diseased liver tissue is removed, hemostasis is achieved, and the liver bed is dried and prepared for the donor tissue. The donor liver is placed in the prepared liver bed. Anastomoses are created between the donor hepatic vessels and the appropriate recipient vessels. The donor bile duct is approximated to the recipient bile duct or to a limb of small bowel for drainage. Drains are placed and the abdominal incision is closed." This description identifies that the native liver is removed (OptumInsight 2015a, 457).

61. **a**   Code 36147 describes the work of accessing and imaging the AV shunt. Ultrasound guidance is coded separately as 76937, based on a coding note with 36147. Code 75791 is not assigned, based on a code note with 36147 (*CPT Assistant*, March 2010, 20(3), 3).

62. **c**   The only true statement listed there is the fact that surgical preparation codes can be used with graft, flap or skin substitute codes. They are used for wounds to be healed by primary intention, are not the same as debridement codes, and can be used with wounds to be treated by negative-pressure wound therapy (*CPT Assistant* March 2008, 18(3), 14–15; Kuehn 2015, 117).

63. **b**   Code 31660 describes the procedure specifically as "bronchial thermoplasty" (*CPT Professional Edition* 2015, 173).

64. **c**   The approach is thoracoscopic, or VATS. Two lesions are removed on the same side along with margins, therefore these are therapeutic wedge resections. The second lesion is ipsilateral, or on the same side; therefore, codes 32666 and 32667 describe this case. Code 32670 is not appropriate because these are two lesions and not two complete lobes are removed (*CPT Professional Edition* 2015, 177–178).

65. **c**   The sacral pressure ulcer is excised in preparation for two myocutaneous flaps, transferred from the buttocks on each side. Code 15936 describes the excision, and the myocutaneous flaps are not free grafts, but transfer flaps, coded as 15734 and 15734-59 (*CPT Assistant*, November 1998, 11(8), 6–7).

66. **d**   26418, 26418, 26540—Repair of both the extensor tendons is coded with 26418, therefore, two of the same code are required. The repair of the collateral ligament is coded with 26540. The capsulodesis code is not assigned because a capsulodesis procedure is a capsule fusion and not the repair of the ligament. The arthroplasty code is not assigned because arthroplasties are repair or replacement of a joint, not the ligament (*CPT Assistant*, December 2000, 12(10), 14).

67. **a**   64635, 64636—Injection of a destructive agent into a facet joint nerve is coded with the code series 64633–64636. The fluoroscopy guidance is not coded separately, based on a coding note found at 77003. Code series 64493–64495 and 0216T–0218T are not used for injection of destructive agents, and the Category III codes are not applicable because they require ultrasound guidance (*CPT Professional Edition* 2015, 375–376).

68. **c**   94727, 94728, 94729—All three of these codes should be assigned to correctly code these tests. Code 94726 is not coded because Plethysmography is an alternative test to the gas dilution method for determination of lung volumes. This is the only acceptable combination to describe the services that were provided, based on the coding notes found at codes 94726–94729 (*CPT Professional Edition* 2015, 604).

69. **b**   33141, 33508, 33518, 33533—This is a combination arterial and venous coronary artery bypass graft. Therefore, the combined arterial-venous grafting codes are used with the arterial grafting codes. Code 33518 is assigned for the two venous grafts (greater saphenous to obtuse and circumflex) and code 33533 is assigned for the one arterial graft (left internal mammary artery). The harvesting of the greater saphenous vein is included in the graft procedures, however the surgical video-assisted endoscopic harvesting is coded separately with 33508. The transmyocardial revascularization is coded with 33141 because it is performed at the time of another open cardiac procedure, based on the coding note found at 33141 (*CPT Assistant*, Winter 1992, 04(2): 12–13, Winter 1995, 04(5): 12–13, and November 1999, 11(9): 14 and 18).

70. **d**   Z51.11, C56.9, C78.00, C79.31—Code Z51.11 would be the first-listed code to indicate that the reason for the encounter is chemotherapy. The codes indicating the neoplasm sites would also be reported. In the Alphabetic Index, reference the main term Carcinoma with subterms papillary, serous, unspecified site which references code C56.9. The secondary sites (lungs and brain) can be located in the Neoplasm Table (Schraffenberger 2015, 149; *ICD-10-CM Official Guidelines for Coding and Reporting 2015*, 1.C.2.e.2.; Optum 2015 *ICD-10-CM for Hospitals*).

71. **d**  96413, 96417, 96367, J2405, J9045, J9267 × 25—This is an IV chemotherapy administration for greater than 30 minutes, which qualifies as up to 1 hour. The second infusion is also chemotherapy, for an additional hour as a sequential infusion. The third infusion is not chemotherapy and is coded as sequential infusion of a new drug. The drugs are each coded as only one unit because they did not exceed the infused amount over the amount listed in the code description (Kuehn 2015, 271–273).

72. **b**  K80.00, R00.0, Z53.09—When a surgery is planned but cancelled, the code for the condition is still coded first. In addition, the contraindication is also coded, as well as Z53.09, to indicate the cancelled surgery (Schraffenberger 2015, 60).

73. **c**  C61, N40.1, R33.8—In addition to coding the BPH with lower urinary tract symptoms (LUTS), code the adenocarcinoma and per the instructional guideline at N40.1, an additional code is assigned for the urinary retention (Optum 2015 *ICD-10-CM for Hospitals*, code N40.1).

74. **d**  Status asthmaticus is an acute asthmatic attack in which the degree of bronchial obstruction is not relieved by usual treatments such as epinephrine or aminophylline. A patient in status asthmaticus fails to respond to therapy (Schraffenberger 2015, 270–271). Only a physician can diagnose status asthmaticus. If a coder suspects the condition based on the symptoms documented in the record, the coder should query the physician about the documentation for status asthmaticus.

75. **d**  The malignancy (breast cancer) is the primary diagnosis. If the patient is being treated for the management of chemotherapy-induced anemia associated with the malignancy and is admitted or treated only for the anemia, the appropriate anemia code is listed after the malignancy code (Schraffenberger 2015, 148; *ICD-10-CM Official Guidelines for Coding and Reporting 2015*, 1.C.2.c.1).

76. **d**  Each time a questionable service is provided, an ABN must be provided (Kuehn 2015, 318–322).

77. **b**  Linking informs the payer which diagnosis is associated with each procedure on the claim (Kuehn 2015, 322).

78. **d**  The Stark Legislation limits referrals when the provider has a financial interest (Hazelwood and Venable 2014, 230).

79. **a**  The outpatient coding guidelines indicate that for an "outpatient" encounter, diagnoses preceded by "questionable", etc. are not to be coded as confirmed. Instead the signs and symptoms are coded (Schraffenberger 2015, 96 and 99; *ICD-10-CM Official Guidelines for Coding and Reporting 2015*, IV.H).

80. **b**  Medicare uses unique procedural codes to identify claims for services when colonoscopy is performed strictly for colorectal neoplasia screening in patients with average risk ("G0121, Colorectal cancer screening; colonoscopy on individual not meeting criteria for high risk") and high risk ("G0105, Colorectal cancer screening; colonoscopy on individual at high risk") for colon cancer. This patient has no history and is therefore not high risk. In these cases, G0121 is reported instead of the standard CPT diagnostic colonoscopy code when there is no need for a therapeutic procedure (*CPT Assistant*, January 2004, 07(14), 4–25).

81. **b**  When the coder compares the procedure description to the diagnosis description, there is a difference between the location of the foreign body; therefore, the diagnosis was not correctly linked to the procedure.

82. **c** Allowing the physician to select the codes for an audit will not ensure a representative sample (Kuehn 2015, 372).

83. **a** None of the claims in the list are correct; therefore, the problem is CPT coding accuracy. A three-level cervical laminectomy is coded as 63045, 63048, 63048 (Kuehn 2015, 196–198).

84. **a** This production report does not contain any entries for new patient E/M codes. It is highly unlikely that all patients that have not been seen previously were seen at the request of another healthcare provider. Therefore, the physician may require education on the definition of new patient visits (Kuehn 2015, 56–57).

85. **c** Electronic spreadsheets can be used to facilitate data collection and analysis. The advantage of spreadsheets is that charts and graphs can be formulated as the data are being analyzed (LaTour, Eichenwald Maki, and Oachs 2013, 516).

86. **a** Encryption is the process of transforming text into an unintelligible string of characters that can be transmitted via communications media with a high degree of security and then decrypted when it reaches a secure destination (LaTour, Eichenwald Maki, and Oachs 2013, 99–100).

87. **a** An electronic health record's scheduling system often prompts the staff to do a benefits eligibility inquiry, which will identify the extent of the benefits and the amounts of copay (LaTour, Eichenwald Maki, and Oachs 2013, 122–124).

88. **a** AHIMA's Code of Ethics are ethical principles that are based on the core values of AHIMA. "Coding an intentionally inappropriate level of service" violates "IV—Refuse to participate in or conceal unethical practices or procedures and report such practices." Specific guidelines are also listed in the Standards for Ethical Coding: "8. Refuse to participate in or conceal unethical coding practices or procedures. Coding professionals shall not: code an inappropriate level of service." (AHIMA House of Delegates 2011; Hazelwood and Venable 2014, 247).

89. **d** There are certain exceptions where the minimum necessary requirement does not apply and the individual or the individual's personal representation is one of the exceptions (LaTour, Eichenwald Maki, and Oachs 2013, 133–134).

90. **d** Both HIPAA and substance abuse laws deal with the confidentiality of substance abuse records (Brodnik, et al. 2012, 339).

91. **a** The notice should be given at the initial contact (LaTour, Eichenwald Maki, and Oachs 2013, 244).

92. **b** Data security is the result of effective data protection measures (LaTour, Eichenwald Maki, and Oachs 2013, 383–384).

93. **a** The Centers for Medicare and Medicaid Services (CMS) and the National Center for Health Statistics (NCHS) provide the official guidelines for coding and reporting using ICD-9-CM. These guides have been approved by the four organizations that make up the Cooperating Parties for the ICD-10-CM: The American Hospital Association, AHIMA, CMS, and NCHS (Schraffenberger 2015, 92; *ICD-10-CM Official Guidelines for Coding and Reporting 2015*, 1).

94. **b** When offenses are discovered, they should be investigated and corrective measures undertaken. Physician practices should develop indicators that would signal a problem. Corrective action may include refunding overpayments from a third-party payer or even self-reporting to the government (Hazelwood and Venable 2014, 231–232).

95. **c** Developing, coordinating, and participating in coding training programs falls under the area of monitoring compliance efforts of the practice, whereas the other answers are actual risk areas identified by the OIG (Hazelwood and Venable 2014, 231–232).

96. **c** Medicare defines "abuse" as involving billing practices that are inconsistent with generally acceptable fiscal policies. This usually results from inadvertent coding or billing mistakes and is not considered fraudulent (Hazelwood and Venable 2014, 231).

## Exam 2 Case 1

| | | |
|---|---|---|
| **DX1** | J18.9 | Pneumonia, unspecified organism |
| **DX2** | F17.209 | Nicotine dependence, unspecified, with unspecified nicotine-induced disorders |
| **PR1** | 99204 | Office and other outpatient E/M, new |
| **PR2** | 96374 | IV push |
| **PR3** | J1956 | Levofloxacin (Levaquin) 250 mg |
| **PR4** | J1956 | Levofloxacin (Levaquin) 250 mg |

## Exam 2 Case 2

| | | |
|---|---|---|
| **DX1** | R19.7 | Diarrhea, unspecified |
| **DX2** | R11.0 | Nausea |
| **DX3** | S40.811A | Abrasion of right upper arm, initial encounter |
| **DX4** | S40.812A | Abrasion of left upper arm, initial encounter |
| **PR1** | 99214 | Office and other outpatient E/M, established |
| **PR2** | 90471 | Immunization administration, 1st vaccine |
| **PR3** | 90714 | Tetanus and diphtheria toxoid vaccine |

## Exam 2 Case 3

| | | |
|---|---|---|
| **DX1** | E10.10 | Type I diabetes mellitus with ketoacidosis |
| **DX2** | K59.00 | Constipation, unspecified |
| **PR1** | 99255 | Inpatient consultation |

## Exam 2 Case 4

| | | |
|---|---|---|
| **DX1** | O03.88 | Urinary tract infection following complete or unspecified spontaneous abortion |
| **PR1** | 99284 | Emergency department E/M |

## Exam 2 Case 5

| DX1 | S76.112A | Strain of left quadriceps muscle, fascia, and tendon, initial encounter |
|---|---|---|
| PR1 | 27664 | Repair extensor tendon, leg; primary, without graft, each tendon |

## Exam 2 Case 6

| DX1 | C90.00 | Multiple myeloma not having achieved remission |
|---|---|---|
| PR1 | 36558 | Insertion of tunneled centrally inserted central venous catheter, without port or pump; age 5 or older |

## Exam 2 Case 7

| DX1 | Q12.0 | Congenital cataract |
|---|---|---|
| PR1 | 66982 | Extracapsular cataract removal with insertion of intraocular lens prothesis |

## Exam 2 Case 8

| DX1 | E10.9 | Type 1 diabetes mellitus without complications |
|---|---|---|
| DX2 | K30 | Functional dyspepsia |
| DX3 | K21.9 | Gastro-esophageal reflux disease without esophagitis |
| PR1 | 91034 | Esophagus, gastroesophageal reflux test, nasal catheter pH electrode |

# Exam 3

1. **b** Retrovir is an antiretroviral that is used to treat viral infections including HIV infection, which causes AIDS. For more information on Retrovir, see http://www.drugs.com/cdi/retrovir.html.

2. **d** Leon-Chisen 2015, 227.

3. **a** The histology of a neoplasm identifies the structure of the cells and the tissue that comprises the tumor new growth. The histology of tissue is determined by a pathologist and documented in the pathology report (LaTour, Eichenwald Maki, and Oachs 2013, 250).

4. **d** Abnormal findings from laboratory results are not coded and reported unless the physician indicates their clinical significance. If the findings are outside the normal range and the physician has ordered other tests to evaluate the condition or has prescribed treatment, it is appropriate to ask the physician whether the diagnosis code(s) for the abnormal findings should be added (*ICD-10-CM Official Guidelines for Coding and Reporting* 2015, III.B, page 100; Schraffenberger 2015, 402).

5. **c** Progress notes are chronological statements about the patient's response to treatment during his or her stay at the facility (Kuehn 2015, 10).

6. **b** Vital signs are recorded as part of a physical examination (LaTour, Eichenwald Maki, and Oachs 2013, 247).

7. **d** When two or more sites are described as "metastatic" in the diagnostic statement, each of the stated sites should be coded as secondary or metastatic. A code should also be assigned for the primary site as 199.1, primary site unknown (Leon-Chisen 2015, 450).

8. **a** A normal heart pumps at least one half or 50% of the blood in the left ventricle with each heartbeat (Schraffenberger 2015, 243).

9. **a** Hemophilia A, also known as classic hemophilia, is the most common type of coagulation defect and occurs as a result of factor VIII deficiency (Hazelwood and Venable 2014, 41–42).

10. **a** Square brackets are used only in the Tabular List to enclose synonyms, alternative wordings, abbreviations, and explanatory phrases (*ICD-10-CM Official Guidelines for Coding and Reporting* 2015, I.A.7, page 8; Hazelwood and Venable 2014, 11).

11. **c** The use of a colon simplifies tabular entries and saves printing space by reducing repetitive wording (Hazelwood and Venable 2014, 11).

12. **b** For categories Z38.0, Z38.3, and Z38.6, the place of admission is coded as well as the type of delivery (*ICD-10-CM Official Guidelines for Coding and Reporting* 2015, I.C.16.a, 60; Schraffenberger 2015, 393).

13. **c** Epstein-Barr is a commonly known viral infection. The other choices listed are bacterial infections (Hazelwood and Venable 2014, 20).

14. **b** Code assignment for HIV depends on whether the patient is symptomatic or asymptomatic (Hazelwood and Venable 2014, 24–25).

15. a  ICD-10-CM defines "sequela" as the temporary or permanent condition that follows the acute phase of an illness or injury. In this case, "scarring following a burn"—the scar is the permanent condition following the injury (burn) (*ICD-10-CM Official Guidelines for Coding and Reporting* 2014, I.B.10, 14; Hazelwood and Venable 2014, 181).

16. d  ICD-10-CM provides the following coding guideline for burns: Classify burns of the same local site, but of different degrees, to the subcategory identifying the highest degree recorded in the diagnosis (*ICD-10-CM Official Guidelines for Coding and Reporting* 2014, I.C.19.d.2, 69; Hazelwood and Venable 2014, 189).

17. c  Category T31 is based on the classic "rule of nines" in estimating body surface involved: head and neck—9%; each arm—9%; each leg—18%; anterior trunk—18%; posterior trunk—18%, and genitalia—1% (Hazelwood and Venable 2014, 190).

18. b  ICD-10-CM refers to medications (prescription or nonprescription) taken in combination with alcoholic beverages as a "poisoning" as opposed to an adverse effect (Hazelwood and Venable 2014, 196).

19. d  In ICD-10-CM, mechanical complications include the mechanical breakdown/displacement, leakage, mechanical obstruction, perforation, or protrusion of the device, implant, or graft (Hazelwood and Venable 2014, 210).

20. a  In ICD-10-CM, hypersensitivities or allergic reactions that occur as qualitatively different responses to a drug, which are acquired only after re-exposure to the drug is the definition of an adverse effect (Hazelwood and Venable 2014, 197).

21. d  A greenstick fracture is classified as a closed fracture. The sites of the fracture are the shafts of the tibia and fibula (Hazelwood and Venable 2014, 182).

22. a  There are two sites to be coded—abdomen and right forearm—both second-degree burn since this was the highest level of burn for each site (*ICD-10-CM Official Guidelines for Coding and Reporting* 2015, I.C.19.d,2, 69; Hazelwood and Venable 2014, 190).

23. d  Because the patient was postoperative, the postoperative infection code (T81.4XXA) should be coded, as well as a code for the cellulitis of the leg, which identifies the specific type of postoperative infection present. Under code T81.4, there is a note to the coder to identify the infection (Hazelwood and Venable 2014, 205–206).

24. b  Crescendo angina is a type of unstable angina (Schraffenberger 2015, 237).

25. d  According to the E/M Service Guidelines, both the time spent counseling or coordinating care and the total time of the visit must be documented (*CPT Professional Edition* 2015, 7–8; Kuehn 2015, 51).

26. d  Chronic obstructive asthma is a chronic form of asthma coexisting with chronic obstructive pulmonary disease. Intrinsic asthma is caused by the body's own immunological response (Schraffenberger 2015, 270–272).

27. b  If a patient admitted with glaucoma and the stage progresses during the admission, assign the code for the highest stage documented (*ICD-10-CM Official Guidelines for Coding and Reporting* 2015, I.C.7.a.4, 39).

28. **d** The CPT codes assigned for the cases scheduled as cervical discectomies are all from the lumbar section; therefore, coders would find a review of spinal anatomy helpful in their code assignments.

29. **c** Patients who have undergone kidney transplant may still have some form of chronic kidney disease because the kidney transplant may not fully restore kidney function. Code T86.10 should be assigned for documented complications of a kidney transplant, such as failure or rejection. It should not be assigned for post kidney transplant patients who have CKD unless a transplant complication such as transplant failure or rejection is documented (*ICD-10-CM Official Guidelines for Coding and Reporting* 2015, I.C.14.a.2, page 50–51).

30. **a** External cause codes for child and adult abuse take priority over all other external cause codes (*ICD-10-CM Official Guidelines for Coding and Reporting* 2015, I.C.20.f, page 78).

31. **b** According to the ICD-10-CM Coding Guidelines, if the format limits the number of external cause codes that can be used in reporting clinical data, report the code for the cause/intent most related to the principal diagnosis. If the format permits capture of additional external cause codes, the cause/intent, including medical misadventures, of the additional events should be reported rather than the codes for place, activity, or external status (*ICD-10-CM Official Guidelines for Coding and Reporting* 2015, I.C.20.e, page 78).

32. **d** Massive doses of steroids is the only answer listed that is a primary cause of metabolic alkalosis. Other causes include hypokalemia, gastric vomiting or suctioning, and diuretics (Hazelwood and Venable 2014, 93–94).

33. **c** A guideline in the Pregnancy, Childbirth, and the Puerperium chapter clearly lists the postpartum period to be 6 weeks after delivery (*ICD-10-CM Official Guidelines for Coding and Reporting* 2015, I.C.15.o.2, 58; Schraffenberger 2015, 323).

34. **c** Labor and delivery refers to the way the female organism functions to expel the products of conception from the uterus through the vagina to the outside world. Labor is divided into four distinct stages; the third stage is referred to as the placental stage (http://www.healthguidance.org/entry/14764/1/stages-of-Labor.html).

35. **b** The ICD-10-CM code book defines a young primigravida as a female younger than 16 years old at time of delivery (ICD-10-CM Code Book, subcategory O09.6).

36. **a** A Z code would not be used because there is a specific code that more adequately describes the scenario listed (Schraffenberger 2015, 322–323).

37. **a** ICD-10-CM classifies both pathological and traumatic fractures. When coding pathological or spontaneous fractures, the fifth character identifies the specific site, and the sixth character demonstrates laterality. These fracture codes require a seventh character to identify the episode of care (Hazelwood and Venable 2014, 120–121).

38. **c** The depth of a decubitus ulcer is identified by stages I–IV. It is important to remember the definition of each of the stages so that an accurate code can be assigned (Schraffenberger 2015, 354).

39. **d** Adverse effects of, or reactions to drugs can occur in situations where the medication is properly administered and correctly prescribed is the definition of an adverse effect. In this case, the patient took the medication as prescribed and had a reaction (Hazelwood and Venable 2014, 197).

40. **b**    Erb's palsy is the only condition listed that is a perinatal condition and not a congenital anomaly (Hazelwood and Venable 2014, 158–166).

41. **c**    The patient has a recurrent hernia with obstruction and this is captured in the diagnosis code (Schraffenberger 2015, 287–288; *CPT Assistant* Nov. 1999, 24; March 2000, 9).

42. **a**    Intractable migraine is defined as headaches with duration of greater than 72 hours (Leon-Chisen 2015, 207).

43. **a**    Lacerations of the same site grouping and same complexity are added together for coding with the most complex repair listed first (Kuehn 2015, 114–115; CPT Professional Edition 2015, 75–77).

44. **c**    –LT and–RT are used to describe that x-rays are performed on each side (Kuehn 2015, 225).

45. **c**    Excisions of lesions are coded separately and simple repair is included (Kuehn 2015, 112–113; *CPT Professional Edition* 2015, 71).

46. **d**    According to the Coding Guidelines, the service is a chemotherapy IV infusion of the initial substance, a sequential chemotherapy infusion, and a therapeutic injection (*CPT Professional Edition* 2015, 621–626; Kuehn 2015, 271–273).

47. **b**    A joint aspiration is an arthrocentesis (Kuehn 2015, 126).

48. **b**    The triangle ▲ is used to mark code descriptions that have changed (Kuehn 2015, 16; *CPT Professional Edition* 2015, 5).

49. **d**    Prolonged pregnancy is defined as pregnancy beyond 42 completed weeks of gestation (Schraffenberger 2015, 323).

50. **a**    According to the Surgery Guidelines, the consultation to determine the need for the procedure is always excluded from the surgical global (*CPT Professional Edition* 2015, 62; Kuehn 2015, 105).

51. **c**    According to the Coding Guidelines, the –26 modifier is required because the pathologist is not employed by the facility and is billing separately. Each specimen must be reported separately (*CPT Professional Edition* 2015, 540; Kuehn 2015, 245–246).

52. **c**    The requirements for a consultation on a patient not covered by Medicare are met (Kuehn 2015, 61–63).

53. **b**    A removal of a portion of the patient's kidney is a partial nephrectomy (*CPT Assistant*, January 2003, 01(13): 9–21).

54. **c**    This is an unstable finger fracture that requires manipulation but not percutaneous pinning (normally a day surgery procedure), or code 26725. In addition, the x-ray is of the fingers, not the hand, or code 73140.

55. **d**    Tympanoplasty with mastoidectomy is coded with one code, 69641 (*CPT Assistant*, August 2008, 18(8): 4).

56. **b** A central venous catheter tunneled through the subclavian vein and terminated in the superior vena cava is coded as a tunneled centrally inserted central venous catheter, 36558 (*CPT Assistant*, December 2004, 12(14): 6–13).

57. **c** The only necessary information listed in the options is the reason for the thyroidectomy. CPT provides codes that describe thyroidectomy for malignancy and those without a stated reason (*CPT Professional Edition* 2015, 347).

58. **d** The femoral-femoral bypass is performed with material other than a vein (prosthetic graft); therefore, the correct code is 35661. Venous options are not appropriate. The thromboendarterectomy is performed on the common femoral artery. This is the picture found at code 35371 in the *CPT Professional Edition* 2015, 215.

59. **a** Code 62369 describes all of the work involved by the pump technician. Physician skill was not required and reprogramming was performed. Based on the coding notes found at 95991, code 62369 is the correct code (*CPT Professional Edition* 2015, 618).

60. **c** A segmentectomy is the removal of one unique segment of a lobe of the lung (supplied by a bronchus, and two arteries, a pulmonary artery and a bronchial artery, which run together through the center of the segment). This is in the code series of procedures performed using a thoracoscopic approach to the chest (*CPT Professional Edition* 2015, 177–178).

61. **b** Based on a coding note at 27407, cruciate ligament reconstruction is coded as 27427; however, this was performed using an intra-articular method with a graft and therefore, code 27428 is chosen. The meniscal repair is performed using an open approach, and code 27403 is assigned (*CPT Professional Edition* 2015, 143–144).

62. **b** One of the uses of the molecular pathology procedures is to test for histocompatibility antigens. The tests in this section are qualitative, not quantitative, and there are only two tiers of tests. The Bethesda System is used to report cytopathology results, not molecular pathology (*CPT Professional Edition* 2015, 480; *CPT Changes 2012: An Insider's View*, 147).

63. **c** This is a temporary urethral stent and is coded with 53855 (*CPT Assistant* February 2010, 20(2): 7).

64. **c** A tethered spinal cord is an intradural lesion; therefore, code 63271 is the only correct option for an intradural lesion of the thoracic spine cord (Spina Bifida Association of America 2011).

65. **b** 22630, 22632, 22842, 22851, 22851, 20937—The lumbar interbody fusion is coded as 22630 for the first level and 22632 for the second level. The spinal instrumentation is coded with 22851 for the three to six segments. The insertion of the cages to form the fusion is coded as 22851 for each level, or two times. The harvesting of the iliac crest bone for the morselized graft inside the cages is coded as 20937. This is coded only once even though it is used in two cages because it is only harvested once (*CPT Assistant*, January 2001, 01(11), 12; Kuehn 2015, 128).

66. **a** J15.212, Z22.322—When the patient has a MRSA infection and the physician documents MRSA colonization, both codes can be used (*ICD-10-CM Official Guidelines for Coding and Reporting* 2015, I.C.e.1.a,b,c, 24–25; Schraffenberger 2015, 117–118).

67. **c** E10.10, E10.65, K04.7, E86.0—A diagnosis of "diabetic" ketoacidosis is coded to E10.10, Type 1 diabetes mellitus with ketoacidosis without coma. Ketoacidosis is a complication of type 1 diabetes, type 2 diabetics seldom develop ketoacidosis. A diagnosis of DKA should be classified as type 1 diabetes. The poorly controlled diabetes, abscessed tooth, and dehydration should also be coded (Schraffenberger, 2015, 163).

68. **b**  T86.19, C80.2, C64.1—A malignant neoplasm of a transplanted organ should be coded as a transplant complication. Assign first the appropriate code from category T86.-, Complications of transplanted organs and tissue, followed by code C80.2, Malignant neoplasm associated with transplanted organ. Use an additional code for the specific malignancy (*ICD-10-CM Official Guidelines for Coding and Reporting* 2015, I.C.2.r, page 31).

69. **a**  L89.621, L89.612—Codes from category L89, Pressure ulcer, are combination codes that identify the site of the pressure ulcer as well as the stage of the ulcer. The ICD-10-CM classifies pressure ulcer stages based on severity, which is designated by stages 1–4, unspecified stage and unstageable. Assign as many codes from category L89 as needed to identify all the pressure ulcers the patient has, if applicable (*ICD-10-CM Official Guidelines for Coding and Reporting*, 2015, p. 47).

70. **d**  A41.9, R65.21, J96.00—Even though the blood cultures were negative, the septicemia can be coded based on the physician's clinical findings. The signs and symptoms are not coded, only the confirmed diagnoses (*ICD-10-CM Official Guidelines for Coding and Reporting* 2014, I.C.1.d.1.a.i; *ICD-10-CM Official Guidelines for Coding and Reporting* 2015, I.C.1.d.1.b, pages 19–20; Schraffenberger 2015, 127–128).

71. **d**  99203, 94640, 94664, J7620—This is a new patient. The E/M requires 3 out of 3 components. Detailed, Comprehensive, and Moderate determine a 99203. The nebulizer is 94640. The MDI teaching is 94664, and the combination of Albuterol and Atrovent is J7620, which is not coded as two individual codes (Kuehn 2014, 50, 267–268, 291).

72. **a**  74178 and 72196—The combination code for the CT of the abdomen and pelvis together is used (74178), along with the individual code for the MRI of the pelvis with contrast media (72196). It is inappropriate to code the CT of the abdomen separate from the CT of the pelvis when both are done together (OptumInsight 2015a, 641, 646).

73. **b**  Patient may have several chronic conditions that coexist at the time of hospital admission and qualify as additional diagnoses. If there is documentation in the record to indicate the patient has a chronic condition, it should be coded. Chronic diseases treated on an ongoing basis may be coded and reported as many times as the patient receives treatment and care for the condition(s) (*ICD-10-CM Official Guidelines for Coding and Reporting*, Section IV: Diagnostic Coding and Reporting Guidelines for Outpatient Services, subparts I and J, 2015, 103).

74. **c**  The *ICD-10-CM Official Guidelines for Coding and Reporting*, Section IV, subpart H. Diagnostic Coding and Reporting Guidelines for Outpatient Services indicate that when a physician qualifies a diagnostic statement as "probable," the condition qualified with that statement should not be coded as if it existed. Rather, the condition should be coded to the highest level of certainty such as the signs and symptoms the patient exhibits. The history of cholecystectomy has no relevance to the current encounter and should not be coded Per the *ICD-10-CM Official Guidelines for Coding and Reporting* 2015, 103, Section IV: Code All Documented Conditions That Coexist, subpart J.

75. **b**  Medicare covers colorectal barium enemas only in lieu of covered screening flexible sigmoidoscopies (HCPCS code G0104) or covered screening colonoscopies (HCPCS code G0105; CMS 2015).

76. **d**  When the coder compares the procedure description to the diagnosis description, there is a difference between the type of immunization being coded and the shoulder pain is linked to the cholesterol. Therefore, the diagnosis was not correctly linked to the procedure (Kuehn 2015, 322).

77. **c** The –76 modifier is used to indicate that a procedure is repeated by the same physician on the same day (Kuehn 2015, 300–301).

78. **d** National coverage determinations (NCDs) or local coverage determinations (LCDs) are guidelines that specify what conditions or diagnoses are needed to justify specific services identified by CPT codes (Kuehn 2015, 318–322).

79. **b** The goal in claims submittal is to submit each claim as a clean claim, which means it contains all of the required and accurate information. A clean claim is essential in order to receive timely and accurate reimbursement (Kuehn 2015, 325–329).

80. **c** For Medicare, a nonparticipating physician who does not accept assignment may not bill the patient more than the Medicare limiting charge, which is 115% of the Medicare approved amount (Kuehn 2015, 316).

81. **c** In the hospital charges displayed, 8/13/20XX and 8/14/20XX are incorrectly coded with initial hospital service codes. The patient was seen in consultation on 8/12/20XX and took over the patient's care for the remainder of the admission; 8/13/20XX and 8/14/20XX should have been coded using subsequent hospital service codes (Kuehn 2015, 59–61).

82. **a** The coder chose the incorrect medication. Depo-Provera is used for estrogen replacement. The testosterone cypionate is a different medication.

83. **c** Statements A, B, and D are actually disadvantages of using e-mail in the healthcare setting. However, using e-mail to clarify treatment instructions and medication administration is beneficial to patients and healthcare providers. E-mail communication is increasingly common in healthcare settings. The AHIMA developed a Practice Brief on provider–patient e-mail security, which lists the advantages and concerns of e-mail communication (Burrington-Brown and Hughes, 2003).

84. **b** A database is a structure that allows for the storage of data about multiple entities (in this example, patients) and the relationship among the entities (LaTour, Eichenwald Maki, and Oachs 2013, 368, 377).

85. **b** An encoder is a computer software program designed to assist coders in assigning appropriate clinical codes. An encoder helps ensure accurate reporting of diagnoses and procedures (LaTour, Eichenwald Maki, and Oachs 2013, 444).

86. **c** Electronic spreadsheets can be used to facilitate data collection and analysis. The advantage of spreadsheets is that charts and graphs can be formulated as the data are being analyzed.

87. **b** Because the physician requesting the record is not listed as the surgeon on this case (or as the attending physician), the physician must have an authorization signed by the patient in order to review this record. This scenario is based on confidentiality and the patient's right (or invasion) of privacy (LaTour, Eichenwald Maki, and Oachs 2013, 353).

88. **b** The hospital does have a right to deny access if such access could possibly endanger the life or safety of a patient or another individual (Roach 2006, 161).

89. **c** The HIPAA Privacy Rule recognizes and incorporates the principle of "minimum necessary." Generally, only the minimum necessary amount of information necessary to fulfill the purpose of the request should be shared with internal users and external requestors (LaTour, Eichenwald Maki, and Oachs 2013, 133).

90. **d**   The HIPAA Privacy Rule does not provide access to the patient for the following: oral information, psychotherapy notes, and information compiled in anticipation of, or for use in, a civil, criminal, or administrative action or proceeding (LaTour, Eichenwald Maki, and Oachs 2013, 319).

91. **c**   Reliability refers to the consistency of any data set (LaTour, Eichenwald Maki, and Oachs 2013, 383).

92. **b**   An amendment to the Federal False Claims Act offered financial incentives to informants, or "relators," who report providers to the government who are committing fraud. This reporting is known as a qui tam action (Hazelwood and Venable 2014, 229).

93. **b**   The Stark Law prohibits physicians from ordering designated health services for Medicare patients from entities from which the physician has a financial relationship (Brodnik, et al. 2012, 438).

94. **d**   The OIG sets forth an annual work plan (Brodnik, et al. 2012, 446).

95. **c**   Sending in a claim twice is an example of abuse (Brodnik, et al. 2012, 430–431).

96. **c**   Congress authorized the establishment of Safe Harbors which are exceptions to the Federal Anti-Kickback Act (Brodnik, et al. 2012, 435–436).

## Exam 3 Case 1

| DX1 | R04.0 | Epistaxis |
|---|---|---|
| PR1 | 99282 | Emergency department E/M |
| PR2 | 30901 | Control nasal hemorrhage, anterior, simple |

## Exam 3 Case 2

| DX1 | A41.59 | Sepsis |
|---|---|---|
| DX2 | N39.0 | Urinary tract infection |
| DX3 | B96.89 | Infection with *Providencia stuartii* |
| PR1 | 99253 | Inpatient consultation |

## Exam 3 Case 3

| DX1 | S22.42XA | Rib fractures |
|---|---|---|
| DX2 | S27.321A | Pulmonary contusion |
| DX3 | S27.2XXA | Hemopneumothorax |
| DX4 | S32.502A | Pubic rami fracture |
| PR1 | 99223 | Initial hospital E/M |

## Exam 3 Case 4

| DX1 | N20.0 | Renal calculi |
|---|---|---|
| PR1 | 50080 | Percutaneous nephrostolithotomy or pyelostolithotomy |

## Exam 3 Case 5

| DX1 | E26.01 | Conn's syndrome |
|---|---|---|
| DX2 | I10 | Hypertension |
| DX3 | E87.6 | Hypokalemia |
| PR1 | 60650 | Laparoscopy, surgical, with adrenalectomy, partial or complete |

## Exam 3 Case 6

| DX1 | D05.12 | Carcinoma in situ of breast |
|---|---|---|
| PR1 | 19302 | Mastectomy, partial; with axillary lymphadenectomy |

## Exam 3 Case 7

| DX1 | Q40.0 | Congenital hypertrophic pyloric stenosis |
|---|---|---|
| DX2 | Q89.09 | Thrombosed accessory spleen |
| PR1 | 38120 | Laparoscopy, surgical, splenectomy |
| PR2 | 43659 | Unlisted laparoscopic procedure, stomach |

## Exam 3 Case 8

| DX1 | S05.52XA | Intraocular foreign body |
|---|---|---|
| PR1 | 65265 | Removal of foreign body, intraocular; from posterior segment, nonmagnetic extraction |
| PR2 | 66852 | Removal of lens material; pars plana approach, with or without vitrectomy |
| PR3 | 92071 | Fitting of contact lens for treatment of ocular surface disease |

## *Exam 4*

1. **c** The PDR is the authoritative source of FDA-approved information on prescription drugs. It includes information on more than 3,000 brand name and generic drugs, as well as information on usage, warning, and drug interactions.

2. **a** The operative report is written or dictated by a surgeon immediately after surgery and includes the names of the surgeon and assistants, technical procedures performed, findings, specimens removed, estimated blood loss, and postoperative diagnosis (LaTour, Eichenwald Maki, and Oachs 2013, 250).

3. **c** Physicians' orders drive the healthcare team. Orders may be for treatments, ancillary medical services, laboratory tests, radiological procedures, drugs, devices, restraints, or seclusion (LaTour, Eichenwald Maki, and Oachs 2013, 246–248).

4. **b** The location of the donor site is not needed to code grafts as the harvesting of the graft is included in the graft code. However, if the donor site requires skin grafting or local flaps, an additional code would be reported (Kuehn 2015, 115–118).

5. **c** New patient and established patient definitions do not apply to emergency department codes. It is necessary that the three key components are described. Time is not an issue in emergency department coding, and any physician can use these codes (Kuehn 2015, 63–64).

6. **b** The *Official ICD-10-CM Coding Guidelines* are published quarterly in *Coding Clinic*, which is published by the Central Office on ICD-10-CM Coding of the American Hospital Association (http://www.cdc.gov/nchs/data/ICD10cmguidelines_2015%209_26_2014.pdf).

7. **c** In scenario "a" the patient was asymptomatic and no further evaluation or treatment was carried out. In scenario "b" the bundle branch block was an isolated finding, which had no implications for the patient's care. In scenario "d" the nausea and vomiting is simply a symptom of the gastroenteritis (Leon-Chisen 2015, 36–37).

8. **c** Aplastic anemia is a condition in which there is a deficiency of red blood cells because the bone marrow is failing to produce them (Leon-Chisen 2015, 195).

9. **d** An eponym is defined as the naming of a disease, condition or structure, after the name of the person who discovered or first described it (Definition retrieved from: http://www.merriam-webster.com/medlineplus/eponym).

10. **a** In the Tabular List, a colon is used after an incomplete term that needs one or more of the modifiers that follows so that it can be assigned to a given category or code (*ICD-10-CM Official Guidelines for Coding and Reporting 2015*, I.A.7, page 9; Hazelwood and Venable 2014, 11).

11. **c** Both volumes of ICD-10-CM use parentheses to enclose supplementary words or explanatory information that may or may not be present in the statement of a diagnosis or procedure (*ICD-10-CM Official Guidelines for Coding and Reporting 2015*, I.A.7, page 9; Hazelwood and Venable 2014, 11).

12. **b** In ICD-10-CM, a symptom is defined as any subjective evidence of disease reported by the patient to the physician (Hazelwood and Venable 2014, 172).

13. **d** The *Official Guidelines* state that the code for the underlying cause (infection or trauma) must be sequenced first (*ICD-10-CM Official Guidelines for Coding and Reporting 2015*, I.C.1.d.1.a; I.C.1.d.1.b, 20–21; Hazelwood and Venable 2014, 22).

14. **a** This occasion of service was only for the radiation therapy; therefore, it is sequenced before the code for the neoplasm (*ICD-10-CM Official Guidelines for Coding and Reporting* 2015, I.C.2.e.2, page 28; Hazelwood and Venable 2014, 35).

15. **c** The diagnosis of hypercholesterolemia is to be sequenced first, followed by the obesity (Leon-Chisen 2015, 168).

16. **b** In ICD-10-CM, alcohol dependence is classified to subcategory F10.2 with the fifth character of this subcategory specifying the presence of intoxication, intoxication delirium, alcohol-induced mood disorder, psychotic disorder, and other alcohol-induced disorders (Hazelwood and Venable 2014, 56).

17. **a** The acute condition is sequenced first followed by the chronic condition (*ICD-10-CM Official Guidelines for Coding and Reporting 2015*, I.C.7.a.3, page 40; I.B.8, page 14; Leon-Chisen 2015, 58).

18. **b** The primary diagnosis is the pernicious anemia with the agammaglobulinemia and gastritis being associated with the anemia and therefore placed after the anemia code (Schraffenberger 2015, 176–177).

19. **a** The ICD-10-CM coding guideline for hypertensive heart and chronic kidney disease states "Assign codes from combination category I13, Hypertensive heart and chronic kidney disease, when both hypertensive kidney disease and hypertensive heart disease are stated in the diagnosis. Assume a relationship between the hypertension and the chronic kidney disease whether or not the condition is designated. If heart failure is present, assign an additional code from category I50 to identify the type of heart failure. The appropriate code from category N18, Chronic kidney disease, should be used as a secondary code with a code from category I13 to identify the stage of chronic kidney disease." Additionally a code should also be assigned for the diabetic polyneuropathy (*ICD-10-CM Official Guidelines for Coding and Reporting* 2015, I.C.9.a.3, 41).

20. **d** Code J01.80 is the correct answer. This code is used when more than one sinus is involved (*ICD-10-CM Code Book* 2014, Alphabetic Index – main term Sinusitis).

21. **b** This code is used because there was no mention of hemorrhage or perforation and was also without obstruction (Hazelwood and Venable 2014, 103–104).

22. **a** In this case, both the code for the cystitis and the organism *(E. coli)* code must be used (Hazelwood and Venable 2014, 128).

23. **a** A sequela is a residual condition that remains after the termination of the acute phase of an illness or injury (*ICD-10-CM Official Guidelines for Coding and Reporting* 2015, I.B.10, page 14; Schraffenberger 2015, 45–46).

24. **d** Heart conditions are assigned to a code from category I11, Hypertensive heart disease, when a causal relationship is stated or implied. Heart conditions with hypertension without a stated causal relationship between the hypertension and the heart conditions are coded separately (*ICD-10-CM Official Guidelines for Coding and Reporting 2015*, I.C.9.a.1, 40; Schraffenberger 2015, 229).

25. c    When a patient has bilateral glaucoma and each eye is documented as having a different type or stage, and the classification distinguishes laterality, assign the appropriate code for each eye rather than the code for bilateral glaucoma (*ICD-10-CM Official Guidelines for Coding and Reporting*, 2015, 39).

26. c    The pain associated with the migraine would not be coded and there is a symptom code for the abdominal pain and the chest pain. Category G89 can be used to code neoplasm related pain (Schraffenberger 2015, 203–204).

27. a    When two or more sites are described as "metastatic" in the physician's documentation, each of the sites would be coded as secondary or metastatic. A code would also be assigned to the primary site, if known, or coded to C80.1 when it is not known (Leon-Chisen 2015, 450).

28. d    Intractable is a term used to describe status asthmaticus (Hazelwood and Venable 2014, 90).

29. a    The diagnosis states that it was an accidental poisoning therefore the correct ICD-10-CM code is T40.2X1A (Schraffenberger 2015, 450–451).

30. b    A concussion is a transient loss of consciousness after a traumatic head injury. A contusion is more severe injury than a concussion. It refers to a bruise of the brain with bleeding into brain tissue, but without disruption of brain continuity. A laceration of the brain results in some destruction of brain tissue. A subdural hematoma is the formation of a hematoma between the dura and the leptomeninges (Hazelwood and Venable 2014, 186).

31. c    Rheumatoid arthritis is an autoimmune disease and is not a type of osteoarthritis (Leon-Chisen, 2015, 297–298).

32. b    Preexisting hypertension is always considered to be a complicating factor in pregnancy, childbirth, or the puerperium and is classified in category O10, Pre-existing hypertension complicating pregnancy, childbirth, and the puerperium. Code O10.013 is assigned to report pre-existing benign essential hypertension when the patient is in the third trimester. A note in the Tabular at the beginning of Chapter 15 defines the third trimester as 28 weeks, 0 days until delivery. An additional code to identify the weeks of gestation is also assigned. An additional note at the beginning of Chapter 15 states to use an additional code from category Z3A, Weeks of gestation, to identify the specific week of the pregnancy (Schraffenberger 2015, 329, 248).

33. c    Fertility preservation counseling is listed under Category Z31, Procreative management therefore it is not related to Z30, Contraceptive management (Schraffenberger 2015, 347–348; 512–513).

34. d    Do not assign a code from Category P55 unless there is provider documentation of isoimmunization or hemolytic disease (Leon-Chisen 2015, 370).

35. a    The definition of Prinzmetal angina is angina that occurs when the patient is at rest, apparently without any stimulation, such as during the night (Schraffenberger 2015, 238).

36. d    History of a TIA is not considered a late effect of a cerebrovascular disease (Leon-Chisen, 2015, 401).

37. c    Internal fixation devices include pins, screws, staples, rods and plates (Leon-Chisen 2015, 492).

38. b    Cellulitis is not a sequela of an injury (Schraffenberger 2015, 352).

39. c    *CPT Professional Edition* 2015, 70–72; Kuehn 2015, 112–113.

40. d    The patient receives 600 mg of Rocephin. The HCPCS code description for J0696 is 250 mg. Therefore, 3 units of Rocephin must be reported (250 mg 1 250 mg 1 some of the third unit of 250 mg) (Kuehn 2015, 271–272, 291).

41. c    The documentation states that the laceration was closed with one simple stitch. This does not support the assignment of the code for a complex repair that was listed on the encounter summary (*CPT Professional Edition* 2015, 75).

42. b    The skin graft is coded as 15271 and the supply is coded as Q4101 x 21 units. Twenty-one units are reported because the wound is 21 sq cm (7 x 3) (Kuehn 2015, 115–118).

43. d    Replacement casts are coded separately (*CPT Professional Edition* 2015, 156; Kuehn 2015, 130).

44. c    One combination code is required to describe the angiography along with the left heart catheterization (Kuehn 2015, 262–264; *CPT Professional Edition* 2015, 574–577).

45. a    All of the work described is included in code 29881 (Kuehn 2015, 130–131).

46. b    The procedure described is a colonoscopy with biopsy and is coded as 45380 (Kuehn 2015, 162–163).

47. d    When the office only performs the x-ray (the technical component), and the physician reading the x-ray is from another group, the TC modifier is applied to the x-ray code (Kuehn 2015, 224–225).

48. a    Index entry under Repair, Anal fistula (*CPT Professional Edition* 2015, 919).

49. c    The only correct answer of these four is C, stating that you code all the laceration repairs (by adding together the lengths of those of the same site and complexity) and listing the code for the most complex repair first (Kuehn 2015, 114–115).

50. a    When the treatment is directed toward the secondary site only, the secondary neoplasm is listed as the principal or first-listed diagnosis even if the primary malignancy is still present (Leon-Chisen 2015, 459).

51. b    Detoxification is the active management of withdrawal symptoms in a patient who is physically dependent on alcohol and/or drugs (Schraffenberger 2015, 193).

52. c    *Dorland's Medical Dictionary*—computerized tomography, 1919 and CPT Professional Edition 2015, 408.

53. c    Refer to the chart in CPT to see that 115 minutes of critical care is coded using three codes (*CPT Professional Edition* 2015, 24).

54. b    Modifiers would not be appended to unlisted codes because these codes describe new or unclassified procedures that have no standard description. Therefore, the description does not need to be modified (Kuehn 2015, 296).

55. c   Removal of the leads is coded separately from the insertion of the new leads (*CPT Assistant*, Summer 1994, 02(4): 10–26).

56. b   The abscess is aspirated through a burr hole, described by CPT code 61150. The stereotactic guidance is coded as 61781 because the abscess is of the brain, or intradural, meaning inside the dura layer (in the brain). The *Coder's Desk Reference* describes this procedure exactly as: The physician uses a burr drill or trephine to create a hole in the cranium through which a brain or intracranial lesion or abscess is located. An abscess or cyst may be drained. The physician incises the scalp and peels it away from the area to be drilled. In 61140, a lesion biopsy is obtained using a forceps or curette. In 61150, a catheter is placed through the hole and into a brain abscess or cyst for drainage. Report 61151 for subsequent drainage of the abscess or cyst through the original burr hole (OptumInsight 2015a, 559).

57. b   The code description for 0123T described the procedure performed through the ciliary body. The surgeon failed to identify the location of the procedure in the documentation (*CPT Professional Edition* 2015, 661).

58. d   This procedure is performed using a laparoscopic approach, therefore either 58545 or 58546 could be the correct answer. However, only 58546 describes the removal of 7 intramural myomas, even if the total weight is not over 250 g (*CPT Assistant*, January 2004, 01(14), 26).

59. b   The repair of the ruptured spleen is coded as 38115 because the code description states "with or without partial splenectomy" (*CPT Assistant*, Summer 1993, 02(3), 5–12).

60. d   Extracapsular cataract removal by phacoemulsification and IOL implant is coded as 66984 (*CPT Assistant* September 2009, 19(9), 5).

61. c   Diagnostic bronchoscopy is included in the surgical bronchoscopy; therefore, 31622 is not coded in this case. Code 31628 correctly describes the transbronchial biopsies. Code 31629 is performed through a special biopsy needle called a Wang needle, which is not documented on this case (*CPT Assistant*, September 2004, 09(14), 8–10).

62. a   The thoracoscopic method determines the code series in this case. Code 32658 describes the removal of the clot from the pericardium (pericardial sac) (*CPT Assistant*, Fall 1994, 03(4), 1–6).

63. b   A PICC line is a peripherally inserted central venous catheter, and coding is based, in part, on the age of the patient (*CPT Assistant*, May 2005, 15(5), 13–14).

64. b   56821, 57420, 58110—The colposcopy of the vulva with biopsy is coded as 56821. The colposcopy of the vagina (without biopsy) is coded as 57420. Code 58110 is used to code the endometrial biopsy in addition to a colposcopy (*CPT Professional Edition* 2015, 334–336).

65. a   50365, 49422—Code 50365 includes the recipient nephrectomy and all the anastomoses required to transplant the kidney. The peritoneal dialysis catheter is a tunneled catheter and is coded with 49422 (*CPT Assistant* April 2005, 15(4), 10–12).

66. a   B26.9—The signs and symptoms are not coded. Infectious parotitis is classified as mumps (Schraffenberger 2015, 94, 401).

67. c   T45.511A, T39.011A, R31.9—Coumadin with an over-the-counter drug not prescribed by the physician is considered a poisoning. The hematuria is also coded (Schraffenberger 2015, 450–451).

68. b   S02.91XB, S06.332A, W12.XXXA, Y92.6, Y99.0, Y93.H3—The dizziness and headache are not coded because they are signs of the skull fracture. Separate codes are needed for the fracture and for the internal brain injuries. In addition, external cause codes can be used to show how the accident happened and the status of the patient when he was hurt (Schraffenberger 2015, 422–423; 425; 469–470).

69. d   Z40.01, Z15.01, Z92.3, Z85.3—Because the patient was previously treated for right breast cancer and was then diagnosed with the BRCA1 genetic mutation, the mastectomy is considered prophylactic. The personal history code, as well as the irradiation hazard, must also be coded (Leon-Chisen 2015, 133, 463).

70. c   99393, 90460 × 4, 90461 × 4—This is a preventive medicine visit, coded based on age. Vaccines were administered after counseling to patient of age 6, therefore, the 90460–90461 series of administration codes are used (Kuehn 2015, 71, 256–257).

71. b   22554, 22585 × 2, 22846, 20931— The three anterior interbody fusions are coded as 22554, 22585, and 22585. The segmental instrumentation spans 4 segments and is 22846, without a –51 modifier. This is an add-on code and does not require a –51 modifier. The structural allograft is 20931 (Kuehn 2015, 128–129).

72. a   Assign a diagnostic code for mitral regurgitation. If the diagnostic test has been interpreted by a physician the coder can assign a diagnosis (*Official ICD-10-CM Coding and Reporting Guidelines for Outpatient Services*, IV.K).

73. a   Assign codes for malignant melanoma of forearm, hypertension. Code chronic conditions if they affect the patient's treatment. The hypertension was being treated with a current medication and for this reason the hypertension is coded (*ICD-10-CM Official Guidelines for Coding and Reporting 2015*, III.A, page 99–100; Schraffenberger 2015, 97–98).

74. d   Do not assign a code for this condition because this is a frequent condition in the elderly, is asymptomatic, and there is no documentation of treating the condition so it should not be coded (Schraffenberger 2015, 99).

75. d   Assign a code for the chief complaint as the reason for the visit in the absence of a diagnosis or defined problem, the chief compliant should be coded as the reason for the visit (Schraffenberger 2015, 110–112).

76. a   Healthcare Common Procedural Coding System (HCPCS) book or Physician Fee Schedule Relative Value File. This file contains all of the HCPCS codes and CPT codes, along with their relative values (CMS 2015).

77. b   A cast application is included in the closed treatment of the trimalleolar ankle fracture (*CPT Professional Edition* 2015, 98–99; Kuehn 2015, 130).

78. b   The –25 modifier should be assigned to the E/M code if a significant, separately identifiable E/M service is performed by the same physician on the same day as a procedure (Kuehn 2015, 297).

79. c   The service distribution report is frequently used for this purpose (Kuehn 2015, 344).

80. c    The immunization administration code is missing from the list of codes. Immunization administration must be coded along with the vaccine (Kuehn 2015, 256).

81. c    The charge summary is sometimes called the office service report and contains a summary of all billing data entered for the practice on one day (Kuehn 2015, 347–348).

82. c    In this example, 10 splints are no longer available in stock. The coding manager can only assume that these splints were provided to patients and that physicians did not code them. Therefore, the appropriate action is to talk with the physicians about the use of supplies and the need for coding (Kuehn 2015, 344).

83. c    Unbundling is the practice of coding services separately that should be coded together as a package because all parts are included within one code and therefore one price. Unbundling done deliberately could be considered fraud (Kuehn 2015, 351).

84. d    Electronic data interchange (EDI) is the electronic transfer of information such as health claims transmitted electronically in a standard format between trading partners. EDI allows entities within the healthcare system to exchange medical, billing, and other information and to process transactions in a manner that is fast and cost-effective (LaTour, Eichenwald Maki, and Oachs 2013, 90–91).

85. c    An intranet is a private information network that is similar to the Internet. Its servers are located inside a firewall or security barrier so that the general public cannot gain access to information housed within the network (LaTour, Eichenwald Maki, and Oachs 2013, 925).

86. b    Interoperability is the ability, generally by adoption of standards, of computer systems to work together (LaTour, Eichenwald Maki, and Oachs 2013, 925).

87. d    An audit trail is a record that shows who has accessed a computer system, when it was accessed, and what operations were performed (Brodnik, et al. 2012, 307).

88. a    A designated record set is maintained in whole or in part, by or for the covered entity to make decisions about individuals (Brodnik, et al. 2012, 499–500).

89. d    All of the statements listed are true about a legal health record (Brodnik, et al. 2012, 167–168).

90. b    HIPAA provides for criminal penalties for healthcare professional who "knowingly and willingly" attempt to defraud any health program (Hazelwood and Venable 2013, 231).

91. c    The OIG investigates and prosecutes individuals who overbill Medicare and also develops an annual "work plan" that lists specific "target areas" monitored in a given year (Hazelwood and Venable 2013, 230).

92. c    Receiving kickbacks in exchange for referring patients to specific facilities is one of the examples listed under the definition of fraud (Hazelwood and Venable 2013, 231).

93. a    Providers who voluntarily report fraudulent conduct need to use the Provider Self-Disclosure Protocol form (DHHS 1998, 10).

94. d    Validity refers to the accuracy of the data (LaTour, Eichenwald Maki, and Oachs 2013, 382–383).

95. b    Disclosures used for treatment do not need to be disclosed (Brodnik, et al. 2012, 243–244).

96. c   *Qui tam* legislation has been widely used in the application of the Civil False Claims Act
        in battling healthcare fraud and abuse. It was also reinforced through passage of the Health
        Insurance Portability and Accountability Act (HIPAA) and the Balanced Budget Act (Hazelwood
        and Venable 2014, 229).

## Exam 4 Case 1

| | | |
|---|---|---|
| DX1 | M48.04 | Spinal stenosis, thoracic region |
| DX2 | M70.61 | Trochanteric bursitis, right hip |
| DX3 | M70.62 | Trochanteric bursitis, left hip |
| DX4 | M65.331 | Trigger finger |
| PR1 | 99214 | Office and outpatient E/M, established |
| PR2 | 20600 | Injection, small joint |
| PR3 | J3301 | Triamcinolone medication, 10 mg |
| PR4 | 20610 | Injection, major joint |
| PR5 | 20610 | Injection, major joint |

## Exam 4 Case 2

| | | |
|---|---|---|
| DX1 | K80.50 | Biliary colic |
| PR1 | 99244 | Outpatient consultation |

## Exam 4 Case 3

| | | |
|---|---|---|
| DX1 | S22.42XA | Multiple rib fractures |
| DX2 | S27.1XXA | Hemothorax |
| DX3 | S52.002A | Ulnar fracture |
| DX4 | S20.319A | Abrasions, chest wall |
| PR1 | 99223 | Initial hospital E/M |

## Exam 4 Case 4

| | | |
|---|---|---|
| DX1 | J44.1 | COPD/chronic bronchitis |
| DX2 | C91.11 | Lymphocytic leukemia, B-cell, in remission |
| PR1 | 99214 | Office and outpatient E/M, established |

## Exam 4 Case 5

| DX1 | I65.21 | Carotid stenosis |
|---|---|---|
| PR1 | 35301 | Thromboendarterectomy with or without patch graft; carotid, vertebral, subclavian, by neck incision |

## Exam 4 Case 6

| DX1 | H05.112 | Orbital pseudotumor |
|---|---|---|
| PR1 | 68510 | Biopsy of lacrimal gland |

## Exam 4 Case 7

| DX1 | T86.11 | Kidney transplant rejection |
|---|---|---|
| DX2 | N18.6 | End-stage renal disease |
| DX3 | T86.12 | Kidney transplant failure |
| PR1 | 50370 | Removal of transplanted renal allograft |

## Exam 4 Case 8

| DX1 | L03.116 | Cellulitis, leg |
|---|---|---|
| DX2 | E11.51 | Diabetes, type II |
| PR1 | 99213 | Office and outpatient E/M, established |
| PR2 | 96374 | IV push |
| PR3 | J0696 | Rocephin 250 mg |
| PR4 | J0696 | Rocephin 250 mg |
| PR5 | J0696 | Rocephin 250 mg |
| PR6 | J0696 | Rocephin 250 mg |

# REFERENCES

The following resources are referenced in the answer key:

Abdelhak, M. 2016. *Health Information: Management of a Strategic Resource,* 5th edition. St. Louis, MO: Saunders Elsevier.

Amatayakul, M. 2013. *Electronic Health Records: A Practical Guide for Professionals and Organizations,* 5th edition, 2013 update. Chicago, IL: AHIMA.

American Health Information Management Association. 2013. Standards of Ethical Coding. Chicago: AHIMA.

American Medical Association. 2015. *CPT Professional Edition 2015*. Chicago: AMA.

American Medical Association. 2013. *Medicare RBRVS: The Physicians' Guide*. Chicago: AMA. Retrieved from https://commerce.ama-assn.org/store/catalog/productDetail.jsp?product_id=prod1230 035&navAction=push.

American Medical Association. 2012. *CPT Changes 2012: An Insider's View*. Chicago: AMA.

American Medical Association. *CPT Assistant*, 1990 through 2014 editions. Chicago: AMA.

Brodnik, M., L. Rinehart-Thompson, and R. Reynolds. 2012. *Fundamentals of Law for Health Informatics and Information Management* 2nd edition, revised reprint. Chicago: AHIMA.

Centers for Disease Control and Prevention, Medicare and Medicaid Services and the National Center for Health Statistics. 2015. *ICD-10-CM Official Guidelines for Coding and Reporting 2015*. Retrieved from: http://www.cdc.gov/nchs/icd/icd10cm.htm.

Centers for Medicare and Medicaid Services, Department of Health and Human Services. 2015. Physician Fee Schedule Relative Value. http://www.cms.gov/Medicare/Medicare-Fee-for-Service-Payment/PhysicianFeeSched/index.html.

Chabner, D. E. 2014. *The Language of Medicine,* 10th edition. St. Louis, MO: Saunders Elsevier.

Department of Health and Human Services (HHS). 2011 (August). *The Guide to Medicare Preventive Services for Physicians, Providers, Suppliers and Other Healthcare Professionals*. http://www.cms .gov/Outreach-and-Education/Medicare-Learning-Network-MLN/MLNProducts/downloads//mps _guide_web-061305.pdf.

Department of Health and Human Services. 1998 (Oct. 30). *Federal Register*, 58400 (63:210). http://www.gpo.gov/fdsys/pkg/FR-1998-11-02/content-detail.html.

*Dorland's Illustrated Medical Dictionary*, 30th ed. 2003. St. Louis, MO: Saunders Elsevier.

Hazelwood, A. and C. Venable. 2014. *Diagnostic Coding for Physician Services*. Chicago: AHIMA.

HealthGuidance. 2014. *Stages of Labor*. Retrieved from http://www.healthguidance.org/entry/14764/1 /stages-of-Labor.html.

Kuehn, L. 2015. *Procedural Coding and Reimbursement for Physician Services: Applying Current Procedural Terminology and HCPCS*. Chicago: AHIMA.

LaTour, K. M., S. Eichenwald Maki, and P. Oachs, eds. 2013. *Health Information Management Concepts, Principles, and Practice*, 4th edition. Chicago: AHIMA.

Leon-Chisen, N. 2015. *ICD-10-CM and ICD-10-PCS 2015 Coding Handbook with Answers*. Chicago: American Hospital Association.

MedlinePlus 2014. *Medical Dictionary*. Retrieved from http://www.merriam-webster.com/medlineplus /eponym.

Nunn, Sandra. "Managing E-Mail as Records" *Journal of AHIMA* 79, no. (September 2008): 54-55.

OptumInsight. 2015a. *Coder's Desk Reference for Procedures 2015*. Salt Lake City, UT: Optum.

OptumInsight. 2015b. *ICD-10-CM for Hospitals: The Complete Official Code Set 2015*. Salt Lake City, UT: Optum.

Repka, M. X. 2011 (Nov. 16–18). CPT and RBRVS 2012 Annual Symposium. http://www.ama-assn.org /resources/doc/cpt/06-2011-opthalmology-repka.pdf. Chicago: AMA.

Roach, W. et al. 2006. *Medical Records and the Law*. Sudbury, MA: Jones and Bartlett.

Schraffenberger, L. 2015. *Basic ICD-10-CM/PCS and ICD-9-CM Coding*. Chicago: AHIMA.

Schraffenberger, L. A. and L. Kuehn. 2012. *Effective Management of Coding Systems*. Chicago: AHIMA.

Spina Bifida Association of America. 2011. Tethering Spinal Cord. http://www.spinabifidaassociation .org/site/c.liKWL7PLLrF/b.2700295/k.6B9E/Tethering_Spinal_Cord.htm.

*Stedman's Medical Dictionary*. 27th edition. New York: Lippincott and Williams.

Stine, Kevin and Matthew Scholl. "E-mail Security: An Overview of Threats and Safeguards." *Journal of AHIMA* 81, no. 4 (April 2010): 28–30.